Effortless Wealth

A Guide for Developing Your Wealth Consciousness

LAURIE LAMANTIA

LALA Unlimited
154 Easy Street
Carol Stream, IL 60188
847.640.8923
LALA Unlimited

Scripture taken from the King James Version of the Bible.

ISBN: 978-1-944923-03-7 (sc)
ISBN: 978-1-944923-02-0 (hc)
ISBN: 978-1-944923-01-3 (e)

Library of Congress Control Number: 2019901444

Lulu Publishing Services rev. date: 04/12/2019

Dedication

In deepest appreciation to Abraham-Hicks, Yogananda
Tricia Fiske and my many teachers who have
generously shared their wisdom
so this process could exist.

Thank you

Acknowledgment & Appreciation

- CCs - Thank you for our years of love, collaboration, and co-creation.
- Pillars – Thank you for your eternal sisterhood.
- Besties – High School sisters always there, always great fun!
- Sweetie – You are truly a wonderful life partner – thank you!

Contents

Prelude

Before we start into this journey, I wish to tell you something that, once you hear it, you might not need to even read this book.

This book's purpose is to give *your mind* something to work through so *it can agree* that you can have the wealth you desire and to realize that wealth is not something you acquire, it is something you already possess.

Over the course of all my research and learning about prosperity, wealth and abundance I have come to see two truths:

1. That prosperity, wealth and abundance are all around us and always flowing to us – freely and unconditionally.
2. We do not believe this – especially when it comes to agreeing to it for ourselves. There is also an important correlation: we believe that we must "do" something to earn prosperity, wealth and abundance, and unless we work to have them, they will not be ours.

This book and every book written like it, from *Think and Grow Rich* to *Rich Dad, Poor Dad,* are written to help you realign your thoughts to unlock the riches that are *already here* for you. *Please take a moment and contemplate that.*

All the books, processes and wealth recipes are given to you to help you realize *the wealth which is always flowing to you* and this book is no different - except in one important way. I want you to assume as you read this *that wealth is already yours!* I realize this idea of not having to struggle to achieve wealth may sound bizarre, but it will become clearer as you keep reading.

This experience is meant to help you create a vibration or atmosphere around you that is welcoming of your wealth. As you think and feel wealthy, you will be creating an energy field around you that attracts and allows wealth. You will feel differently, and ultimately you will be inspired to act differently.

People with wealth consciousness approach the world very differently than people with poverty consciousness.

This whole book is meant to give you the clarity and ability to start agreeing to your wealth, and help you ease into agreeing to experience the wealth that is and has been available to you already...always and in all ways.

"You came to this earth for 3 reasons: To experience your <u>freedom</u>,
to seek your <u>joy</u> and witness your <u>expansion</u>." – Abraham

EFFORTLESS WEALTH:
Investing in Your Wealth Consciousness

Chapter 1: Expand the Definition of Wealth, Investing and Effortlessness

Invest - Before You Invest

This is an investment book, but not the kind you might be expecting, where I give stock tips, industry analysis, or real estate wisdom. There are already many books you can read for that advice. This is an investment book of the highest order, one where you will be putting your wherewithal on a sure thing, the only thing you have control of and the most important investment you can and ever will make. You will be *investing in yourself and developing your wealth consciousness to make high quality life-energy choices.*

Most people I know spend a great deal of time and energy learning about financial investing and money management. They listen to tapes, go to seminars and they invest a great deal of time efforting for their wealth. But in truth, all of this *effort* is usually in vein because deep down, most people believe their lives are limited by scarcity and fixed-pie agreements that go unquestioned. If we invest our money with "scarcity-agreements" at the foundation of our investment strategy, we are not making the highest and best use of our investment energy. We are much better served by investing in wealth consciousness first and learning how to invest our life energy effectively - *then* invest our money.

As you develop your wealth consciousness it is important to learn to see yourself as a powerful investor that invests your life energy. How and what you *invest* your life-energy in is how you create your life experience. Through our time together as you read this book, we are building the groundwork of your wealth consciousness and developing your skills as an investor. And this groundwork is the bedrock of a rich wealthy life portfolio. Ultimately, you will have much better results - really!

"In investing, what is comfortable is rarely profitable."
- Robert Arnott

Expand Your Definition of Investing

Traditional investing is the process of putting money into an account - be it a bank account, 401K, IRA, or some other repository where your "wealth can grow". Growth is an assumption of investing; we're told to invest early and often and be patient as we watch our balance increases. In business school, we are taught about investing: specifically Return on Investment (ROI) - maximizing the outcome based on the input. Essentially, that is what I am teaching you to do in this book, except instead of money investing, I am teaching *energy investing*. More specifically, you will learn how to consciously invest *your life energy*. As you do, you will experience all manner of ROI, from joy to health to fun and money too. This notion of energy investing might not be comfortable to you yet, but it will be profitable.

Recently, I was sitting on an airplane and was writing a bit. As I wrote, the gentleman next to me asked what I was writing. I told him it was an investment book. Well as the law of attraction would have it, he was an investor! I am writing about investing, and bam, an investor is sitting next to me. He assumed I was writing a classic financial investment book about finding good companies in which to invest and my philosophy about management styles, competition, ROI and all the other things that make up a traditional investment strategy. I said, "Well I am not writing that kind of investment book, I am writing

> The point of this book is to help you see yourself as a powerful investor who creates, and as one who is getting clearer and clearer about where you are investing your life energy and getting clearer and clearer about what you truly want to invest in.

about energy investing." To his credit he was not only intrigued, he was genuinely interested and we talked for much of the 3-hour flight about energy investing—what it is and how to go about doing it on a daily basis. It was very clarifying for me and for him, I hope.

He was a very disciplined financial investor in that he does his industry analysis, EBITA (earnings before deduction of interest, tax and amortization expenses) calculations, long term growth prospects, competitive analysis, etc. and *then* decides to focus the money in his fund on the *prospects with the highest rate of returns.* Classic investing.

I said that is exactly what energy investing is all about. Becoming a disciplined energy investor means learning how to invest *your* life energy into the experiences that you believe have the greatest rate of return and not to put any more energy into the past hurts and worries, as these are sunk costs...energy used on past experiences. The key is to focus on investing your precious life energy in the here and now and future desires.

As I shared these thoughts with my flight companion, he made an amazing connection between our investing conversation and his personal life. He was worried about what was going on with his son as a result of a divorce that he was in the middle of. As he told me the specifics I could tell it was an energy drain for him. I asked him, "If you were to make a feeling-energy investment, how would you invest your feeling energy right now?" He said he would just focus on his son and how much fun they have together. He would envision them enjoying each other's company and continuing to do so. And he would not put any additional energy into the thoughts and feelings (like the struggle with his wife) that did not have the high rate of return that the feelings about his son did! BAM. WOW. YES! This is investing your life energy into what you want – high rate of return energy investing. He got it and so will you!

> *"Be patient with yourself. Self-growth is tender; it's holy ground.*
> *There is no greater investment."* —Stephen Covey

Expand Your Definition of Wealth

When most of us hear the word 'wealth,' we think of money or financial wealth. That's fair, but for the purposes of our discussion here I want us to expand our definition of wealth from little "w", which means money and/or finances, to Wealth with a capital "W", as in the huge, unlimited world of abundance and fun that is always flowing as a part of life: a wealth of opportunity, a wealth of health, a wealth of possibility, a wealth of fun, a wealth of love. When I say Wealth, I want you to think, **WUW: Wealth-Unlimited-Wealth**! Fulfilling, ever-powerful, always flowing energy available to me – *unconditional* energy that makes everything possible!"

Throughout this book, I capitalize the "W" in wealth to call out the concept of Big-Wealth. To me, Big-Wealth is this unseen Wealth-Energy surrounding us always and in all ways. The capitals are reminding us of this Magical-Unseen-Force-of-Aliveness that is flowing around us, to us and through us, whether we believe it or not.

I purposely use all kinds of different terms for this Big-Wealth-Energy like *Creative-Gloriousness, Allness, Great-Wealth-of-All-That-Is, Spirit, Great-Plenty-Source, Wealth-Spring because I* don't want us to get caught up on terms, or get caught calling it just one thing. I wish for us to grow a general *felt-sense* (feeling in your body and idea in your mind) of this WUW, Unlimited-Wealth-Energy – that is around you always. Can you feel how expansive and paradigm shifting the idea of *Magical-Unseen-Force-of-Wealth-Energy* is?!

And a big benefit of this new perspective on Wealth is that as we develop our Big-Wealth consciousness our little-wealth money will flow.

Wealth First – Then Money

Wealth first – then money! Let me say that again for emphasis because it is really something I want us to be clear about: Wealth consciousness first – then money. We will discuss money a great deal in this book, but at this point, I would like us to untangle Wealth and money. Wealth is always flowing; money is only one form the flow takes. When you feel Wealthy (Big W), money and all manner of good things flow to you and your life becomes even more magical. You get money and a whole lot more! How sweet is that?

Think of it like this: Do you wonder if water is available to you? When you turn on the faucet do you wonder if the water will flow out of the spigot?

I bet not. The Wealth I am talking about is like water from the faucet - always available to flow to you when you turn on *your* faucet – but you need to learn how to turn on the flow! As we invest in our Wealth Consciousness, we are learning how to turn on our faucet. This will lay the foundation for success in all things including financial success. Hopefully, you will come to agree that there is an abundance of Wealth all around you and experience life the way it was meant to be experienced, prosperously and joyfully.

> *"There exists a great unseen stream of power, which may be compared to a river, that every person who has accumulated a great fortune has recognized the existence of."* – Napoleon Hill, *Think and Grow Rich.*

Feel Wealthy then take Action

An important corollary to the idea of "wealth first, then money" is to *feel wealthy first then take action*. At first it may seem that much of this book is about just changing the way you think and feel. But that's just part of the change that will transpire. As our wealth consciousness grows, our actions and our outcomes change.

For example, in the past you might have worried if you should speak up in a meeting, worried your position or opinion did not matter – but after you are on your wealth journey for a while, you feel more confident and comfortable sharing your ideas, because you feel the abundance of possibilities that come from you being you in that situation.

Or in the past, you might have had an inspiration to do something or call someone, but then your mind jumped in and said – *oh that is not going to work* and you did not follow the inspiration. (Believe me, I do it to myself all the time. I think *you know maybe buy some amazon stock* – but then I think, *no too expensive.* Then bam it goes up $50 – rats.) But as you develop your wealth consciousness you feel expansive and inspired. You feel like, *hey why not see where this leads* and *you follow the inspiration* because it feels exciting and filled with potential. Over time, these new actions, and new behaviors on your part will yield unexpected outcomes and fresh results.

For example, I am taking a chance with writing a children's book. I had been telling my friends about some of my ideas and they were like – write it! I just feel inspired to open my heart in that way...and I am excited to see how it all unfolds – but so far it has been pretty magical.

Wealth consciousness inspires action, wealth consciousness helps paint our days with possibility. And wealth consciousness has us taking action with a different energy behind it. Over time, you'll see that scarcity-based action is not nearly as powerful as wealth-based inspired action.

I know for me, when I feel wealthy and empowered I walk through my day differently than when I feel small and disempowered. When I feel like Big-Wealthy-Laurie I don't worry about little things that crop up, I just deal with them and move on. When someone makes a jerky comment, I think, *"awe your having a bad day, hope it goes better"* and I move on. At work, I just know what I am doing is moving things forward in a productive, profitable way. When I am Big-Wealthy-Laurie I am so confident and capable, and I am having so much fun throughout my day!

When I am little-scarcity-Laurie, I worry, I go-negative and I doubt myself a lot. I am not happy with where I am and who I am. Contentment, satisfaction, forgit-about-it! I can be a real drag and I feel like a drag. In fact, I drag myself around doing what I *have to* do, and "should" all over the place (if you get my drift). When I am out of wealth-alignment I feel sad and out-of-sorts.

My intent is to help you develop your wealth consciousness so you have a practiced felt-sense of wealth and so Big-Wealthy-You is online more of the time. Because ultimately, by thinking and feeling in wealthy ways, your actions and outcomes will change accordingly.

I understand you might be thinking, we can't just think about being rich and then expect someone to ring our doorbell with a million-dollar check (but stay open to the possibility ☺). We can't just think about having a great presentation at our meeting without actually putting in the work into preparing for it. But, what I want you to realize is that actions backed by wealth-focused thinking feel different and have different results. As you feel different, the outcomes will be greater.

Realize, you are putting in *the work* by learning to adjust your felt-sense vibration to wealth. Realize, learning to think and feel wealthy is *the work*. Because this wealth-based thinking and feeling investment manifests itself in our behavior. When we vibrate wealth, joy, contentment, confidence, etc., it colors everything we do for the better. We are vibrating wealthier, people see us in a different light and the wealth flows.

> *"Wealth is the ability to create anything you desire."* - Deepak Chopra

Wealth is...

Throughout this process, my key premise is that Wealth is always around us, in all ways. It is the great unseen stream of power energy, ever flowing. It always has been and always will be. It is inherent in everything, everywhere. The Wealth-Energy is the building block of life and it cannot be contained, nor limited *and* you can tap into it.

Wealth is an abundance or profusion of anything and everything. Is there not an abundance of cells in your body, a profusion of energy in your environment and plenty of microorganisms all around you? In spring, there is an abundance of blooms, in summer there is plenty of heat, in fall there is an abundance of leaves falling and in winter there is plenty of snow. What is behind all this plenty? The Great-Plenty-Source!

But many of us pinch ourselves off from this Wealth-Source. This is what I call scarcity: when we pinch our connection to Wealth off through worry, fear, doubt, not-enoughness-thinking and the many scarcity-based agreements our world has allowed to take root. You can feel when you are doing this. Your body will give you indicators, like you will feel tight, stressed or you will feel heavy. You will have a felt sense (a mind-body knowing) that you are giving into scarcity consciousness. As you catch yourself in these heavy, worried feelings you are at a wonderful point to choose a new thought that is more wealth aligned, like, *I will find a new way*, or *wealth is here now - relax*.

You can make a decision right now to embrace the ever-present Wealth-Source that is always flowing into your life, by accepting that it is here for you always and in all ways and let it flow through you – take a breath and let it flow.

> *"Our key to transforming anything lies in our ability to reframe it."*
> – Marianne Williamson

Why Consciousness? Wealth Consciousness

I want to talk a bit about consciousness as it is the foundation from which your creative investment journey takes place. As many teachers have said, you create your reality. **And it is your consciousness that shapes your reality.** *As you think, so it is you experience.* More specifically, what you vibrate (think and feel) is what you attract more of, and deliberate conscious energy investment plays a major role in what you vibrate.

Your thoughts coalesce energy into physical reality into physicality. Because thoughts are things – they are actions. Thoughts and feelings are vibrations that bring energy together, that bring the Wealth-energy together. Thus consciousness, the focus of energy thought forms, brings together reality (realities). It is like mixing an energy cake and the energy ingredients (like fear or joy) affect the result (aka taste).

I know this sounds a bit woo-woo, but our consciousness is the framework of how we perceive things and it is what creates our experience. This is why your Wealth Consciousness is paramount to your experiencing wealth. As we journey through this book, we are investing in creating the body-mind-framework that focuses your life energies in the direction of wealth. As you develop your wealth consciousness you will feel differently, you will think differently and your new mind-body energy will vibrate in a different way attracting new opportunities and inspiring you to make wealth-aligned choices and actions.

At first, this might seem Pollyannaish, as most of us are not Wealth-aligned but scarcity-aligned. But as we journey forward, you will build momentum and start to vibrate differently and life will show up differently. It has to, it is the law of attraction in action – which we will explore more throughout our journey together.

Wealth creation is the capacity of every human to focus (invest) their life-energy and consciousness in the direction of their desires in a loving, effort-less way that feels specifically aligned to them. Your Wealth Consciousness will move you into a state of mind and body that shifts your frame of reference from poverty to prosperity and a whole lot more.

"Your mind is a garden. Your thoughts are the seeds. You can
grow flowers. Or you can grow weeds." - Anonymous

Now let's discuss money. Because honestly that was the reason I went on my wealth journey! I was tired of money making me feel bad and I wanted more money. And my guess is, that is a real desire of yours and why you picked up this book.

M-O-N-E-Y

I have a friend who does not use the word money, she spells it out m-o-n-e-y like my grandma used to do with the word candy, c-a-n-d-y, so us kids would not know she was talking about something we wanted. I know we all want m-o-n-e-y and the more the merrier.

But most of us approach the subject of money from scarcity consciousness...*I don't have enough and I want more.* As I discussed previously, this consciousness – the scarcity consciousness – is not a framework that will create an abundance of anything much less money. Scarcity consciousness creates more scarcity, wealth consciousness creates more wealth – more WUW!

Money and financial wellbeing is something I know you can experience – and as you realign your consciousness to turn on the Wealth-Source and realize your creating power – it will be, it must be.

"Abundance is not something we acquire, it is something we tune into."
– Wayne Dyer

A note about the million dollars: Many of us think about what we want to create in our lives and assume we need money to make it happen. Moreover, we limit the definition of wealth to tons of cash. (That is ok, but we can be much more expansive about our definition of Wealth.) This limited definition of wealth as money is why we always fall back on, "I cannot do this unless I have money...I need to win a million bucks!" We stop ourselves in our tracks before we even begin to invest in the wealth creation process. But the Wealth Consciousness we are creating is not limited by money. Money is only one way in an infinite field of possibilities to help you experience the life you desire. We are in the throes of expanding our understanding of Wealth and our relationship to it. As we expand our understanding and experience, we expand our ability to flow our desires into our lives including but not limited to money.

> "To me, money is defined as, My Own Natural Energy Yield."
> – John Randolph Price in The Abundance Book

A Bit About Effort-Less-Ness

If you picked up this book, my guess is you were intrigued by the title *Effortless Wealth*. You might have said, "Effortless wealth" is not possible, or thought, "Oh, wouldn't that be nice –

– effortless – haha". Either way you did not really think wealth could be all that effort-less.

Most of us have an unconscious, unquestioned assumption that there has to be a great deal of effort, a.k.a., hard work in creating wealth *because it is hard to come by,* and that we need to be deserving of wealth.

This is a double-doubt whammy to our wealth: Can I work hard enough? Am I deserving enough?

These doubts and negative feelings hinder our enjoyment and experience of wealth. If we want to succeed in this life, we must work hard and if we want wealth, it requires difficult effort and scarifies...feel familiar?

I carried these feelings around like a club in my mind. I pushed and bullied myself to work harder, do more and be better and earn the right to deserve wealth. The pressure would become intense and I would get exhausted. I would fall into depression. This difficult, pressure-filled effort turned what I was doing into drudgery. It became an internal nag that sucked the life right out of anything and everything I was doing and my results were marginal.

What I have come to learn is that all of that "pressure" and difficult efforting was actually working against my desires for wealth. Actually, it made my journey feel harder, take longer and made it not much fun. Because the more I efforted, the more I wondered why I was putting myself through this. Was all the work going to pay off? The doubt was working against me, too.

For now, at this point in the process, let's give ourselves permission to ponder: Does wealth have to mean hard work and difficult efforting? What if we approached everything we do with an excitement that what we are doing is bringing us closer to the wealth we desire by tapping into the power of the Wealth-Source? What if you believed Wealth was not scarce, but easily available? What if we knew everything was working out? Wouldn't that change things quite a bit?

The beauty of effortlessness is you get to have what you desire and you get to enjoy the process along the way. The need for pushing, forcing and fear-based action falls away. The joy of effortlessness is in knowing the power you have and investing it with clarity and purpose and WUW is available for you.

I promise that as you move forward on this journey and dig in deeper, you will find that effortlessness is a whole lot more fun than difficult efforting and that flowing and inspired action is more peaceful than forcing and pushing; it is like you are going to be going to the *School of Magic* instead of the School of Hard Knocks that so many of us have been enrolled in.

> *"Love gives us in a moment what we can hardly attain by effort after years of toil."* —Goethe

Note: Throughout our journey together I give "investment tips" like the one that follows. These are ideas for you to put into practice to develop your wealth consciousness and approach life from a wealth perspective.

◎ Investment Tip: Use The Effort-Less Approach

Feel the difference between the Effort-Less Approach and the School-of-Hard-Knocks approach.

How do you feel as you read down the words in the left column? How do you feel as you read down the words in the right column?

School of Magic - Effortless Wealth Approach	School of Hard Knocks Approach
• Grace & Ease	• Have to
• Positive Expectation (knowing life is on your side working to bring you what you desire)	• Must
	• Should
	• Can't unless
	• Attack
• Available abundance	• Defend
• Allowing Prosperity	• Force
• Peaceful Fulfillment	• Take because of scarcity
• Contented Action	• Compete because of not enough
• Plenty to go around	
• Want to	• Push because of inadequacy
• Would love to	
• Won't it be great when	• Hard work because no pain, no gain
• Joy-filled effort	
• Enthusiastic Play	• Get your share of the pie
• Flowing	• Money does not grow on trees
• Inspired Action	
• Satisfaction	• Difficult efforting
• WUW	

Both columns can get you to the same place…really, they can. I am making the case that the left column of Effort-Less Wealth will get you there faster, with less stress, better health, more fun, more joy, intact relationships and children that still love you.

The right column of the School-Of-Hard-Knocks gets you stress headaches, health issues, broken relationships, anger management classes, in-fighting at work, frustration when things do not go as expected, loss of friends, sleepless nights and estranged children and spouses.

You might still do the exact same actions and have the exact same plan, but your vibration and felt sense using the left column will yield faster, better results. Play with the Effortless Approach and see how you feel today.

> *"All achievement and all earned riches have their start with an idea…*
> *a state of mind that requires little or no hard work."*
> – Napoleon Hill, *Think and Grow Rich*

Understand how you feel as you take action

Have you heard the notion that it is not so much what you say, but it is how you say it? The same goes for energy investing. ***It is not so much what you do but how you feel as you do it.*** Many of us get caught up in doing and taking action – almost mindlessly. Being busy almost seems like a competitive sport these days and I agree it feels better to do something than to do nothing.

But taking action while you feel miserable or poor is not nearly as powerful as doing the same action when you feel empowered and hopeful. The law of attraction matches how you vibrate or how you feel. So even if you are doing what you think is the *right thing*, if you are feeling scarcity/fear/worry while you do it you are not getting the maximum return from your actions. If you can, take a few breaths – even something as simple as breathing can adjust your energy – then take a moment and feel the Wealth-Source around you, available for you to tap into it. Remember, you are consciously learning to shift your consciousness and your energy in your chosen direction. So maybe the wisdom of the 7 Dwarfs can help:

Whistle while you work. Feel good and empowered as you do what you are doing and make the most of your energy investing.

An effort-less energy investing example...

I love the business creation story of Playboy creator Hugh Hefner. Mr. Hefner had an inspiration to create a magazine and a life approach that embraced sexuality and sensuality and provide men with a classy venue for their natural urges. To get clear about this new approach, he locked himself in a room and spent 3 days writing his philosophy and what he wanted to create with this new enterprise he was undertaking. In essence what he wrote was his vision statement and what he created in his mind and body was his "success story". He invested his life-energy into a powerful success vibration of **this-is-what-it-feels-like energy** to bring his vision to reality. What he did was immerse himself in the idea until it became a done-deal in his mind and body (What I call feelizing – feeling and visualizing. We will discuss this more in Chapter 9). He said that 3 weeks later he was able to purchase the Playboy mansion by taking out a mortgage and raising money from investors and what would later become known as Playboy, he was off to the races. Heff said that the time he spent creating the vision statement - feelizing the successful wealth experience - was what set the whole thing in motion. He was clear and then it all took off...with relative ease and effortlessness. [1]

> *"The object isn't to make art, it's to be in that wonderful state which makes art inevitable."* ~Robert Henri

Be in that Wonderful State Which Makes Wealth Inevitable

Heff was in that wonderful state which made his art inevitable. And that is what I wish for you too as you explore and read; to cultivate that wonderful state which makes your wealth inevitable. Some call it being "in the zone", others call it "in the flow" and I am calling it "Wealthy". Investing in our wealth consciousness facilitates us into that wonderful state where we feel joyful, playful and excited about the magical possibilities of our lives. And

---

[1] Example taken from E! True Hollywood Story: Hugh Hefner and the Playboy Empire.

inevitably from that consciousness springs wealth of all kinds, from financial wealth to a wealth of health, enjoyment and many other forms of wealth.

◎ Investment Tip: Play with Gently Down the Stream

Sometimes, we are taught songs and rhymes as kids that actually are little instructions for how to live life. One of the classics is: "Row, row, row your boat gently down the stream, merrily, merrily, merrily, merrily life is but a dream." This is a perfect song instructing about effortlessness, about creation and about life. First, the tune is pretty catchy, you have to admit. It is just fun to sing...so that is something right there, you feel good when you sing it. Then it says "gently down the stream," which implies that the stream is supporting you, the stream of life is there, gently bringing you down to a new destination, effortlessly. Just row and go with the flow, merrily are magical instructions for creating. And finally, the life is but a dream...so don't take it so seriously.

Play with rowing gently down the stream by relaxing your face muscles right now and feel ease in this moment. Ease in this moment is a wonderful way to put yourself in that inevitable state. Play with going with the flow by being gentle and kind to yourself right now. Play with doing whatever you are doing, merrily. Enjoy singing the little tune. Play with not taking it all so seriously and see how that makes you feel; see how wealthy that makes you feel.

"You will be effortlessly filled with as much as you can open yourself to receive." –Bryant McGill

Remember…

- Expand your definition of investing to include that it is a way to consciously focus your energy.
- Expand your definition of Wealth to include it is an abundance or profusion of anything and everything.
- You can develop the ability to be in that wonderful state that makes wealth inevitable.
- Wealth does not require hard work and difficult effort.
- Wealth Consciousness creates a wealthy reality.
- Wealth Unlimited Wealth (WUW) is here for you always and in all ways.

Frequently Asked Questions

1. **How can I make the leap to believing that wealth is already here waiting for me?** To be honest, is it not that big of a leap once you start developing your Wealth Consciousness. Nor is it hard to imagine you have the power to attract wealth once you understand magnetics and the power of the law of magnetic attraction. As I invested in understanding these unseen forces and how I could use them, I felt very comfortable making the leap that Wealth is already here and I can turn on my faucet to allow it – and hopefully at some point you will be too.

2. **So Big Wealth is different than little wealth, whaaa?** Big Wealth is an abundance or profusion of anything and everything and as we open our faucet to it and direct it with our thoughts, words, and feelings, we create our unique wealth reality. Everything is orchestrated through your consciousness. Your consciousness – how you invest your attention, energy and focus in a particular direction – draws it into your reality. Little wealth is the way we usually think of it: wealth equals money…exclusively.

3. **So, what is the connection between Big Wealth and money?** Money is Wealth-Energy physicalized into a particular form. Just like you can use flour to make a cake, or a biscuit or paste; the same basic building block can have different intended outcomes. Your wealth consciousness directs the Big-Wealth-energy building blocks to create money or any other creative vision you have (more on this in the Awakening Chapters).

4. **What should I think of myself as, creator or investor?** Yes, both! You are a creator investing your life energy. And you can look at yourself as an investor that creates by the way you invest your energy. (We will discuss this in Chapter 5 – Awakening to Who You Really Are.) As you think of yourself as a *creator* who is *investing* and an *investor* who is *creating*, empowerment is the key. Feel empowered as you think of yourself as a creator investing in your desires, and feel like all that, as an investor creating your wealthy life!

5. **These concepts hurt my brain already…**Great! That means you are *in it* and considering these new ideas about how to think of Wealth. This all hurt my brain too for a long time, because it was so counter to what I was taught about life and wealth…and it is uncomfortable. But if you stick with it, you will feel so free and alive!

Investment Strategy: I am open to a new definition of Wealth

Invoke This…

Hello, Big Wealth Unlimited Wealth - WUW! I welcome you into my world and into my life! It feels awesome to know that I am connected to you always and in all ways. I am appreciating the continual, unconditional contribution and flow to my well-being.

Hello, Wealth-Energy! I am open to seeing Wealth in a new expanded way that includes abundance, prosperity and unlimited possibility. Wow, that feels so good!

I see how Wealth is available right here for me, sharing with me, caring for me, inspiring me, and holding me dear.

I am ready to see myself as a powerful creator that invests my life energy with intent, focus and clarity.

I am excited to awaken to a new definition of Wealth. And I am excited to experience Wealth, my Wealth, unconditionally.

What a fun Wealth journey we are on! WUW!

These investment strategies appear throughout the book at the end of each chapter to assist you in speaking in a new, powerful way about your connection to Wealth. Think of them as invocations of sorts. Read them with the intention to invoke your experience of True Wealth. Speak them out loud several days in a row or when you need to readjust your vibration to help reinforce developing your wealth consciousness.

Chapter 2: The Easy-Does-It Investing Process

The Easy-Does-It Process is a play-filled approach to Wealth Creation, where we remember that at the essence of all of life is unlimited abundance, and unconditional prosperity available to us - just because. Easy-Does-It is meant to help you relax and feel less resistant and thus allow more enjoyment, more wealth and all things good to flow! Sweet- right?!

Introduction to the Easy-Does-It Investing Process

We are undertaking a journey that is different than the traditional hard-effort, action-oriented approach many take to wealth. The *effortless approach* is based on flow and ease, allowing and enjoying. To this end, the Easy-Does-It investing process helps us look at ourselves and at life from a playful vantagepoint. Throughout this journey, we are going to play with learning to allow our wealth. We are going to enjoy seeing the world in a new way, and we are going to expand our ability to invest our life-energy in a conscious and clear way. The Easy-Does-It approach reminds us to be *easy* about it and encourages us to relax, so we see how life can surprise and delight us

Part of the Easy-Does-It-Process is creating a Wealth Habit where you see and agree that life is a magical, unlimited, abundant, unconditional playground for desire-fulfillment. The process helps you to use your creating tools *that have always been within* you to attract to you all you desire and more.

Fundamental to the Easy-Does-It-Process is the belief that you are a powerful creator with the ability to consciously focus your energy on the things that you feel will move you closer toward the life you want to be living.

An understanding of the basics of magnetics is very helpful to allow yourself to embrace this experience. We are going to invest in understanding and utilizing the unseen energetic system that is at work all around us, always: The Law of Attraction. Like the law of gravity, the Law of Attraction is always operating whether we are conscious of it or not. The Easy-Does-It process helps you work with and capitalize on the power of this Law of Attraction.

So as we continue on, it is powerful to embrace these 3 wealth concepts:

1. Unlimited Wealth (WUW) is flowing (to you) - always and in all ways.
2. Wealth is unconditionally available (to you).
3. You allow this Wealth into your life by cultivating an *allowing vibration*, by efforting less and enjoying more, by agreeing to it and by listening to your inner guidance system to choose actions, experiences and things that feel uplifting. Easy ☺.

The Stages of the Easy-Does-It Investing Process

The Easy-Does-It process is written as a linear process, but don't let that hold you back. Just jump in and use the process however it feels good to you. Think of it as more circular, like a wealth wheel, jumping in where you are at this moment. Use it as a living process that you move in and through over the course of your ever-expanding prosperity journey. The seven stages of the Easy-Does-It Process are:

1. AWARENESS – of what are we feeling/believing right now
2. ALCHEMIZE – transforming old beliefs to new energy
3. AWAKEN – to new understandings of ourselves and life
4. ALIGN – to the WUW unlimited wealth all around
5. ATTRACT – clarifying what you want
6. ALLOW – welcoming what you have intended
7. AMAZE – noticing what is flowing in

Awareness
Of Your Past

Alchemize
Your Beliefs

Awaken
Your Power

Align
Your Energy

Attract
Your Dreams

Allow
Your Desires

Amaze
Yourself

- **AWARENESS:** We start by understanding where we are at right now by becoming aware of what we think, feel and believe about Wealth and our ability to have it. In the "awareness" stage of the Easy-Does-It process, we will create a base-line understanding of our current wealth belief system and reality. This is very helpful because we cannot change that which we do not know we are agreeing to. There is so much clarity that comes when we become aware of how we have been feeling about (thus investing in) wealth and money. These are topics that take up a tremendous amount of our energy, but in which we rarely invest consciously to understand and transform our behavior and beliefs from an energy investment perspective. It is through *awareness* that we get clarity on how we might be scarcity investing and getting in our own way.

- **ALCHEMIZE:** Once we have clarity and awareness about beliefs and agreements that might be keeping our Wealth at bay, we can consciously transform our energy. By working through a few exercises to alchemize our old beliefs, we can let go of the stuck beliefs and free that stifled energy and make it available to invest in the new Wealth experience we desire.

- **AWAKEN**: One of the most powerful things we can do is give ourselves the opportunity to awaken to some new ways to look at life from a Wealth perspective and build our new Wealth Consciousness. We will discuss the creating technologies (covered in Chapter 5) that facilitate our creative urges. We will also explore many new ideas about life and wealth that will support your Wealth Consciousness Portfolio.

- **ALIGN**: Next, we will see how to align our vibration to Wealth. This is really about seeing Wealth and feeling wealthy. Once we awaken to the truth of Wealth's availability and accessibility in our life, it will be easier to relax into trusting life and allowing all manner of Wealth to flow to us. Aligning to Wealth is the way we cultivate feeling Wealthy in a conscious, deliberate way.

- **ATTRACT**: The next "step" is to invest our energy toward creating the wealth we wish to experience. In this stage, we will consciously engage the Law of Attraction and work through some investment tools and processes to help us attract the wealth we desire by applying the creation technology tools in a focused way.

- **ALLOW**: The next step is allowing, which is flowing with life in grace and ease to *allow* the wealth we have intended to come to us... because not only do we need to intend to be wealthy, we need to agree to it, we need to allow it. In the Allow step of the Easy-Does-It Process, we will talk of what it feels like when we partner with life, working with its abundant nature and welcoming it to benefit us.

- **AMAZE**: The last "step" in the process is really noticing the amazing changes that are happening as a result of this investment strategy. You will be amazed at the things that are happening in your life and you will amaze yourself at how much fun you are having creating.

The Easy-Does-It investing process helps you consciously apply yourself in a mindful way to create the wealth experience you are intending.

Invest in Keeping a Wealth Journal

As we are discussing, it powerful to set your intention to feel wealthy and then notice the wealth tat comes. A while ago, I wanted to teach myself to win the lottery. So, over the course of a month, I played the lottery every day and journaled about it. As I played and journaled, I learned many things about how my mind worked, how I felt about the lottery and winning and losing, so much came to me. It was such a valuable experience.

One of the most wonderful things I learned is that *I win the lottery every day.* (Every day, I virtually won the lottery because I had unexpected experience that made me go "wow, thank you, that was great!") Things like, getting an extra cookie with the lunch I just bought, to a cat letting me pet it for 5 minutes, to enjoying a jet-ski ride on a lake. These things feel like lottery wins to me. And by journaling about my lottery journey and capturing those "lottery wins" in my wealth journal...I noticed lottery-like wins. And as the law of attraction works – what you put your attention on grows. See and feel lottery-wins get more lottery wins! Nice!

This is what the wealth journal will do for you. As you intend to feel wealthy, it is powerful to notice wealth experiences as they happen to us every day and write them down. Then you see how much wealth you are experiencing and agree that you are wealthy!

Your wealth journal will become a great repository of wealth feeling and experiencing and *you will notice that you have become the wealth you seek.* Investing in writing into your wealth journal will yield great dividends over time in cultivating your wealth consciousness and thus effortless wealth.

Throughout this book, there are many journaling questions and opportunities for you to explore your thoughts and feelings about what you are learning. Take time to capture your experiences in the journal – you will be glad you did – I promise you.

If you like, decorate your journal to make it feel good and make it something you are creating, something wonderful, special and enlivening.

One other idea is that you can purchase a ready-made **Effortless Wealth**

Journal at TheAbundanceCenter.com. The journal workbook has all of the questions in this book with space to write your thoughts. Bonus – it is a coloring book so you can feel playful as you reflect on your wealth journey.

> *"Listen, dear journal, I will tell you what I will tell no one else."*
> — Ella Gertrude Clanton

Invest secretly for now

You may feel that this is a whole new way to look at the world, and in many ways, it is the opposite of how most of us have been taught or come to believe. Austerity, debt-crisis and all the other fear-factor stuff out there creeps into our psyche and reinforces the scarcity messages. So initially, I am asking you to work through this Easy-Does-It investment journey, secretly. Keep your wealth journey to yourself. You will be tempted to discuss these ideas and concepts with friends, family and people you want to help...but don't—at least not yet. Give these new ideas enough time to root in your own fertile backyard before exposing them to the judgment and assessment of others. Just for a bit, maybe six months, do this investing in the privacy of your own heart and mind.

> *"Deep calm and ease are the state that allows you to move beyond the limitation of your rational mind."* –**The Four Desires** by Rod Stryker

We are creating the "eyes" to see

One of my teachers was telling a story of a student who was learning to "manifest". The student was saying how she was looking for an apartment and of the 23 she looked at, none were good enough. The next day she meditated in the morning before she went out apartment hunting. As she meditated, she felt herself connect and align with the peaceful expanded feeling that comes from meditation and she felt uplifted as she set out for the day. This time, she found just the right place, right away. The student later asked the teacher, "Did I manifest this apartment?" And the teacher responded, "Actually, you manifested the eyes to see it."

As we take this wealth journey, we are investing in the ability to see the wealth that is already here waiting for us. We are investing in the eyes to see the world in a new way. By cultivating your wealth consciousness and understanding that Wealth is here, and always has been...you are creating the eyes to see that which is already here for you.

"Your inner eye is seeing more clearly now...your sense of knowing is becoming more "realized." – Mystery of the Universes, Book Three

We are expanding the pie and creating more pies!

We have all heard the idea that there is a "fixed pie" of opportunity or money and that there is only so much to go around. And if you do not get your piece of the pie you will be left out or miss out (FOMO).

But this is a very old notion. Why do we have to agree to only one pie? Why do we have to assume there is a limitation to the amount of wealth, opportunity or anything else for that matter?

Effortless wealth says, *"I will make more pies!* I love pie and want apple, blueberry and peanut butter pie. I don't have to be limited to just one slice – I can have my cake and eat it too (I know I am mixing my pastry – but you get it right?!)

There are many benefits to cultivating your wealth consciousness. There is the obvious benefit that you will experience more wealth in wonderful new ways and as we expand our wealth consciousness we expand the overall wealth pie and make more pies. The people we interact with will have access to more wealth. The companies we work with and do business with will have access to more wealth. Ultimately, we expand the wealth capabilities of the globe. One of my teachers says that you cannot have world peace until there is prosperity for all. I know that as we develop our wealth consciousness we are making more and more prosperity available for all. More pies! More Pies! Sweet!

"Personal transformation can and does have global effects. As we go, so goes the world, for the world is us. The revolution that will save the world is ultimately a personal one." — Marianne Williamson

Remember...

- The Easy-Does-It-Process will help you powerfully develop your wealth consciousness.
- A journal will help you document your journey and help you capture insights, observations and new understandings.
- It is ok to keep this journey your secret for now.
- You are investing in the eyes to see the wealth all around you. The more you expand your wealth consciousness the more you expand the pie and make more pies for everyone.
- Easy-Does-It means effort-less and enjoy more.

Frequently Asked Questions

1. **Does the journal have to be written or can I type it into my computer?** Do whatever works for you. Some people find it is more clarifying to slow down and write and draw in a journal. Others find it easier to capture ideas directly into their computer and just get the ideas out – fast. Just do something! Make the investment. Send the message to your psyche that this is important and you are making an important investment for your wealth-being.

2. **Does Easy-Does-It matter?** Well for the purposes of our work together yes, very much. But you can keep banging it out. I respect that. I did it for years. My mind would not let me try easy-does-it. I felt like I was being weak or cheating. But over the years, I have been learning that easy-does-it is the more powerful way. Give it a try and see...

Easy-Does-It
Investing Process

A

Awareness
Of Your Past

Alchemize
Your Beliefs

Awaken
Your Power

Align
Your Energy

Attract
Your Dreams

Allow
Your Desires

Amaze
Yourself

Chapter 3: Invest in Awareness!

Awareness is taking time to reflect on past and current wealth beliefs and experiences, so we are clear about what we have come to *agree* to with respect to wealth, richness and prosperity. We cannot change what we are not aware of. This reflection will create a baseline understanding so we are not constantly re-investing based on past agreements but based on new agreements aligned with our new wealth intentions.

You are an Investor Creator

You are a powerful energy investor, and up to this point, your accumulated beliefs and agreements (past investments) about wealth have created your current wealth experience. Please, try not to over react about this. It just is what it is, and the exciting part is that as you gain more awareness about your wealth beliefs, you will feel more powerful to make wealth-supporting investments going forward.

So, it makes sense that if you have been thinking thoughts that are not in alignment with feeling wealthy, it is valuable to become *aware* of them and then decide if you will choose to agree with them going forward. Do you want to continue to invest your valuable life energy into old scarcity beliefs? There are no right and wrong thoughts by the way...only thoughts and beliefs that will bring you closer to what you say you would like to experience or not.

Understand Your Definition of Wealth

One evening I was out with friends and asked them if they felt rich. Did they feel wealthy? As we started to talk, a couple of things came out. First, some of them had not thought about what their definition of wealth was. Second, several of them felt wealthy but not necessarily "rich" with lots of money. My one friend said, "Well, I guess it depends on what you think wealthy is." These are important aspects of wealth: Have you thought about it? Do you know what your definition is? What do you deep in your heart define wealth to be? How do you feel about wealth? What about you as wealthy?.

What I have noticed is that **there is a polarity around defining wealth. Some make it completely monetary**: "I will be really wealthy when my net worth is over $10M." **Others define wealth expansively**, but do not include money. They say, "I don't need money, the love of my family makes me truly wealthy." Either way, both definitions revolve around money at their core. There is no right or wrong answer. But I will caution you that it is ok to include money along with all the other wealth you desire. Allow yourself to create a wealth definition that is expansive and inclusive. This is your definition, so what you want is all that matters right here, right now. So, take a moment and define wealth for yourself...write it down in your Wealth Journal and date it. Over time it might change, you might want to add or modify your definition...that is ok, but for now, use this space for your definition of wealth today and come back in the future and write your definition then.

Wealth Journaling:

• My definition of wealth right now is...

Date:_____

Understand Your Assumptions About How Wealth Comes About – For You

As you think about your definition of wealth, it is beneficial to also think about how you believe wealth comes about. If you think about it, you probably have some deep beliefs about how wealth happens. So we are going to spend a bit of time understanding how you believe wealth happens and what assumptions you hold around *your ability to have and create wealth*. What you believe is possible for you; what it will take for you to have the wealth you desire; who/what outside force will have to cooperate; and if you even think it is possible for you to be wealthy.

"I have concluded that wealth is a state of mind, and that anyone can acquire a wealthy state of mind by thinking rich thoughts." - Andrew Young

Wealth Journaling:

1. What assumptions/beliefs do you have around what it takes to experience wealth? How does wealth happen? What beliefs do you hold about how people end up wealthy? What do people do to be wealthy?
2. What assumptions do you hold around your ability to create wealth? What are you going to have to do to be wealthy? What are you going to have to sacrifice? Can *you* ever be wealthy?
3. What assumptions do you have about the wealth you are creating? What is an appropriate amount of wealth? Do you have to do certain things once you have wealth?
4. What stories did you hear about money and wealth when you were a kid? What how did your dad feel about it? You mom? What money messages did you get?
5. What is your earliest childhood memory about money?
6. How do you feel about the words: Wealth? Money? Richness? Prosperity? The 1%?
7. How do you really feel about you being wealthy?

It is interesting to note if any of your journaling falls into some of these patterns:

If you feel …

- "I do not create much."
- I do not have that kind of power to create."
- "Other people might be able to do this but not me."

All of these fall in the "I am not able to" category.

If you feel...

- "I have to have the right education, contacts, family, upbringing to have wealth."
- "I have to be the right gender, race, religion."
- "I have to have enough money, time, energy, opportunity."

All of these fall in the "I don't have enough of the right stuff"category.

If you feel ... "My wealth desires...

- "...should not be too grand or greedy."
- "...should be responsible and respectable."
- "...should fit some measure of "doing good".

All of these are judgments about what is appropriate to create.

If you feel...

- "It is up to God to decide if I am to be wealthy."
- "It is up to my boss to give me a raise."

These fall in the "it is up to an outside force" (It is not in my hands) category.

What did you notice?

Did any of your journaling show that you feel *"I am not able to"* have the wealth I desire? Or *"I don't have enough of the right stuff"* to create wealth? Or *the wealth I seek needs to be appropriate*? And/or that you are not in charge of your wealth experience as *"it is up to an outside force"*? These are scarcity agreements and it is time to be clear about them and prepare to let them go.

Wealth Journaling:

1. What did you notice? As you review the journaling, what themes did you notice?
2. Did any of the above categories resonate with you?
3. Did any of your experiences fall into similar categories? Which was most predominant?
4. If not, how would you frame them?

"People say that what we are all seeking is a meaning for life. I don't think that is what we are really seeking. I think that what we are really seeking is…the rapture of being alive. That's what it is all about."
– Joseph Campbell

Unquestioned Scarcity Agreements

So now we have a basic understanding of your definition of wealth; how you feel about it; what you believe is possible for you; what it will take for you to have the wealth you desire; who/what outside force will have to cooperate; and if you even think it is possible for you to be wealthy.

Now we'll explore some general scarcity agreements, or the beliefs people hold around wealth, how it comes about, who can have it and who cannot. This is meant to help you unlock some additional scarcity beliefs you might be holding that you do not know you even believe.

For example, if you picked up this book, the idea of effortless wealth – either the effortlessness part or wealth part might not seem possible to you. There is an **unquestioned scarcity agreement** in here…that there has to be a great deal of effort in the creation of wealth. Many of us hold this belief, the unquestioned scarcity agreement that wealth takes difficult effort and you need the right ideas in the right place with the right contacts in the right circumstance and that requires great effort. But what if difficult effort is not what is really needed? What if enthusiasm, inspired action, joyous momentum, and play were used instead of difficult effort? Play your way to wealth (hey that sounds like a great book title!). Change the belief that it has to be difficult and drastically change the experience and outcome.

Clarity is Power

A scarcity agreement is an unquestioned assumption, a rule, a belief, that we hold subconsciously that is a part of the way we look at life and a perspective from which we live life. These are things we have come to agree to as fact and live our lives in alignment with. What I have seen is that people hold onto their scarcity agreements and then create lives that fit within this "set of rules". Thus, they limit what can be, by obeying assumed rules and expectations. Don't do this to yourself. ***Don't limit what can be, by obeying rules that don't exist.***

In this segment, we are going to be questioning these old scarcity agreements we have been making (or might be making) around wealth and how it comes about. Then, we will take the beliefs we just assume to be true and ask, *"Is this really true? Do I want to continue to agree to it going forward? How would I change it?"*

> *"The Power of trying. Want to try something new, but not sure it's worth it? Trust me: it is."* - Jason Feifer editor *Entrepreneur.com*

The 10 Unquestioned Scarcity Agreements

I have boiled the scarcity assumptions into 10 scarcity agreements.[2] This is not meant to be an exhaustive list of all the unquestioned scarcity assumptions we humans make around wealth. We don't have that kind of time, nor should we spend that kind of time! What you need is to get clear about *your* agreements (as quickly as possible), release/modify/change them (as quickly as possible) and then move on (as quickly as possible). Notice I mention as quickly as possible. We humans love drama and trying to fix stuff, but really there is nothing to fix. We go to therapists, talk it over with our friends and family and essentially keep reinforcing the belief. Bluck - better to see it, choose anew about it and move on from it - just that quickly - it is possible – allow it.

The key to remember here is you have been investing in these scarcity

---

[2] The concept of 10 agreements are patterned from similar concepts in the book <u>Conversations with God</u> by Neale Donald Walsh.

assumptions by your agreement. **As we agree with something we invest in it** by reaffirming it and abiding by it in our expectations and actions. Are these what you want to keep investing in? What might you want to invest in going forward?

Please have your wealth journal ready as you read the following section to jot down notes about how you feel as you read each of these agreements. *Also note, in the next chapter (Chapter 4) we will learn a way to let these energy investments go.*

10 Unquestioned Old Scarcity Agreements

1. *Scarcity Agreement #1* – **There is a separation between you and wealth.** Many of us believe that wealth is outside of us, that we are separate from it and different from it. What this creates is a feeling of the need to go out in search of it, to try to obtain it and make it ours. It also creates the misunderstanding that some can have it and some cannot. This separation anxiety grows more acute the more we see our wealth at a distance. Separation is part of the human experience; it makes the human game very interesting. But from the larger energetic perspective, we are all part of an energy ocean. This energy ocean, call it Love or Wealth, permeates everything, is in everything, is the creative building block of everything. And this "Wealth-Energy" creates interconnectedness; a oneness that unites everything together. So, there is no separation between you and wealth. You are actually Wealth-Energy personified.

   ❖ Better to invest in a new wealth agreement that there is no separation between you and wealth and that you are made of the same energetic building blocks as the Wealth-Energy.

Wealth Journaling:

- Do I agree wealth is separate from me? When have I felt this?

- Do I want to continue to agree to this going forward?
- If I made a new choice about me and my wealth connection what would it be?

2. *Scarcity Agreement #2* – **There is judgment around wealth.** Judgment creates assessment that there is a right way and a wrong way to create wealth and a right way and a wrong way to be wealthy. For many of us, we judge harshly because we have been judged harshly and we fear the reprisal that comes from that judgement. We become afraid to have what we want or be what we are drawn to in our *hearts*. With social media – judgement has become a national past time. And that judgement of what is good, what is better and how is best can really suppress our true desires and heartfelt urges. But the Wealth-Energy truly is judgement free. It is hard for us to imagine but energy is energy. How we use it, is at our discretion. And when we follow our heartfelt urges and listen to the calling of our souls, we will find we are creating wealth scenarios and experiences that are a win, win, win for all involved.

   ❖ Better to invest in a new wealth agreement that there really is no judgment around what you want. What you want is what you want...and it is ok to want what you want - judgment-free.

Wealth Journaling:

- Have I judged others wealth? Have I been judged harshly? What has been the effect on my wealth due to this?
- Do I want to continue to agree to this going forward?
- If I followed my heart – what would I do and feel?

3. *Scarcity Agreement #3* - **You are not worthy to have wealth.** The roots of worthiness are deep in our cosmology. Many of us are told we are born flawed, or inadequate in some fundamental way. Or that we need to be deserving of wealth. From the get go, we are not sure we are worthy of the wealth or the good things we desire. So, we decide we will *earn* our way and thus we will be worthy and

deserving of wealth. And if we are not experiencing wealth, we must be doing something wrong, or are just not worthy of wealth.

Or, we think we need to have the "right stuff" in order to experience wealth. And many of us are not sure if we do. Do we have what it takes to be wealthy? Many of us limit ourselves because we feel we do not have the right education, or the right contacts, or the right family or upbringing. Some feel we have to be the right gender, race and/or religion. If we don't have enough money, time, energy, opportunity, luck, we will not be wealthy. What is interesting about all of these judgments is that they are based in scarcity. All of these fall in the "I don't have enough of the right stuff" category. Well, I hope you are sitting down, because I want to tell you a huge secret: You were born with the right stuff. You are not inadequate in any way. Wealth is available for all of us equally, unconditionally.

For many of us, we end up in an endless cycle of feeling inadequate and then trying to prove our worth. It almost feels like an epidemic in our culture. But the unquestioned assumption that you are NOT worthy and not doing enough triggers the law of attraction, which feels our vibration and attracts more experiences of "not worthy, not doing enough." This makes it feel like you can never get ahead. Don't go there any more - just don't. You are worthy of all good things, period. You are a glorious being, born from the wealth of all goodness and have the essence of amazing. It is time to agree to your greatness and let this whole question of worthiness go - it is so last century...really.

❖ Better to invest in a new wealth agreement that your worthiness is not the question. Agreement is what is needed. Agreement that you have equal-access to the Wealth-Energy. Forget the question of: "AM I good enough?" And start declaring, "YES, I AM!"

Wealth Journaling:

- How have I let unworthiness and/or feelings of inadequacy get in the way of my wealth experience?

- Do I want to continue to agree to this going forward?
- If I made a new choice about me and my wealth worthiness what would it be?

4. *Scarcity Agreement #4 –Wealth is conditional.* Conditionality is so ingrained into believe systems: *if you want this you need to do that.* You can only have wealth *if* X happens. Conditionality is different than consequentiality. Conditionality says certain things must be present **before** we can experience our desires. Consequentiality is an **end**-result of our actions. The problem with conditionality is that you are always chasing some magical combination of conditions under which you will "get wealth." To be honest this made me very angry in the past. I felt frustrated and all kinds of not-so-good things because it seemed I could never line up this required set of conditions (whatever they were).

   What I have come to know is that wealth is always flowing, unconditionally. I have made a deep journey into the underling building blocks of life and have found them to be incredibly loving and wealth promulgating. When we can know this and feel it deeply, we become less worried about chasing after some magical set of conditions and become more enticed by feeling wealthy and allowing the results of that wealth-essence materialize into our reality.

   ❖ Better to invest in feeling wealthy no matter what the outside conditions are. Wealth-Energy is always flowing, well-being is always flowing. Don't let your current reality conditions dictate your future wealth experience.

Wealth Journaling:

- What conditions do I think need to be present for me to experience being wealthy?
- Do I want to continue to agree to these going forward?
- If I made a new wealth investment about conditionality, what would it be?

5. *Scarcity Agreement #5* - **Sacrifice is necessary to have wealth.**
Many of us believe that we must sacrifice something to have wealth,
whether it is freedom, integrity, family, health - something must be
given up. It feels like the tyranny of the OR. You can have wealth
OR freedom; wealth or integrity; wealth or a happy family, wealth
or your spirituality, but you cannot have both. In fact, many believe
money and the other desires of life are mutually exclusive. Many
believe the way you make money is by having a job and sacrificing
yourself to it, to get paid thus giving up freedom. Others believe
they have to do "unmentionable things", like cheat, lie or some other
forms of putrid behavior which is a sacrifice of their integrity to
have real money; ultimately holding themselves apart from wealth
because they do not want to do "rotten things". There is something
inside of us that seems to "require a transaction" of some sort for
our minds to agree we can have the things we desire...I will give
this, to get that. But sacrifice is not required. There is no fixed pie
of abundance. You expand the wealth-pie just by desiring wealth.
Abundance abounds unconditionally.
   ❖ Better to invest a new wealth agreement that sacrifices are not
   required. You have an unlimited access to the unlimited Wealth
   WUW -Energy.

Wealth Journaling:

- What sacrifices have you made or think you need to make to
experience wealth?
- Do I want to continue to agree to these going forward?
- If I made a new prosperity choice about sacrificing, what would
it be?

6. *Scarcity Agreement #6* - **Scarcity and limitation exist.** This is
fixed-pie-syndrome. Many of us believe there is only so much
money/love/resources to go around. And this not-enoughnesss
thinking is so prevalent and pervading in our world that we just
keep agreeing to it, automatically. But limitation, inadequacy and

the corollary concepts of lack, shortage and only-so-much-to-go around, keep us in scarcity consciousness. The concept of "scarcity" has its place: it helps us make decisions and get clarity. It helps us choose and understand our preferences, but beyond that it has gotten way too much play. It is one of the most powerful reasons we will not allow ourselves to believe in wealth for ourselves, much less wealth for all. Being powerful creators means we can expand the pie, create more pies and create more than enough. **Use your wealth consciousness to take the limitations from the WUW unlimited Wealth-Energy and remove the conditions from unconditional Wealth-Energy.** This is your opportunity to invest in "more-than-enough", unlimited-pies, bounty, abundance and the truth that you are always prospering, growing and creating!

❖ Better to invest in "Wealth Goggles" to see the abundance of plenty all around you and see how much wealth is everywhere. And invest in creating new realities of more-than-enoughness, expanding pies and unlimitedness. Before Roger Bannister in 1954, the four-minute mile did not seem possible. Once he broke the "rule" that it is possible, the four-minute-mile became a new norm. You are a powerful wealth creator; allow yourself to make experiencing Wealth in all its forms your new norm!

Wealth Journaling:

- How has the agreement in scarcity and limitation impacted my beliefs as to what is possible for me?
- Do I want to continue to agree to these going forward?
- If I made a new expanded choice about the impact of scarcity on me, what would it be?

7. *Scarcity Agreement #7* – **Because wealth is hard to come by, difficult effort is required.** In order to have wealth you must work hard and make scarifies, right? Many of us believe that effortlessness is not possible because there has to be a great deal of difficulty in the creation of wealth. Just look at all of these agreements we are

discussing, from "there is a right way and a wrong way", to "sacrifice is necessary", to "wealth is conditional". And we've spent our lives hearing sayings like, "Do you think money grows on trees?" "No pain, no gain." We have seen people try really hard to have wealth only to feel they have not "made it". All of this leads us to conclude that wealth is hard to come by and rightly so. Many of us have struggled and continue to struggle for our wealth. And so by the law of attraction, struggle creates more struggles.

This is why this book is called Effortless Wealth. Effortlessness, flow, enjoyment, create more effortlessness, flow and enjoyment. I know at this point all of this might just sound like platitudes, but as we become conscious investors of our energy, when we decide we are going to invest in new ways, one of the big agreements we need to start to alchemize (transform) is the difficulty with which our wealth comes. Remember, we are creating the eyes with which to see. See that abundance, prosperity, and love is around us always and in all ways. Now, we are creating the eyes with which to see it. We are investing in a new way of agreeing to the world so we can experience it in a whole new way. And at some point very soon, you too will have created the wealth consciousness to "see" the wealth all around you and "agree" that it is there for you to enjoy...freely and effortlessly.

❖ Better to invest in the new wealth agreement that effortless flow yields better results. Intend to notice the magnificent unlimitedness and the sheer magnitude of power that is churning out everything from billions of new cells in our body, to unconditional solar power, to go-zillions of cosmic dust particles, all without one bit of effort on our part. Wealth is always wealthing - see it everywhere and be dazzled!

Wealth Journaling:

- How has the agreement in difficult effort impacted my experience of wealth?
- Do I want to continue to agree to these going forward?

- If I made a new effort-less choice about how to experience wealth, what would it be?

8. *Scarcity Agreement #8 - **Wealth will impact you negatively.*** We have all seen or heard stories of "wealthy people gone bad" using money as a tool to control or manipulate or just be nasty. From Scrooge to Gordon Gekko in the movie *Wall Street*, wealthy people are usually not all that beloved. And we have all seen those scary stories about lottery winners having terrible things happen to them after they "got the money". From the negative press, to the ugly uses of money - why would anyone want to be wealthy? It sounds like risky business. In fact, so risky, we are probably better off not having the hassles. And deep down, we might just be saying just that and unconsciously feeling we don't want wealth because of how it will change our lives and make people see us differently or treat us differently. If we become wealthy, we will lose our friends and become one of those lonely, miserable rich people we don't like or people will just like us for our money. So, best to keep myself where I am, we may think. But, it is in our very best interest to create a new reality for ourselves around all of this. You are a powerful creator! You don't have to agree to create any of this negativity! You get to create yourself into the kind of wealthy person you want to be. And you can start by envisioning yourself as the uniquely wealthy person you are! See it, feel it, believe it. You are on a unique wealth creation path that is fresh and uncharted. Allow yourself the grace and magic of becoming the wealth (and wealthy person) you seek.
   ❖ Better to invest in the new wealth agreement that you get to create your wealth experience, your way, and that you will be a unique wealth way-shower who operates from a deep sense of connectedness to their inner wealth-spring.

Wealth Journaling:

- Has the unquestioned agreement around the negative effects of wealth impacted me? How?

- Do I want to continue to agree to these going forward?
- If I made a new prosperity choice about wealth's impact on me, what would it be?

9. *Scarcity Agreement #9* - **Your wealth needs to be appropriate.** Many of us believe there is appropriateness about the amount of wealth we are creating and the appropriate uses of the wealth; it should not be too grand or greedy. We should be responsible and respectable using it. It should fit some measure of "doing good and have a higher purpose." All of these are judgments about what is appropriate to create. One of my teachers says, "God does not judge if seven Rolls Royces are too many - we do!" And this gets right to the heart of how we limit ourselves with these rules of appropriateness we are agreeing to. What I have found is that when you let go of all these rules, you let the possibilities flow. We relieve ourselves of the assumed burdens of wealth and the resistances we may have to prosperity. And when resistance releases - good things flow.

    Better to invest in the new wealth agreement that as a creator you determine what is appropriate and that if you desire it, there must be a reason. Agree to honor the yoga tenant of "do no harm", then invest your life energy freely.

Wealth Journaling:

- Do I feel my wealth need to be appropriate? Has this agreement impacted my experience of wealth?
- Do I want to continue to agree to this going forward?
- If I made a new choice about how to experience wealth, what would it be?

10. *Scarcity Agreement #10* - **An outside force can withhold your wealth from you.** We have come to agree that it is up to some outside entity to decide or distribute wealth to us – from the company we work for to God. What this creates is the feeling that our wealth is not in your hands (it is in my boss's hands) and is not really up to us. Deep down, we feel our wealth can be withheld from us because we do not

deserve it; we have not earned it, or have done something wrong, so we cannot have it. We may have concluded that life does not want us to be wealthy. Or we were told by a well-meaning other that wealth is not possible for all of us. Or that the 1% are hoarding it.

For a great many of us, we have an unquestioned assumption that is up to God to decide if we are to be wealthy. And many of us think God has a grudge about money (because someone once said money is the root of all evil, or something like that). So we assume God probably does not want us to be wealthy?!

All of these agreements and their many corollaries are assumptions about how you will get wealth and if you will experience wealth. And this is one of the most powerful assumptions to address head-on, because your wealth is your choice. Wealth is never withheld. Whether you experience wealth is within *you* to agree to. And when you decide to be wealthy you will be. It is law. When you decide to invest in knowing you have free, equal access to the Wealth-Energy, just watch as all of life supports you to make this truth a physical tangible manifestation of the decision you are making and have made: that you have decided unequivocally that you are wealth and wealth is yours.

❖ Better to invest in the new wealth agreement that *you—not an outside force—decide* about your wealth experience. You are your wealth creator and your wealth cannot be withheld - ever. Make a fervent declaration that this is so and a new wealth reality will start to fill in around you.

Wealth Journaling:

- Have I agreed that some outside force has the power to withhold my wealth? What is this force? Why would it withhold from me?
- Do I want to continue to agree to this going forward?
- If I made a new choice about my wealth experience, what would it be?

What you might be noticing with all of these scarcity agreements is that much of what we have come to agree to in our society about wealth and success makes life much harder than it needs to be and makes experiencing wealth much harder than *it was meant to be.*

We are in the process of becoming *aware* of the difficulty and old hard knocks approach to wealth. This awareness will start the process of release and renewal inherent on the path of easy-does-it wealth investing.

More Wealth Journaling:

- As you review these unquestioned assumptions, which ones stand out for you? What is the biggest unquestioned assumption that is between you and being rich? Write it down and get clear about it. We will be using your response in the Alchemize Chapter.
- Are you going to keep unconsciously investing in these old agreements? What if you keep agreeing to these?
- When are those times when that little voice inside your head says, "I can't be wealthy because...?" Note these and say, "I am not going there anymore!"
- Which of the new investment strategies jumped out to you as one you feel strongly about?

Don't Box-In Wealth

All of these old scarcity agreements put a box around wealth and limit the unlimited potential we all have to create wealth or anything else we desire. These unquestioned assumptions are the ultimate in-the-box-thinking. It is important to see them in order to expand our ability to enjoy the wealth we seek. Because before you can consciously create wealth, you need to really believe you can. There are going to be times when the little or not-so-little voice in your head says, *wealth is hard to come by, life is difficult, wealth is for some and not for others, I need to find the right way*, or whatever old agreements you have made to this point. They are part of your old portfolio and we are investing in a new wealth portfolio that believes wealth is available to all, unconditionally. **Your experience of wealth gets to be uniquely an expression of you, with no rightness or wrongness because wealth is never withheld.**

New Wealth Agreements

Now is a perfect time to get down a starter list of the new wealth agreements you might want to consider for your life going forward. We It is all in your journal – take a moment to summaries them now. If we were to just look at the old scarcity agreements and flip them to be the NEW WEALTH AGREEMENTS. They would read like this:

1. There is *no separation* between you and wealth.
2. There are *no judgments* around the wealth you desire.
3. You are *totally worthy* to have wealth, in fact worthiness is not even a consideration.
4. Your wealth is *un-conditionally* yours *and there is plenty for all.*
5. Sacrifice is *not* necessary.
6. Scarcity and limitation *do not exist.*
7. Wealth is *easy to come by.*
8. Wealth will impact you *as you decide.*
9. Your wealth *does not need to be appropriate.*
10. Your wealth *can never be withheld* from you.

Wouldn't it be great if these were your new unquestioned wealth agreements?

Wealth Journaling:

- Which of the above **new** agreements would you be willing to embrace? Why do you think?
- Which of the above new agreements feel just plain wrong? Can you feel into why?
- How would you rewrite the new agreements in a way that you can embrace?

> What you have come to believe and what you agree to, create your experiences in life...And you decide what you are going to believe and agree to by the ideas you continue to invest in.

Use this space to create your list of new wealth agreements:

MY NEW WEALTH AGREEMENTS

- I deserve wealth, unlimited wealth.
- I love money and money loves me.
- Abundance and wealth are my birthright.
- I am wealth, abundance and joy.
- Money flows and comes to me easily & frequently.
- I have a surplus of money always.
- I decide to receive wealth & money
- Wealth is un-conditionally mine
- I rest, play and enjoy money with pleasure
- I am wealthy now!

Have you been keeping yourself poor?

Can you see how all of these unquestioned assumptions might be exactly what has been keeping your wealth at bay? This probably is a very tough question for you and might actually make you angry. You may be thinking: *What are you talking about? I am not keeping myself poor, I would never!* This is good; anger is energy – great transformative energy that can take you in fresh directions (mostly because you're sick of what keeps triggering your anger in the first place).

What I have seen over and over is that **we keep ourselves poor (resist our natural prosperity) because we are honoring the teachings and feelings of someone or something in our lives.** Sit with this for a moment. Out of love or respect for someone or something in your life, have you *agreed* to stay poor or just break-even or just make ends meet because that is what you saw your mother, father, or family do? It is out of a "child's love" for the parent that many don't want to excel forward? If you think this is not you, you might be very surprised to find it is.

I realized after a dinner with my dad several years ago that for all his years in business he really only wanted to break even...not too much, not too little. We were talking about his business and he said, *"I don't need much, just enough to pay my bills."* I realized later that this was a break-even energy investment on his part. He was pouring life energy into his business and it made enough money to break even at the end of the month. And I was doing that with my business, too. I was thinking, *well as long as I cover my "nut" I am ok.* What?! What?! What?! OMG, I thought, I am doing what my dad did. That is how he thinks and feels and I am doing the same. I was honoring his values and approach and I did not even realize I was doing it!

And I have seen many others do the same thing of honoring their heritage instead of forging forth past the past:

- An adult daughter keeps herself working very hard but really only just scraping by because that is what her mom had to do to give them a life start here in America after World War II.
- An adult male keeps himself poor because if he does financially better than his dad they will not have a relationship because his father will feel threatened.

- A mother keeps herself poor so she does not have to tell her addicted child she cannot give him money (she can't she has none) just like her mom did to her.

We end up unconsciously feeling that, since our parents struggled, we have to as well. My family did not have much money but we were happy. If I have money I might not be happy. I will honor my family by staying "within their means". Harv Eker calls these habits your wealth blueprint in his very well written book, **Secrets of the Millionaire Mind: Mastering the Inner Game of Wealth.** Your wealth blueprint keeps you unconsciously following a wealth approach created long ago.

The amazing thing is we do not realize we are doing it. Birds of a feather flock together. We keep ourselves poor so others, our friends, etc. still like us - so we can keep flocking together. It is a decision we made when we were very young and now it is a part of us. It is ok. See it, feel it, acknowledge it. It was something you decided long ago and are now maybe "seeing" for the first time. And that which is brought into the light of day can be worked with.

Wealth Journaling:

- Have you been honoring someone in your family or heritage because that is what has been done? How?
- Have you been keeping yourself poor? Why? Do you want to continue to?
- How would you like to move forward and do instead?

◉ Investment Tip: Invest in Possibility

Worry is a wasted energy. Fear and its brothers worry, doubt and guilt all create emotion in us that can attract what we don't want to have happen because sometimes "what we fear, we draw near." Better to come from a place of possibility and attract what you want. Take any fear statement you have and move it to a possibility statement. Instead of, "I am afraid I will fail." Say, "There are many possibilities on the horizon and any one of them can bring me the success I desire." Learn to invest in possibility by finding fresh statements that speak to your success.

The agreement of postponing life until …

One scarcity habit many have is that we agree we cannot enjoy life until…fill in the blank: *until I have a great job, until I have the right house in the right neighborhood, until my kids are grown, until college is paid for…*The mental rut is laid and then when we do have the house, we are so used to putting off life, we are so used to sacrificing for wealth, that we keep doing it. Even when we have achieved what we put off life for, we end up putting a bigger goal out there and then chase that. This is the classic "who moved my cheese problem,"[3] where we think someone or something is moving the fulfillment of our goals just out of our reach, only we are the ones moving our own cheese.

So many of us put life on hold *until* we have enough money. But that day never seems to come. That is because the more we live the more desires we create. We ultimately are not satisfied in the moment because there is still more to accomplish and experience. **Don't dish on today because you don't have what is coming tomorrow.** You will have it. Don't stress yourself out with the classic "I am not wealthy until I have a million dollars in the bank." When you get to a million, a million will not seem like enough. So, then you make the goal $2 million, then $10 million. Start loving your life now and the wealth you have now. This is a sure way to enjoy the wealth of the moment.

Wealth Journaling:

- Have you been postponing life? How?
- What do you think needs to happen before you can enjoy yourself?

"There is no path to happiness. Happiness is the path."
– Thich Nhat Hanh

---

[3] Concept from the book *Who Moved My Cheese* by Spencer Johnson.

When investing, change is inevitable

When we are engaged in conscious investing, we are engaging essentially in a process of change. Creating brings about change - it has to - it is the nature of creativity. Life is change. When things do not change, they become stale, stagnant and smelly. In our book *Breakthrough Teams for Breakneck Times* my co-author and I talk of making change into a core competency. That is, it is important to change for change's sake – getting used to it and developing our change muscle for when we really need it. Make change your friend and make little changes every day so you are comfortable with it.

Interestingly, when we create and invest in our new wealth agreements, we are creating something new... a new life experience, a new job, a new business, or a new relationship. One day when I was meditating I heard loud and clear: *for things to change something needs to change!* I wanted these new life experiences but I was holding on to old habits and thought patterns. I was not willing for some things to change. I was afraid. I was worried about my security and the things I liked in my life. I was worried that I would lose what worked. This is a very human thing and it is understandable. It is also where some good old-fashioned mind management is worth instigating. Try to catch yourself in these old fear thoughts and reinvest your thoughts into the changes you are choosing to make, into the new agreements you are practicing, into the new possibilities about Wealth and your connection to it.

> *"I really don't like the word change, I prefer the word adjust,*
> *it does not feel so scary to me."* – Ted LaMantia

Wealth Journaling:

- What am I afraid to lose if my desires happen? What change do I fear most?
- What am I ready to have change?
- What am I willing to change to symbolically show I am ready for things to start moving in the direction I say I want to go?

◎ Investment Tip: Mind Management

Your thoughts, a.k.a. your mind is a creating tool because thoughts are things. They are vibrations that pull experiences to you. But many of us have not really learned to manage our minds and choose our thoughts. To me, this is the reason for the saying, *your mind is a terrible thing to waste.* If you don't manage your mind, you waste your life energy. This investment tip asks us to learn how to manage our minds, so we are creating consciously. Mind management requires:

1. Understanding the role and power of the mind and your thoughts.
2. Learning and practicing how to turn it on and off! (meditation is one of the best ways).
3. Deciding what you are going to focus your thoughts on (journaling is powerful).
4. Consciously focusing your thoughts on what you want – not on what you don't (again, journaling is effective).

Learn to use your mind wisely and you will become one powerful creator!

What scarcity agreement are you ready to let go of?

Find one thing that you are really ready to let go of. This might be the agreement that you are not able to have wealth, or some other very specific memory that seems to stand between you and your desired wealth experience. We will use this belief as fodder for alchemizing in the next chapter.

Wealth Journaling:

The scarcity agreement I am ready to let go of is…

I have to work hard to have money

Please note, this scarcity agreement is one you will play with as we continue our journey.

I will never depend on a man to have money

---

⑥ Investment Tip: I decide!

Sometimes we don't even know that we are doing something until it is mentioned to us. The same goes with experiencing our wealth. Because we usually have many of the unquestioned assumptions from judgments about what is appropriate, to believing we don't have the right stuff, to agreeing to limitation and scarcity, we are virtually saying "NO" to the wealth that is all around us. But these are all agreements we have made.

Stop for a moment and really feel into this. Now is the time to stop the old and make a new investment. Make a new agreement. Start agreeing: *"I now agree I have the power and choice to enjoy to my desired wealth experience."* Right now, you can decide to allow your wealth; you are in charge! No one or nothing outside of you decides - you decide, you allow, you agree! If you can really feel this and own it, you are making a huge leap right over all those old beliefs. Play with this and see how you feel.

Why Not You?

Throughout this chapter, we have been uncovering the reasons we believe wealth is not for us. We are seeing what we have agreed to about what needs to happen in order for us to have the wealth experience we desire. But all that really matters with respect to wealth creation is that you decide you can be wealthy; that success can be yours and it is. The great thing about this process is that YOU are at the center of it as the power investor. What you decide to think about, what you decide to say about your wealth experience, what you decide to believe and agree to and what you do and how you feel when you do it - that is what creates your wealth experience. You are at the helm of that ship. **You decide how wealthy you are going to be.**

> *"The Soul is ever-free; it is death-less because it is birth-less"*
> *– Sri Yukteswar*

Remember…

It is time to invest in these new wealth agreements:

- There is *no separation* between you and Wealth.
- There is *no judgment* around the wealth you desire.
- Your worthiness is not in question with respect to wealth.
- Wealth is *un-conditional.*
- Sacrifice is *not* necessary to have wealth.
- Scarcity and limitation *do not exist.*
- Wealth is *easy to come by.*
- Wealth will impact you *as you decide.*
- Wealth *cannot be withheld* from you.
- You Decide.

Frequently Asked Questions

1. **Why do I have to spend time on this part? Aren't I just investing my attention on the opposite of what I want?** If you are asking this question, you are noticing how the law of attraction is always in action and what we focus on we attract. But we are not meant to dwell here for very long, just long enough to notice our unquestioned agreements. Then we move on. We are not going to spend one more minute here than we need to. And if you can see that all of your old notions are just that—OLD—and you are not going to let them hold you back anymore—yahoo for you. Move on to the attracting step. But what I have seen is the power of awareness combined with alchemizing (the next step in the process) really moves the energy to a new place.

2. **Do I really have to go back and dig up all this old junk?** Interestingly enough, all of these unquestioned assumptions matter, until we decide they don't. We have all had experiences in our past

that shape what we think and believe now. And if those beliefs and experiences serve you (you are experiencing the wealth you desire) then keep honoring them. But if you are not where you wish to be, then it is worth looking at your childhood and the past...briefly. Your upbringing is just the "set up". It is the *start* of the game called life, but it does not have to be the way the game is played forever. Dig only enough to get clarity, then stop, alchemize, reach for something greater and move on!

3. **What do you mean that these agreements are really resistance?** Pick one of the beliefs you have been agreeing to—say, there is only so much wealth to go around. Notice how you feel in your body when you tell yourself this. Do you feel comfortable, at ease and relaxed? My guess is probably not. Well any feeling in your body that makes you uncomfortable, tense, tight, worried, frustrated, anxious etc. acts like a vibrational barrier between you and Wealth. It is like you are a vibrational bubble that your desires bounce off of. That essentially is resistance.

4. **But doesn't God ultimately decide?** In 2006 *Time* magazine published a cover story called, "Does God Want You to Be Rich?" The article went on to discuss the varying viewpoints of different segments of the Christian church. The reason I bring this up is that one of the biggest unquestioned assumptions we hold is that God decides. We want to know what "God thinks" and "God wants". Some people think God is on their side and that God wants for them to be wealthy. Thus, they walk in complete knowledge that they are blessed and honored. But for the vast majority of us who were taught that "money is the root of all evil" or that it is "easier for a camel to pass through the eye of a needle than it is for a rich man to enter the kingdom of heaven" we think God does not look favorably on money and wealth. These little sayings matter because they affect how we feel about our ability to be wealthy. It is worth some deep reflection. If we hold the unquestioned assumption that some outside entity is in charge of our wealth we have given our power away. Free will empowers us to find ways to be prosperous and to share our prosperity freely and joyously.

5. **But doesn't education matter?** We have all heard that Bill Gates did not finish college and there are many multi-millionaires who did not go to college. In fact, one of the powerful findings in the book *The Millionaire Mind* is that education does not matter as much as we think. I am not making the case for blowing off education because I think learning is an important and vital thing we all need to do, all of our lives. But many of us feel that *because* we don't have the *right* education from the *right* school we are disqualified from the wealth we desire. Do not buy into the notion that education or the lack of it means you cannot be wealthy. The data does not support that... and neither should you.

6. **What if I have other agreements I am not aware of?** Don't worry about them! When it is time and if it becomes time, you will start to notice them. But the good news is that as you develop your wealth consciousness, these old agreements start to fade and fall away. You just naturally start replacing old resistant agreements with new wealth-conjuring beliefs. So, relax and enjoy your life.

Investment Strategy:
I Decide about my Wealth Experience

Invoke this...

What a revelation, that the ideas I choose to invest in become the agreements and beliefs I hold which shape my experience in the world.
Therefore, I decide about what I choose to agree to.

What a revelation, that the ideas I have been holding are mine to agree to or not going forward.
Therefore, I decide to agree to new wealth agreements.

What a revelation, that many of the old scarcity agreements are just a product of scarcity-biased thoughts.
Therefore, I decide to invest in thoughts that are wealth-biased.

What a revelation, that wealth is a fundamental building block of life and that abundance abounds.
Therefore, I decide to allow a wealth experience that knocks my socks off!
Yahoo for me!

A

Awareness
Of Your Past

Alchemize
Your Beliefs

Awaken
Your Power

Align
Your Energy

Attract
Your Dreams

Allow
Your Desires

Amaze
Yourself

Chapter 4: Invest in Alchemizing!

Alchemizing is a powerful process of transforming old energy agreements and feelings, which are not serving us any longer, and making the energy available for something greater and aligned with our new wealth investment intentions.

Learn to Release

One of the most difficult things to do as an investor is to know when to get out of certain investments. The Kenny Rogers song puts it pretty well: "You need to know when to hold 'em and know when to fold 'em, know when to walk away, know when to run." We stick with certain investments, even though they are not yielding the results we would like. We get attached to certain approaches even when we know there are more effective methods out there. We get used to spending our energy in a certain way on a day-to-day basis that might not be for our highest and best good, especially when those behaviors leave us without enough energy for our desires and our dreams because they leave us feeling guilty, small or inadequate.

The purpose of the Alchemizing process is to release our energy from old investments (i.e. scarcity beliefs, agreements, habits) and put it toward new ones that are more aligned with our wealth desires. As we let go of the old holdings and old approaches, which in our body usually feels like resistance or stuckness, we can transform the energy that those behaviors occupied to make it available for new experiences. Our work in the last chapter, Awareness, hopefully brought some clarity and insight into your old thoughts and beliefs about wealth, money and how it all comes about. In this step, we are going to Alchemize and transform those deeply held, unconscious and least beneficial scarcity agreements. As we do this, we release the resistance energy that keeps us in the old scarcity patterns.

"Change is hard because people overestimate the value of what they have – and underestimate the value of what they may gain by giving that up." – James Belasco & Ralph Stayer

Releasing Resistance

At this point in our journey, we are becoming aware of the old scarcity agreements that have created our wealth experience to this point. These beliefs are a combination of thoughts and feelings held for a long time. David Hawkins in his powerful book, *Letting Go*, notes that, "**All thoughts are held in your mind's memory bank under a** *filing system* **based upon the** *associated feeling*. **They are filed according to** *feeling tone* – **not fact.** And the thoughts associated with even *one feeling* can run into the thousands!" *So, it is advantageous to pay attention to the feelings – more so than the thoughts.* Addressing your feelings about money and wealth will help you make rapid releasing progress vs dealing with each of the individual thoughts.

If you stop for a moment and feel into these old beliefs they probably feel heavy, confining or limiting. These negative feelings and many others like worry, anger, frustration, blame, shame and not-enoughness – are all a form of *resistance*. Resistance feels like a blockage to the natural abundant Wealth flow that is at the core our of life. Release the resistance and we become available to be in flow and to feel the Wealth of life flow through us.

The alchemizing process assists us in releasing and transforming these resistant blocking energies to allow for your natural Wealth to flow.

*"Handling an issue from the intellectual level will produce thousands of thoughts & scenarios that overwhelm and cause many sleepless nights due to the racing thoughts. All of this is fruitless – **until the underlying feelings are addressed; the thoughts will continue endlessly.**"*
– David Hawkins in *Letting Go: The Pathway of Surrender*

Let go of the old holdings to make room for new

There is a wonderful book called *The Journey Home* by Lee Carroll. It is a story of a young man on his spiritual journey. Before leaving on his journey, Michael Thomas (the hero) packs a sack of important things he thinks he will need on his trip. The bag is filled with photo albums and other mementos of his life...treasures that he has *accumulated* that remind him of his past. On the journey, he faithfully carries the bag through many trials and tribulations. After a great ordeal, he ends up in a terrible storm and is faced with death unless he releases his sack and runs for shelter. After trying desperately to save his mementos he lets them go and runs to safety. He is devastated that he lost the pictures of his beloved mother and father and the other treasures of his old past life.

As he was grieving the loss of his mementos (which was totally appropriate) he heard a voice in his head saying, *the journey you are on requires you to let go of your past baggage so you are free to travel unencumbered.* This of course is a metaphor for our lives... our past, good or bad, is just that - our past.

To move on in our wealth journey, we need to be free from the expectations, assumptions and hurts of our past baggage so we can be free to experience and enjoy the now moment, as it is, as it can be, based on who we are now and who we are choosing to be; not as we think it should be based on who we were.

"Create your future, from your future...not your past. In many ways enlightenment is just that...lightening our load, releasing the old emotional and physical baggage to make room for the new."- Big-Laurie ☺

As we discussed in Chapter 3, over time we have accumulated old scarcity habits, beliefs, feelings, thought patterns, experiences, etc. that become scarcity baggage. It is time to clean out the sack, but as with all things, it is our choice to let the baggage (scarcity agreements and the associated feelings) go. Like the old adage says, *what we resist persists.*

Please note, you do not have to do this. But keep in mind that baggage is heavy and slows us down. Some of us create very elaborate cart systems, like anger or *I can't*, to help us carry our baggage with us from day-to-day because we think we have to or we should or everything will fall apart. We are free to do this, and the older we get the more attached to our scarcity habit baggage we get, interestingly enough. *But it is easier to dance with life, to skip and play, when we are free and light in heart, mind and body.*

It reminds me of a story about Marg, who knew her power to create. She had been consciously directing her energy to attract a new job. After a short time, she found a wonderful job in the industry she wanted, working with people she adored and doing work she found rewarding – perfect. The trouble was that she had to take the train to get to work and Marg was claustrophobic. So much so, that when she was meditating she said, "I really love my new job but we are going to have to find a new one – I cannot stand riding the train anymore!" Then she heard from her inner wisdom, *"Instead of giving up the job you love...why not release the fear of small places? Intend to let that go, use your power of creation to create peace on the train."* What a concept for Marg! Instead of continuing to work around her fear, she could walk right into it, surrender it and transform it.

> *"Let it go, let it go, can't hold it back any more.*
> *Let it go, let it go, turn way and slam the door...*
> *its time to see what I can do to test the limits and break through!"*
> - Princess Elsa in the movie *Frozen*

The Power of Surrender

For many of us, the concept of surrender brings up feelings of defeat and loss. To surrender is to give up and feel the pain of not succeeding. And because we do not want to feel this way, we resist surrendering – which is logical. But if we can release the negative connotations behind surrender, it can become a great tool to open the energy channels because we are letting go of all the stress and resistance around it. As we journey on into alchemizing, feeling the relief that surrender brings is a wonderful way to allow the freshness of wealth to flow. And what I am learning is that if you surrender trying to figure something out, you come to something truly profound and life giving – something can finally become apparent – because we are not blinded by the stuck scenarios. Earlier, we talked about creating the eyes to see; surrender and letting go really provides that spaciousness to finally see.

Surrender is a felt sense of relief. As you let go, you can feel the muscles in your neck and shoulders relax, you can feel the pain in the back of your neck and jaw release. This is only the start of the power of surrender. As the tension goes away, spaciousness comes forward and new possibilities and awareness's come to light. Surrender is a powerful tool because it opens up the natural flow of all things good including wealth.

We have all heard stories of a couple trying to get pregnant, trying all manner of IVF and other means to no avail. Then they finally surrender to the fact it is not going to happen. So, they start to look into adoption and before they know it, not only are they going to receive a beautiful being through adoption but they also find out they are pregnant! This is the power of surrender.

And you might be saying – I can't surrender. I can't give up the fight. If I do terrible consequences will come, like my security will be in jeopardy or things will fall apart...people will get hurt. Yes, I know, I have had all of those thoughts and feelings too. But, now I know two things about surrender:

1. *I can't* usually means, *I won't*. "I can't surrender this because if I do things will fall apart." But really, *I can* surrender the feelings, worries, doubts and all the other heaviness. I could if I wanted to.
2. Once I do surrender, something comes about that solves the problem or helps me move forward in some way that was previously blocked. And the sense of relief feels so wonderful.

A surrender example: I was dealing with an issue in our business. We were asked by our landlord to move our manufacturing facility. This is a huge expense and upheaval! I had been resisting the move and really *fighting* the whole idea. Plus, the alternatives seemed completely unacceptable. I was struggling and pretty angry. Then I got a migraine (well several) and said, *I just cannot do this anymore*. I started the process of surrender. I did some letting go of the fear around the move, I did some letting go of the anger that we were going to have to upheave the operations. I did some releasing of the terror that we were not going to survive the financial burden. To be honest, it took a while. Then after my migraine, I took a day off of work, went to yoga and enjoyed the breathing and releasing of tension. The next day, I went to *my teacher* and did a lot of crying and releasing with her guiding me to let go of what I could.

Two days after my session with my teacher, we got a call about a property that was previously not available that was a good option becoming available for our operations. This is the power of surrender.

Note: I said I did *some* surrendering…surrender is a process and some things that feel really huge or intense might not all go at once. But over time, they loosen and untangle. Be gentle with yourself and remember easy-does-it.

Choosing to surrender might at first feel like loss. But surrender is an important part of the alchemizing process. On the journey to letting wealth flow, we need to stop the fight. We need to release the resistance otherwise we can stay stuck for years – really years. Surrendering is powerful – if you choose to do it.

Recommendation: I highly recommend reading Letting Go: The Pathway of Surrender by David R. Hawkins. It is the best book I have ever encountered about the power and the process of surrender.

What does alchemizing mean?

Webster's Definition of Alchemize: *1. To transmute, to change or alter in form, appearance or nature especially to a higher form. 2. Alchemize, the process of transmuting a common substance, usually of little value into a substance of great value.*

Traditionally, alchemizing is the process of turning lead into gold. It is a transmutation process where you take a base metal and change it into a precious metal usually using fire and heat. The alchemizing process is powerful and transformative, as you are converting energy from one form into a new form. That is what we are going to do here with the old scarcity belief you identified in the Awareness chapter that you are ready to let go of (see your journaling from Chapter 3).

We are going to transform the old scarcity agreement energy, taking the old lead-based thought and feeling and transmuting it into precious new wealth energy. When we do this, we are making the new energy available for new investment, making space for new investments that are more aligned with your now wealth desires. This is important: we are not just going to let go of the old beliefs and feelings, we are going to use the energy from them to new affect.

As we have discussed, the old lead-based beliefs act like resistance, as they do not really feel good or support our new understanding of wealth or our intentions to experience it. For example, one of the old beliefs that you might be transforming is the belief that *wealth is conditional and hard to come by*, in that you must fulfill some prescribed equation of brains, talent, education, hard-work and lineage in order for you to experience wealth. Conditional wealth (which was scarcity agreement #4 in Chapter 3) is actually a pretty traditional view of how wealth comes about.

Now, take a moment and feel into this belief that *"wealth is conditional and hard to come by."* How does that really feel to you? If you are like me, it is frustrating or angering. *How do I get this magical combination of brains, talent and luck and how do I ensure it will work for me?* Frustration, anger, confusion, hopelessness are all forms of resistance. They do not feel good and act as an energy road block to the wealth you would prefer.

So, let's walk through the alchemizing process to transform this old agreement.

"People don't resist change.
They resist being changed." – Peter Senge

The Alchemizing Process

You can use this Alchemizing Process when something comes up that feels like scarcity and old fear energy holding you back. Or when something arises that stirs anger, resentment, inadequacy or hurt. *All of these are messages from your internal wisdom to take a deeper look and to let go of these energy feelings.*

Ideally, you will become skilled at alchemizing old feeling energy into new. *At some point, I hope you will be "so done" with believing in scarcity, you can let it go completely.* You'll just know and feel unlimited, unconditional wealth deep inside. How cool, right? But for now, let's just get good at noticing, letting go and deciding how we want to re-invest ourselves.

The key with this process is your intention. *How strongly do you feel about releasing this old belief and being done with it?* How clear are you about what it is and the way it has been working in your life? How ready are you to let it go? If you have strong intention, good clarity and readiness, this process can be very powerful. Even if you don't, this experience will be helpful and valuable. So please keep going.

The Alchemizing Process Steps:

1. Acknowledge - the old scarcity agreement and feeling
2. Accept it – as it is
3. Release it – symbolically and tangibly
4. Thank it – and become peaceful with it
5. Replace it - by reaching for a vibration that feels better

The alchemizing process is quite simple and can be done as quickly or slowly as you would like. Try not to make this into a big deal. The process is really just meant to help transmute old resistant energy to new, clear, available energy. You will free yourself of the scarcity feelings and be back in free flow—and that takes about as long as a pot of water to boil. Please don't get stuck in a quest to find things that are broken and then fix them. We don't want to get lost in the mind chatter. Nor do we want to spend endless years analyzing these old scarcity agreements. This process is meant to acknowledge the old feelings and approach, release the resistance around it and make space for something new. That is really all there is to it *and there is huge benefit to doing it.* The honoring and clarity that come from going through this process are very powerful, as is the new application of your energy investment into something more aligned with your Wealth Consciousness. There is powerful intent behind this process, so don't lose track of it because it feels weird. It might feel weird, but it is anything but.

"Remember that the mind of a beginner is an open channel for genius"
- Goddess Tarot Card: Princess of Pentacles

Step 1 – Acknowledge It - See the scarcity agreement and its associated feeling(s).

The first step is to **acknowledge** the scarcity agreement and how it *makes you feel* - because we cannot change that which we stay unconscious to. See it as it is - without judgment. Just say hello to it and feel where you are now before trying to move away from it. Don't pretend it does not matter, nor try to skip on to the something greater or move into fixing mode before honoring what is here right now. **This can be the hardest step, because some habits, beliefs and thought patterns are difficult to see and acknowledge.** In the case of Marg, she could have not gotten clarity unless she acknowledged she felt uncomfortable riding the train. They are part of our life goggles and this makes them tricky to detect. But as we are on this journey, things will inevitably come up that need to be let go. You can feel it because something feels bad or scary or disempowering. You run headlong into an old scarcity pattern and it makes you feel stuck, frustrated or poor. Usually, feelings like guilt, worry, doubt and/or inadequacy accompany our old patterns. Another way we hold onto scarcity approaches is pride in being frugal or righteousness in sacrificing yourself are other ways we keep ourselves attached to old patterns.

Wealth Journaling:

An effective way to acknowledge a scarcity belief is to journal about what does not feel good. Did a situation come up that pushed your scarcity/poor/money frustration button? Just start writing with the intent to get clarity on the issue and the feelings inside of it – "unpack it" so to speak. You may also want to journal about the scarcity agreement from the previous Awareness chapter that you chose as the one you are ready to let go of.

Ask yourself:

- *How am I feeling? What brought this up? What other feelings are beneath the initial feeling?*

- *What is it that needs to be transformed for me to move forward and feel ready for prosperity? What seems to keep getting in my way?*
- *What am I thinking, feeling or doing that creates this difficulty around wealth?*

Throughout this journaling time, just write. Notice and acknowledge. Don't censor or worry about being politically correct – the more honest you are about how you really feel, the better the clarity you will get.

Something to note here is that deep inside you might feel you need to keep doing what you are doing or something will go wrong. There is a reason you believe what you believe and do what you do.

So going back to the example we have been discussing, feel the effects of the belief that *wealth is conditional and hard to come by.*

> Acknowledge: *"I am tired of working so hard and never getting ahead. It seems that certain people have it much easier; they have the right contacts and education. They don't work nearly as hard as I do but they have much more than I do. I am so frustrated and angry that it is not what you know but who you know. I feel hopeless I will ever work my way out of this situation."*

The above statements acknowledge the idea that wealth is conditional in that if you do not have the right contacts or education, you are not going to experience wealth. It also shows that hard work and more hard work may or may not lead to more wealth & money.

- Take a moment to notice how you feel in your body as you write all this. Where have you been holding it? In your neck? Your Jaw? Lower back? Your heart? Hips? Ankles? What have these scarcity agreements made you do or feel? Just notice and write.

> Acknowledge: *"Sometimes I make decisions to relieve that mental or physical discomfort knowing that I cannot change where I was born or how I was raised or whom I grew up with. Sometimes I just crack a beer open and watch the game. I feel mad at my fate. And I feel hopeless and unworthy...an outsider with no*

*hope of becoming an insider and no hope of ever getting wealthy…
always a minor league player."*

This is good information and clarity. And from clarity comes wisdom to move forward in a new way. So, let's move onto Step 2 – accepting.

Step 2. Accept It – Accept the truth of how you really feel.

To be **accepting** means to not fight against what is showing up right now. Thus, being present to how you feel in this moment. When we begin the process of accepting, we do not reject our feelings and beliefs, or throw them back, walk away or get angry at them or ourselves. *Nor do we jump into fixing them prematurely.* These feelings are forms of resistance (energy invested into the thing we don't want to experience anymore). Right now, we just notice the feelings that arise as we think of the belief that has come up for alchemizing. We are allowing the truth of it, as it is, without judgment. We are not necessarily agreeing with it, but as we see and feel the belief as it is, we honor ourselves.

"To be totally accepting means to not quarrel with what is showing up right now. It means not to reject it or throw it back or walk away from it but to embrace it, hold it and love it. Should the present circumstance be one, which you now choose to change, simply choose to experience it another way. Your inner experience of it can and will be changed forever, simply out of your decision about it." Conversations with God – Book 1

Wealth Journaling:

Don't pretend that your feelings are not at play. If you feel angry, be angry. If you feel overwhelmed or hopeless, allow yourself to accept that is how you really feel. Right now, it does not matter how it came to you, it is yours – you own it. And as the owner you can alchemize it. Don't feel guilty or give in to inadequacy. Stand tall and know you are in the process of making new conscious investments.

- If you were honest, and it was ok to feel how you feel – you would say you feel _____? Can you give yourself permission to accept how you really feel? Can you just be with it right now?

- What is the message inside of the feeling? Are there any flashes of memories or thoughts that arise as you go deeper into the feeling? Just notice.

Accept: *"I can see how I came to this conclusion about needing to come from the right family, with the right upbringing. My parents did not even care if I went to college. I felt disregarded. I grew up in a neighborhood where that was not important. I see that I did not grow up knowing the right people to open the right doors and this has made me really <u>angry</u> - feeling a <u>victim</u> of the system and honestly, I am very <u>tired</u> of working so hard. I can see how <u>victimized</u> I feel. And <u>frustrated</u> and <u>tired</u>."*

Now that we have more clarity about how we feel, we have more understanding of where our wealth is getting blocked. Steps 1 & 2 gave us clarity, Steps 3 & 4 will help release the blockage and get the energy flowing.

"I have found that if I somehow shut down the Love Vibration – the feeling of complete unconditional love – I am putting a heavy restriction on my visible supply (money)." – John Randolph Price in *The Abundance Book*

Step 3. Release it – symbolically and tangibly

Releasing and surrendering are where we start the energy transformation process. It is valuable to make the conscious decision to release the scarcity feeling/agreement and let it go. This conscious choice makes it clear to our mind and body that *we are ready, willing and able to move on freely.* There are many ways to release in this stage.

In this step, you are taking an action with intention to symbolically and tangibly release the feeling energy of the agreement and let it go. I say symbolically and tangibly because our minds really like solid action; you feel you are taking a solid action to be done with this scarcity belief that feels like it has been holding you back. And the action can be as simple as sitting with the feeling until it dissolves or doing a releasing tool (see the next investment tip)…you decide what feels needed and when.

To start, just sit with the scarcity feeling. If you are worried be worried, if you are scared be scared, if you are disappointed be disappointed. As you do this, you will feel the energy arise and your mind will want to jump in and fix it or justify it. Don't. Just let the feeling be there and feel it. Also notice any other associated feelings that are in there to be "unpacked". After you feel fear, you might then feel anger, then you might feel rage or exhaustion. Let it come, let it be, let it come to the surface freely. As it arises let the energy of the emotion flow (tears, anger, yelling – it's all ok). This is the energy releasing...there is nothing more you need to do really – but notice it, let it flow and let it go. Sit with it and it will start to **dissolve**. Take a few breaths and feel the tension release from your shoulders, neck and torso. Breathe deeply and relax. Give yourself permission to release the tension, release the anger, release the frustration. Feel lighter and lighter.

Sometimes, it is helpful to do something even more transformative. You may choose to write the agreement on a piece of paper and tear it up. Or may want to write it a good-bye note, a *Dear John letter* of sorts, and then you may want to burn it – see the "Burn It" investment tip a bit later. For me burning stuff feels powerful. Here are some other releasing "actions" you can take:

◎ Investment Tip: Releasing Tool Box

It helps to have a set of actions (or tools) you can use that help you quickly release and let go of the unwanted scarcity energy. To use these, start by getting clear about the emotion or feeling that you are ready to release. As you do these "tools" intend to let go of the feeling and its associated energy. Some of my favorite "let-it-go" releasing tools are:

- Taking a shower and letting the water wash away the old feeling
- energy;
- Flushing the crap energy down the toilet (pun intended);
- Drawing a line in the sand and stepping over it; releasing as you do;
- Drawing a chalk box around you and the scarcity feeling, and stepping out of the box with the intent to be free from limitation;
- Burning some sage with the intention to clear the old energy to make way for the new;
- Singing & dancing around to Taylor Swift's "Shake it off".

...you get it. Find ways that work for you to dissolve and release the old gunky energy. Use these tools whenever you feel stuck or worried to release the scarcity energy and old belief patterns.

Wealth Journaling:

- What feels like a good way to release this old agreement?
- What symbolic and tangible action can I take (that will do no harm to anyone or anything) to feel I have released this old belief?

Now with our example of the belief that *wealth is conditional and hard to come by:*

> Release: *I am ready to let this scarcity energy feeling go where I have agreed that wealth is conditional and it is hard to come by. I am writing down all the hurt, loss, worry, anger and resentment. I allow myself to feel the energy of victimization, frustration, hopelessness and exhaustion start to release. I write until I feel release. Then, I take the piece of paper that I wrote the old agreement on and I tear it into little tiny pieces. As I do, I feel the old energy leave me. I surrender the pain, worry, hurt, and limitation. I let them leave me. I intend to surrender what does not work any longer. I surrender the fight. With each tear – I feel freer and freer, lighter and lighter. And now I will burn it for good measure enjoying the release and turn to ash.*

Step 4. Thank it and become peaceful with it

This step is quite beautiful in that we can now see how the scarcity energy was part of our journey which brought us here. We are on the path toward conscious wealth investing and this is a very powerful and exciting path to be on. Somehow this old scarcity agreement served us and we experienced it for a reason. We saw or experienced something in the past that brought us to this old conclusion. We came to believe and act the way we did for a good reason. It may have helped us survive and get through life.

At this point, feel thankful to the old agreement for what it has given you and taught you. Feel thankful for it giving you the gift of insight. As you thank it for helping you, protecting you and giving you what you needed *at the time,* you are alchemizing it from something that was a problem to a friend with a gift. Thank it for showing you the **contrast** to what you *really* want. It was there for a reason and you are thankful for the new understanding and growth it has brought.

To be grateful for something is to stop resisting it, to see it and acknowledge it, even when the gift is not immediately apparent. Gratitude for an experience, condition, or outcome is a powerful tool in the creation of your reality.

You might even want to bless it. Give it your best energy and your highest thoughts. Feel it was a friend come to help you move in a new direction.

For the most part, after we become peaceful and thankful for an issue it is mostly transformed – the energy is transformed from frustration to clarity, from anger to understanding and this takes the disempowerment out of the equation.

Wealth Journaling:

- What has this old agreement given you and taught you? What have you learned about how you feel and how you have been living your life as a result of this old scarcity belief?
- Do you have any new insights, understanding or clarity now that you have worked through this alchemizing process?

From our example that wealth is conditional:

Thank It: *"I can see how these old beliefs about connections and education have been limiting my future. I also see how much I agree to hard work and no pain, no gain. I am thankful I am seeing them for the limitations they are. In fact, what if there are fewer conditions around my wealth than I thought? As I see these, I feel lighter and lighter, freer and freer. I am a unique being with unlimited capabilities and the ability to create my life without the conditions of the past, or of others' experience!"*

Interestingly enough, once thankfulness has permeated your consciousness, peace seems to come naturally.

As we accept the feelings as they are and we become more present to them, something happens without our effort; **peace** starts to flow. Because when we look directly at an issue we have been fighting, ignoring, or trying to fix and acknowledge it without resistance – the resistant feelings can start to dissolve. Peace happens!

Peace puts us in the now and allows us to choose anew. And as we are thankful and peaceful there is a transmutation of energy that happens to transform the energy from "lead" (old scarcity belief) to new energy available for reinvestment in a new golden wealth agreement. Peace essentially raises our vibration to wealth potential. Moving through these energy transmutation steps is how we are alchemizing the energy.

Wealth Journaling:

- Is there a statement that allows you to become peaceful with the old experience and feeling? Below are a couple of new thoughts to consider. Feel free to use one of these or come up with one of your own – either way, try to find a statement that brings you closer to peace – or gives you a bit of relief – around the old scarcity agreement.
  - *"I see why I came to this conclusion. I see what happened in the past. And I see why I thought what I thought and felt what I felt. And now, I am ready for something new."*
  - *"That was then and this is now. Now, I get to decide about how I am going to approach things going forward."*
  - *Maya Angelo said, "When we know better, we do better. With this clarity and insight, I know better and am ready for something even better."*
  - *"That was something that I used to think that no longer applies. And it does not serve me to think it any longer. I don't need to think it anymore – so I am just moving on."*
  - *"I see how these things of the past inspired me or pushed me to where I am now. And maybe they were a gift because I would not be here at the doorway of real Wealth if it were not for them."*

Going back to our example of the belief that wealth is conditional and hard to come by :

> Peace: *"I can see how feeling like I did not have the right contacts made me work even harder to get educated. I pushed myself. But what if the idea that wealth is conditional does not serve me any longer? I can choose to find a new wealth agreement that is more aligned with my new wealth consciousness. I am ready to just move on, in peace."*

Can you feel the flow coming back and the grip of resistance loosening? I hope so. I hope you are feeling freer and freer. So, let's move on to step 5 - replacing.

"When we discover and acknowledge the hidden gift that is there, a healing takes place. Every life experience has a hidden gift."
– David R Hawking in *Letting Go: The Pathway of Surrender*

Step 5. Replace it - Reach for a new wealth agreement that feels better.

The last step of the Alchemizing process is <u>to reach for a new wealth agreement or some new idea or feeling that feels better.</u> Now is the time to reach for a new thought or feeling when it comes to your wealth. Reaching for something greater means making a new investment that feels good to you. You are now going to make a powerful investment in a new idea and a felt-sense of a fresh wealth experience and perspective. Because one of the most effective tools for dealing with an old experience is to give it a different meaning. We take on a different attitude about the past hurt and we acknowledge the hidden gift in it.

Viktor Frankl, a holocaust survivor, shows us in his powerful book Man's Search for Meaning that emotional events and past hurts will change considerably and be healed if a new meaning is placed around them. Viktor chose to give different meanings to the experiences he had in the concentration camps. Viktor said "Everything can be taken from a man but one thing: the last of the human freedoms—to choose one's attitude in any given set of circumstances, to choose one's own way."

We get to decide about how we are going to think and feel as we move forward and this is the power of replacing the old scarcity feeling and agreements with our new Wealth attitudes and feelings.

When we release and let go, our energy rises and gives rise to something higher and a feeling of lightness. You feel better and you feel energized. **You feel and see new possibilities**. You probably experienced something like this as you were doing steps 3 & 4. As we let go and feel better, freshness flows. We move to lightheartedness from which something unexpected arises. You find the gift. Wealth getting access to you! Wealth is able to flow through you without the resistance and energy blocks of the past!

Wealth Journaling:

- If you were to reach for a new wealth agreement that feels better what would it be? What would you start investing in instead of the old limitation?
- What would you rather feel than the anger, frustration or whatever you mentioned in Step 2?

To wrap-up our *wealth is conditional and hard to come by* example:

> Replace: *"I am coming to learn that I am a powerful investor of my life energy. I get to decide my reality and agree that Wealth is all around me! Contacts and effort may be a factor, but my talents, capabilities and energy investments are far more powerful and influential."*

———

You have just alchemized the old scarcity feelings into fresh wealth energy! Nice job! I hope you are seeing how the Alchemizing process can help you take something that has been bothering you, limiting you and creating resistance to your natural Wealth and transforming it into a lighter, freer possibility energy.

The Alchemizing process is seeing and feeling where we have been ignoring, repressing or working around a fear instead of looking directly at it and saying, "I see you, I feel you, I understand you, I know you were in my life for a reason, I release you, I let you go and I bless you – thank you!"

Another Alchemizing example...

This example addresses how we often agree that "big" wealth is harder than "little" wealth to create. My teacher Abraham says, "It is just as easy to create a button as a castle. The process is the same."

Side note: "Abraham" is a collaboration between the married couple Ester and Jerry Hicks and "Infinite Intelligence" referred to as Abraham. Ester is able to "channel" Abraham, which means she can tap into the Abraham consciousness and share their very wise wisdom. I know, I know, this sounds like woo-woo at its craziest. But if you listen to Ester sharing Abraham it is amazing, helpful information. So, my feeling is, if it is valuable helpful information, *use it*. Abraham-Hicks resources have been instrumental in my Wealth journey and maybe they will be for you too. You'll find that I reference them a great deal throughout this book

Back to my story, one day I was creating a great parking spot at the fitness club I go to, as it was the time when all of the classes start thus the parking lot is always really full. As I was creating a great spot, I jokingly said *"and I would like a million dollars."* That kind of caught me off guard. Why did I think it is easier to create a great parking spot than it is to create a million dollars? Because my unquestioned assumption was that "big wealth" is harder to create than little everyday wealth. But to the Unconditional-Wealth-of-All, a million dollars is not that much, but I guess to me it is! So, I want to alchemize this old notion that a million dollars is hard to create.

1. **Acknowledge It** – I found it interesting that as I said, "I would like a million dollars" I had a ping in my gut and a voice in my head that said "hey *it is not that easy – Laurie.*" I felt a million dollars *is* hard to create. And this made me <u>annoyed</u>. So, in that spilt second, I acknowledged the "ping" and the idea and the feeling. It happened fast but I saw it and felt it. This is acknowledging.

2. **Accept It** – To be honest, I have been <u>frustrated</u> that money has not grown as fast as I think it could. So, I assumed the million was <u>difficult</u> for me to create. I have seen many people try really hard and <u>sacrifice</u> a lot and not get there. I felt like my sacrifices have not been enough – which made me really sad and defeated. In fact, I never even thought it was possible for me. *How did all of these thoughts feel?* All of these thoughts made me *feel* sad, small and inadequate. And, if I can accept these feelings I can transform them, these are the feelings I want to release.

3. **Release it** ... I decided I was going to do some surrendering and I would start with the feeling of inadequacy. I took a few deep breaths and allowed myself to feel what I feel. It brought up tears, it brought up hurt, it brought up sadness. I did not follow any of the thoughts around it (e.g. Why do I feel this way? Where did it start? How do I get over it? I don't engage them. I just let them dissolve.) – I feel the feelings as they are. Then I felt weary and tired. I sat with those feelings. Then I felt frustration and again I just let the frustration run its course. After a bit, I felt relief...and it felt odd, I did not "do" anything but let the energy run its course. My face relaxed, my jaw unclenched. I felt a bit better. Then the notion that maybe it might not be that hard to create a million popped into my head. I am good with that and I felt complete at that point.

4. **Thank it and become peaceful with it...** I understand a bit how I came to this belief and I respect myself for having had it to this point. But right now, I am grateful for the relief and the insights. I thank it for the clarity it has brought and the growth it is showing me. I thank it for showing me this old "hard to create" belief and I am ready to transmute it so I can invest in a new agreement. I bless it and myself for this insight.

I am ready for peace. I am ready to release the resistance around difficult wealth. **I breathe and relax. Breathe and relax. I took more breaths, allowed my energy to rise and let myself come to peace. I felt my energy shift.**

5. **Replace It**... I decided to feel I was ready to invest in the new belief that money is easier to come by. I am ready to feel and enjoy the flow, grace and ease of the wealth all around me. Now tears of gratitude start to flow. I like the idea of easy money. Effortless wealth sounds great. I took more deep breaths and enjoyed the excitement that was starting to bubble.

"Believe it can be done. When you believe something can be done, really believe and your mind will find the ways to do it. Believing a solution paves the way to solution."
– David J. Schwartz, Magic of Thinking Big.

The Power of Alchemizing

As we are learning, alchemizing is a powerful capability you have always had at your disposal to transform lower vibrating energies (lead) into powerful higher vibrating energies (gold). This is one of your most basic gifts as a human and now you know it as a power investor. As we consciously apply this process to our day-to-day feeling experiences, we are becoming conscious investors. **Your vital, precious life energy is the real currency!** This process helps you maximize your investments for the greatest returns.

"Our ability to respond to life and to be responsible for our life is a major factor in finding meaning and therefore, fulfillment in life." – Viktor Frankl

---

◉ Investment Tip: Have an Alchemizing Ceremony...

For some of us, having a tangible short ceremony to signify the intention of transforming an old belief and its associated feelings into new available energy can be valuable. So, you might want to have an alchemizing ceremony...maybe using the old scarcity agreement you have been working with in this chapter.

In this "ceremony", what we will be doing is visualizing taking the feelings and thoughts and filling a virtual golden sack with them. Set aside 15 minutes or so, not much more, and intend to transform the energy of the old agreement by visualizing this short process:

- Begin by breathing to a count of 4 or 5. Just breathe in and count to 4 or 5 and then breathe out and count backwards from 5 to 1. Do this for a few moments and allow yourself to get comfortable and relaxed.
- Next, imagine taking the old belief like...*wealth is hard to come by* and feel it. Allow yourself to feel whatever feelings you have around it, like victimization, worry, anger, frustration, apathy and start to put them into the "golden sack". Visualize the golden sack sitting in your navel center and fill it with all of the energy and the emotions that accompany the scarcity feelings. Feel the old hurts, worries, and issues being gathered in the sack. Feel the anger, frustration and hopelessness gather into the sack. Let all of it be gently and effortlessly accumulated in the sack at your navel center. Feel the tension release from your shoulders and back. You might even be carrying the scarcity energy around in your lower back or hips. Allow yourself to release the energy into the sack. Allow yourself to be free of them. Take a few breaths as you allow the energies to gather in the sack.
- Say out loud: *"I put this energy into the golden sack along with the sadness and frustration, the worry and doubts of past. I allow myself to transmute*

these old energy feelings. I allow myself to release all the old investments and let them go to be renewed and transformed."

- When the bag feels "full", pull the golden cord and close the sack. Next, surround it with your love, bless it and thank it. Now we are going to use the white light of transmutation to disintegrate the sack and its contents. Visualize the bag surrounded by a white fire that is transmuting the whole thing - bag and all its contents. Feel the energy being transformed back into new potential. As the metaphorical fire burns, let go of the old energies from you heart, hips, head, and wherever you have felt them lodged.

- Breathe deeply and say, *"I transform this old energy, releasing it, I am at peace."* Sit for a bit, as the white fire engulfs the bag, gently transmuting the energy. Do this as long as needed until you feel freed and released of the old energies. As the fire burns, thank the energies and lovingly release the past investments and agreements, making the energy available for fresh new possibilities.

- Do this until you feel the energy has completely been alchemized back into fresh energy and the bag is completely disintegrated. Breathe and feel the lightness in your body. Feel clear and free. Sit for a moment and enjoy the clarity, freedom and excitement.

- Now gently reach for something greater – you might have something that pops in your mind or just feel that you are now allowing your wealth in…simple and effortlessly.

- You may want to stay in this place of repose for as long as feels good.

If you are uncomfortable with visualizing the golden sack and filling it with energy and seeing the white flame consume it, or if you would like to do something more tangible to really feel the release and symbolically alchemize the energy, you might want to burn the agreement with the following process. My conscious creator group had many powerful experiences when we got together and burned our old beliefs in the fireplace. This was very therapeutic.

◎ Investment Tip: Just Burn It...

You will need pen and paper and a fire pit or fireplace to burn the paper. You can also light a candle and burn the paper by dropping it in a fireproof bowl. Just be careful as the paper flames up quickly. Once you get the fire going, spend a few minutes breathing and becoming present. Settle into the moment. You will be writing down the Alchemizing steps on a piece of paper. – or you can use your past journalings – it is up to you.

- **Acknowledge** the feelings by writing about the old belief and how it has made you feel in the past. Write for a few minutes until you have clarity about it.
- Stop and reread it. See it and **accept** it as it is. Allow the way this belief made you feel and notice what you did as a result - all in the spirit of clarity, understanding and acceptance (please no judging or assessing or comparing, just noticing).
- Spend a moment thanking it for being here and showing up now, as a gift for freedom, change and new opportunities. Take a moment to **thank** yourself for working through this process and being willing to let the scarcity feelings and agreement go.
- Go outside or to your fireplace and light the paper on fire. As you light it and watch it burn, feel the energy be **released** and transformed. As it burns, feel the energies release and peace come as the old agreement transforms. Choose to let go of them from inside of you, around you and beyond you. Release and surrender as the paper burns. Thank it and yourself, feel love in the moment and love of the experience. As the paper burns agree that you are now free of this old belief and its associated feelings and are ready to reach for something greater.
- Breathe and enjoy the relief and release as the fire burns and transmutes the energies making them fresh and available for new investment.
- After you enjoy the release, take a moment and say what you would prefer instead. What do you really want to invest this new energy

toward? Reach for somehting greater and **replace** the old energy with your new investment intention.

"Each of us is born with a ceaseless drive to thrive. Its intensity is never diminished, but it can be overshadowed by hurt, anger, fear grief and our self-defeating beliefs. "– Rod Stryker in **The Four Desires**.

Now you...

Now it is your turn to take one of your scarcity agreements and its associated feelings (the one you most wanted to change from the Awareness chapter would be great) and have an alchemizing session.

Before you start, take a few deep breaths and center yourself. Decide you are ready to alchemize these old scarcity energies and feelings into new fresh available energies. Remember you are the power investor.

1. Acknowledge It

What belief or scarcity agreement have you held around your wealth that you want to transform so you may move forward? What are the associated feelings you have felt around them. Remember, please don't censor or worry about being politically correct – the more honest you are about how you really feel, the freer you will feel as a result.

2. Accept It

How does this belief make you feel? Try to feel it as it is. If any past experiences come forward – just note them...don't get caught in fixing them, analyzing them or over thinking them. But allow the feelings of them to come forward. Accept it as it has been in your life – just as it is.

3. Release It

It is here you may want to fill the golden sack with the energy of the old belief. Fill the sack and allow the energy from your head, neck and shoulders to release and relax. Fill the sack with the feelings and surrender them into the sack. Let them dissolve in the sack. As you fill the sack thank the energy and bless it, allowing it to transform in the white fire of transmutation.

4. Thank it and Become Peaceful with It

Thank it for what you learned and the new clarity it has given you. Thank the feelings and scarcity agreements for being there. They were there for a reason and now you are ready to move forward.

You might want to say something like: *"I can see how I came to this agreement and why I feel what I feel. I had good reason and respect myself for what I decided. I also see how I can move forward in my wealth creating experience because of this new understanding."*

5. Replace It with something greater that feels better

If you were to reach for something that feels better than what you just alchemized, what would you reach for? What would you go for now? What would you start investing in instead of the old limitation? Remember, Easy-Does-It.

◎ Investment Tip: Just Drop It

Have you noticed how singers and entertainers are dropping their microphones at the end of their performance? They finish the song and just drop the microphone as a statement of "there I did it, now I am done – so done – I am complete." You can do the same with this old **scarcity** belief you have been carrying around. Just drop it and walk away. No need for drama, justifications, guilt or anything. Just drop it and move forward, free and clear.

Reach for Something Greater: Give yourself permission to be wealthy

Give yourself permission to be wealthy – really wealthy. If you are reading this book, it means that somewhere deep inside you believe can have real Wealth! And I also know that if you are reading this book somewhere deep inside you have an internal knowing that Wealth is yours and always has been. You are ready! So ready! Alchemizing supports you in aligning with the Wealth that has always been yours, always and in all ways.

"Sorrow prepares you for joy. It violently sweeps everything out of your house, so that new joy can find space to enter. It shakes the yellow leaves from the bough of your heart, so that fresh, green leaves can grow in their place. It pulls up the rotten roots, so that new roots hidden beneath have room to grow. Whatever sorrow shakes from your heart, far better things will take their place."

— Rumi

Remember...

- Alchemizing is the process of transmuting energy from "lead" (old scarcity belief) to fresh energy available for reinvestment in a new golden wealth agreement.
- Alchemizing is easy and does not need to take a long time.
- It is ok to let go of your scarcity baggage.
- Surrender is powerful.
- It is ok to feel how you feel.
- It is ok to be wealthy.
- You are a powerful investor who moves energy to create.
- Energy is the real currency.
- You have the power to alchemize scarcity thoughts and feelings into wealth feelings, effort-lessly.
- Be gentle with yourself as you do this powerful process.
- The Alchemizing process is 5 simple steps: **Acknowledge** the old scarcity belief & feelings that do not feel good. **Accept** them as they are – do not try to fix or avoid them. **Release** the feelings by letting them go and giving them up. **Thank** it for the role it played and come to peace with it. **Replace** it with something greater (invest in a new Wealth agreement).
- Easy-Does-It: less scarcity, more prosperity.

Frequently Asked Questions

1. **How long does this take?** The process can take as little as a minute or so but you might want to make it a bit of a ceremony...maybe 15 minutes. I suggest slowing yourself down and setting aside the time to honor the old and then make room for the new. **The key is to feel the energy shift in your body from tension to relief, from resistance to release.** Think of a garden hose that has a kink in it; once you straighten the hose, the water can flow. The same is true here. The alchemizing process helps get the kink out so your

wealth energy can flow. For me, the more conscious I am and the more present I am when I do these processes, the more I feel I have invested beneficially.

2. **When will the effects be felt?** Trust that this is a powerful process. Even if you are just going through the motions, change is happening. For some, you will feel the release and shift in your body right away. We are all different. But one thing is certain: if you do this process you will be transmuting energies. You are a powerful alchemist moving energies all the time. This process helps you to do it in a conscious, loving, efficient way.

3. **How often do I do this?** Whenever you run into a scarcity agreement or feeling that seems to be at odds with what you are creating. Or when you feel you are ready to release an old agreement for something new. What I have found is I can alchemize something quite quickly now. Once I see it and acknowledge it, surrender the feeling energy then I bless it and say, *this is what I choose now instead.*

4. **What is the difference between baggage, blockage and resistance?** Actually, you can use them interchangeably as they are all ways to look at limitation and resistance, which slows down your natural Wealth flow.

5. **I still feel very strongly about my belief; the process did not seem to work.** Yes, you may need to work with some of your deeply held beliefs and agreements for a while. It took years to agree to them and it might take a bit to fully alchemize them. Don't stress about it. Find the feeling and acknowledge it. Don't let your mind hijack you into trying to figure out a fix. Don't even try to deal with the thing that is stuck – just go general until you feel better. And you don't have to go general on the subject of your belief – go general on any subject that feels better. For example, sometimes when I am trying to find the right answer for a business problem, I go more general to something that I feel good about and that is not stressful to me. I might reinvest my energy by focusing on how well our team works together. Or if I am not feeling all that good about the company, I feel around inside my body until I find something that

feels better like: *"Easy-Does-It Laurie. All is well and all will be well* ☺ *- Ah that feels better."*

6. **I don't want to feel peaceful about it and I don't want to be accepting of it. What now?** Well, thank you for your honesty. That is keeping it real and I respect you for that. Anger or fear are valuable energy in that they can protect us and keep us safe. And making peace can almost feel like a cop out. But the point here is not to let our old scarcity belief keep running the show. We are looking to use it to move forward. The peace aspect is about finally seeing it, acknowledging it and understanding it, instead of running from it, suppressing it or pushing against it. Peace puts us in the now and allows us to choose anew.

7. **I don't really have something "greater" to reach for.** I understand, sometimes we have been thinking and doing what we always have for so long, we are at a loss for what we would prefer instead. **So, go for the feeling!** What feels good? Joy, fun, play are all good feelings. Or you might want to review the New Wealth Agreements from Chapter 3 and pick one that feels juicy to you. Or you might want to consider reaching for the opposite of the belief you were agreeing to. For example, flip the notion that *wealth is conditional* to *Wealth is available to everyone including and especially me!* ☺

8. **I don't want to surrender – it feels weak.** Yes, for many of us surrender has a connotation of weakness and loss. And maybe that is ok. We are "giving something up" ...our old ways of feeling and doing. However, as we alchemize we are gaining something greater: spaciousness, the power to choose anew, freedom from the old, availability for wealth to get in – pretty go stuff I would say.

9. **What if I don't want to let go of my old feelings about wealth? This is a variation on the previous question.** For many of us, we have used these old feelings to keep us safe. We came to them for a reason – a good reason, and do not want to go through that experience again or what our family went through. I get it, really, I do. But is it worth paying the continuing cost of the old feelings and emotions which keep us in this current state of scarcity, worry, overwhelm, and/or anger about wealth? Handling the residual

feelings by letting go and surrendering the emotions allows freedom to move into new wealth feelings and thoughts. It is said that many people spend their lives regretting the past and fearing the future and dreading the now unable to experience joy in the present. This alchemizing process can give you freedom from the regret, fear and dread.

10. **This feels weird (too woo woo), can I skip this Alchemizing thing?** To be honest, I have tried skipping this step. Many times, my mind would not let me. **I find that until a belief and feeling is consciously honored by you and alchemized, it hangs around.** Some part of me realizes these beliefs are a big part of who I was and who I am and on some level they need to be honored, *you* need to be honored. These are not *broken* beliefs. Just old beliefs and that is different. My teacher says, "there is are not better beliefs only different beliefs." The alchemizing process is a powerful way to transform your old energy investments and feelings to invest in something new. If this process seems weird, that's ok. You're trying something new and that can sometimes feel uncomfortable. Try to accept this and just keep going. It may push you out of your comfort zone but you will be amazed by how transformative it feels.

Investment Strategy:
I am a Powerful Alchemist

Invoke This…

- I see now that I am a Powerful Alchemist with the ability to transmute energy.
- I am ready, willing and able to transmute old energies from leaded-scarcity to golden-abundance and from heavy resistance to light free-flow.
- I am a powerful investor of the highest order, deliberately investing my feeling energy into the experiences I desire. I see now that the real currency is energy, and I have a choice about how I invest my energy.
- I know that it is ok to be wealthy and empowered. I relish the enjoyment I have to invest in new vibrations & transmute old worries.
- I am ready to release the old scarcity agreements and feelings to reach for something greater.
- I see the power of releasing and surrender; I feel the spaciousness and lightness that comes from letting go.
- It is wonderful to know that as I release the scarcity worries, wealth (love) naturally comes in to fill the space.
- I know that for every lead-based-fear thought, I can develop the internal presence of mind to catch that thought and alchemize it into a golden, supportive upside thought. Wow, I rock!

A

Awareness
Of Your Past

Alchemize
Your Beliefs

Awaken
Your Power

Align
Your Energy

Attract
Your Dreams

Allow
Your Desires

Amaze
Yourself

Invest in Awakening

What follows are three chapters on Awakening: Awaken to Who You Really Are, Awaken to the Creating Technologies, and Awaken to the Wealth Inherent in Life. These chapters provide the bedrock from which your wealth creation journey flows. Embrace them and you'll set yourself up for wealth creating success.

Why 3 awakening chapters?

As I was growing up, I felt a like a victim-of-the-system of life on earth. Most of the time life felt like a difficult struggle and a WTF experience and I was frustrated and angry – so angry. But as I journeyed forth, I came to understand my life in a new context and in a new way. I felt I awakened to something that I was not taught – a new way of being in the world – a wealth way. That is what I wish for us to explore with these awakening chapters. Awakening to a new understanding of life facilitates new experiences. The combination of the three awakening chapters is meant to help you develop your wealth consciousness by giving you a new foundation for wealth understanding and creation. Seeing life with wealth at its foundation is so important and necessary to make the rest of the easy-does it process possible.

I hope you come to see what I have learned, that there is a "wealth creating system" already in place for you to use. The system exists and is not biased against us. In fact, it is set up for us to succeed – once we understand how it works. We are the deciders of how we interact with the wealth creating system. Awaken the ideas presented in the next 3 chapters and you will be primed to use and enjoy the system.

You can harness the power of this system to your benefit or you can ignore it. If you awaken to its availability, you are well on your way to your new approach and experience of WUW – Wealth Unlimited Wealth!

Chapter 5: Invest in Awakening: To Who You Really Are

The first aspect of Awakening is investing in remembering and appreciating Who You Really Are. This is the most important part of your wealth journey. Remembering, embracing, and appreciating your uniqueness, worth and value, just as you are, is necessary for experiencing true Wealth.

Developing Your Understanding of Who You Really Are

This is the first of three Awakening chapters that set the new foundation for building your Wealth Consciousness. This is a critical point in the process because if you are not awake to Who You Really Are you will not feel empowered or valuable enough to tap into the Wealth that is available to you.

Developing a deep understanding and appreciation of Who You Really Are and what you bring to the table is a vital step in your wealth consciousness journey. Self-awareness and self-appreciation enable us to live fully and joyfully steeped in the truth of our self-worth. And to be honest, I believe that self-worth impacts our net-worth. Because people who have a sense of their innate worth make different kinds of decisions and take actions that honor their value.

Investing in awakening to Who You Really Are is a marvelous adventure because you are going to come to know yourself as you were meant to experience yourself here on earth: *as a powerful investor who creates constantly through the investments you make.*

Awakening has the wondrous benefit of knowing we are glorious amazing beings. Who You Really Are is a soul having a human experience— instead of a human having a once-in-a-while-soul experience. Do you believe you are glorious?

A friend of mine told me a story of how she was in an advanced yoga training with yogis who had been studying the ancient yoga tenants and precepts for years. She said she was taken aback as they went around the room to introduce themselves. Each of the students introduced themselves in an apologetic way saying how they still needed to do much work and that they were still not where they were hoping they would be. My friend said that she was saddened that these advanced yogis, with strong meditation practices and deep commitment to yoga, where still feeling inadequate.

Inadequacy, inferiority, and the similar not-enoughness beliefs we hold about ourselves keep us bound to limitation and from the wealth we wish to experience. This chapter is about acknowledging and appreciating Who You Really Are so these old feelings can start to fade and new possibilities allowed to flow.

"Love is what we were born with.
Fear is what we learned here." – Marianne Williamson

◎ Investment Tip: Gaze Deeply

Can you look in the mirror and see a glorious person? If not please spend time every day to see the glorious person you are. What is animating your body? What leaves when you pass on in death? Gaze deeply into your eyes and stop judging. See the essence that illuminates and animates your body – then you will start to see something you may never have seen. Play with gazing deeply in the mirror and notice what you feel and see.

"Who You Really Are is love personified." – Big-Laurie

Awaken to You as Investor

One day when someone asked what I do for a living, I decided to say, "I am an investor!" That felt bold and a bit dishonest, as I did not have tons of passive income or a big portfolio of cash to invest. Later, I was thinking about that supposedly *bold* statement: *"I am an investor."* I know why I said it. I had been on my wealth journey for a while and I had started buying a couple of condos around my neighborhood. I was considering, *what does it take to allow yourself to be what you say you want to be?* My desire was to be an investor and consider myself a legitimate investor, but my mind was saying, "No, you do not have enough experience and passive income to call yourself that!"

As I continued to contemplate the audacious statement, I realized I am an investor! I am an energy investor, investing my life energy by aligning my vibration to attract the things/experiences I want to create. I had the AHA realization that I am an investor! It is probably the most powerful, accurate truth of what I do and who I am. And I am making the case that you are a powerful investor too—an investor of the highest order.

You are a powerful investor - whether you know it or not

Every day, every moment you are making investment decisions. You are making "energy investments" with THE most valuable investment currency—your life energy. Most people think money is the most powerful investment currency—it is not. You! You are! As you invest your life energy in a way that honors who you really are through the thoughts you choose to think, the words you choose to say, and the things you choose to endeavor in, you are investing in your future experience. You are an energy investor and as you invest yourself, consciously or unconsciously, you are creating your future returns.

Sit with this a bit, because I think if you started to see and feel yourself as an investor, you might make different choices about what you invest in and how you invest. And as every investor is different, so too is what they choose to invest in. There are no right or wrong investments - only what feels in the highest and best good of *you* - *your* dreams, *your* desires, *your* passions – what makes *you* feel you are honoring yourself.

*"Our self-respect tracks our choices. Every time we act in harmony
with our authentic self and our heart, we earn our respect. It is
that simple. Every choice matters."* – Dan Coppersmith

Invest in a Way That Honors You - that is True to You

As I was writing this chapter, I really wanted to share with you how
important you are, as you are. Your unique desires and approaches to how
you live your life enhance the whole of humanity. Because you never know
how you being your unique you will impact another person.

I still remember a man who got up at a seminar I was attending. He had
an idea for solar power. His passion and excitement inspired me. I wanted
to help him in some way. But at the time, I was very engaged in the many
things of my life. As I sat there listening to him, I realized I could invest in
his idea, I could invest in him – by sending him my thought energy of success
and dreams fulfilled. I invested my love energy into him and his idea as he
spoke - and that was an AHA for me. In a very real way, he inspired me in
this whole investment direction! He was investing his energy in a way that
honored him and it inspired me (and he probably will never know it). As he
was honoring himself there was this magical benefit that all around him
were getting! And I got some of that magic.

As you Awaken To Who You Really Are and flow with the natural
things you are interested in, you are investing and your magic will affect the
world around you. As you honor yourself by listening to the urges of your
heart, you will feel drawn to certain things that resonate with you. And if
you allow yourself to follow these urges and invest in them with your life
energy, you craft a very wealth-filled life… one that is uniquely fulfilling to
you in so many ways.

Wealth Journaling:

- As I look over the things and desires in my life that inspired me –
  what thread do I see?
- What things have I invested my energy into up until this point?

- If I were to be honest with myself, the things that are inspiring to me or that I really desire right now are…
- How can I invest my life energy now in a way that honors who I am as a person, and who I'd like to evolve into?

"As we let our light shine, we unconsciously give other people permission to do the same. As we are liberated from our own fear, our presence actually liberates others." – Marianne Williamson

Invest in Appreciating Your Self-Worth

We cannot have an investment discussion without looking at how we feel about ourselves. Most of us are very hard on ourselves, feeling we are not worthy of the good things of life or that we are inadequate.

You are a sure thing! I hope you come to believe this as we work together. The interesting thing is I cannot make you believe in your natural amazingness nor your importance – you need to do the work and invest in yourself and these new ideas and understandings. To tell your truth and be very honest about what you *really* desire; to listen and honor yourself, to respect and appreciate yourself enough to honor Who You Really Are is very courageous. **And to believe you are worthy of good things is at the core of wealth consciousness**.

I believe self-worth and the self-talk that springs from self-worth are the central issues when it comes to honoring Who We Really Are and consequently experiencing true Wealth. Many people feel they are inadequate in some way (see scarcity agreement #3 from Chapter 3) and then try to work to overcome it or just agree to the false premise that they don't matter or are broken in some way. You are not a mistake! Please contemplate the fact that *you are a perfect expression of who you need to be.* You were created uniquely perfectly. Embrace all of yourself – including quirks.

Many of us work really hard to compensate for that deep nagging feeling of inadequacy, insufficiency, and not-enough-ness and some amass huge amounts of money in the process. But the money never fully fills the hole of feeling inadequate, nor do the things money can buy - spouses, houses, cars (people, places, things). These people have money but are not really wealthy.

Feeling worthy, knowing your self-worth is the *key to the kingdom*; because from that feeling of self-worth, we grow in peace and balance. We walk the earth in a different way. As you tap into your birthright of intrinsic value and know that who you are is vital to the earth-plane you shine and as you invest in honoring your internal urges you contribute greatly.

Please don't let this point be lost. How you feel about yourself, what you have come to agree to about your worthiness, is a huge determining factor in experiencing your wealth. **If you do not feel deserving or "worthy" of wealth, no amount of affirming or efforting is going to overcome that. You are the decider about your wealth worthiness.** If it was up to me, I would wave a magic wand and have you know - you are! But it is not up to me. You need to take yourself on the truth journey and come to know Who You Really Are. Your worth is never in question. In fact, Who You Really Are would think this is a crazy thing to even discuss. Because the truth is that in any moment you can remember your magicalness, and in that moment, you will know that the *concept of worthiness does not apply - at all.*

It is my hope that as you honor who you really are and find ways to invest your life energy into the desires of you heart, you will feel truly wealthy. As you invest in appreciating you as you, you become a radiator of inspiration and wealth.

⊚ Investment Tip: Just Because

It is time for you to play with knowing that you are always supported and dearly loved by All-That-Is, just because.

You are deepening your understanding of Who You Really Are and the role you play in the Great Wealth unfolding.

Allow yourself to be the recipient of the love that is always flowing to you - just because. Your Internal Wealth Source is always guiding you, inspiring you, paving the way for you, acknowledging you, honoring you, respecting you, playing with you, co-creating with you, sharing with you, caring for you and has your back - unconditionally - just because.

You are never alone and always supported by your internal wisdom and guidance. Say this over and over, many times a day so the realization seeps into your cells and you feel it. "I am never alone and always supported, loved, guided, trusted, honored, enjoyed, prospering and showered with unlimitedness, just because of Me being Me." Acknowledge that *you* are the object of the love - just because. Play with this feeling of never being alone and always shared with - just because - and see how you feel.

Invest in Your Sense of Value

It is funny how those little scarcity voices jump in to scare us from this journey. Almost daily, I need Big-Wealthy-Laurie to talk to Little-Scarce-Laurie about how this journey is a good idea and a valuable use of our energy. You see, Big-Wealthy-Me knows our sense of value and feels empowered, strong and very rich. But as I go through my days, watching the news, or even just overhearing other's conversations, I get bombarded with "scarcity messages" and then Little-Laurie jumps in and says, "Hey, it is tough out there, what are you talking about with this Wealth stuff?!" Then Big-Laurie needs to jump in and remind me of the WUW unlimited wealth and magic of life. It is from this bigger sense of Self-Value that true Self-Worth happens. The larger truth of Wealth helps us sooth ourselves when our worries and fears come to "talk scarcity" to us.

This process is a journey and making this journey means you are going to look at the world and yourself in a whole new way...*with wealth goggles on.*

What I have come to learn on the awakening journey is that we are all innately valuable – just because.

Your value is not because of what you do, who you know or how you are educated, or any of the other conditional messages about value. You are valuable and valued just because of Who You Really Are. For now, it would be hugely beneficial if you assumed you are valuable and that you are an intricate part of the Wealth Source, the Unlimited Wealth-Spring and as such have access to all of the capabilities and power of the Great-Wealth-Source. How cool is that? Talk about Easy-Does-It! Value yourself and enjoy the benefits! Slow down to go fast; enjoy to enjoy! Yahoo!

⊚ Investment Tip: Flower Power

Please go out and purchase a bouquet of flowers...ones that make you feel wonderful. Bring them home and put them in a lovely vase and stare at them for a bit. Notice the bounty and beauty in each flower, as it is. In each petal there is perfection, abundance, fragrance, miraculous-ness really. How much effort did you put into creating those flowers? Did you have to put any effort into the seed knowing what to do to create the plant? Did you have to tell the flower how many petals to create? How much project management went into that bouquet? Abundance is just there, just because. Why? Why Not! This is the wealth approach of the Great-Wealth-Source: *Of Course! Let's make more!*

Play with noticing how wondrous this bouquet of flowers is and how little effort was required on your part to make it come into being. Notice the unique perfection of each flower, just as it is. Feel the wealth in each flower and let each flower teach you about the wealth that is hanging around waiting for you to notice it.

> *"All flowers have an angel standing over them –*
> *saying "grow, grow!"* – The Talmud

How Have You Been Investing Yourself of Late? Take an Energy Audit.

I have a friend who thinks he is investing in his business. He spends hours and hours "working" at his computer, wringing his hands and looking for clients. But the whole time he *feels* he is not doing enough, he *believes* the economy is not favorable and he is *worried* he will not have enough money for the end of the month. Then he gets distracted and starts surfing the web and checking his Facebook feed. And to be honest, his business has gone nowhere...he gave up.

So, let's do an energy audit of how he invested himself throughout the day

1. **He did not align to Wealth.** He got out of bed with anxiety about the day and did not take time to meditate and align in some way with the Wealth flow. Once aligned with Wealth, he would have felt inspired to action.
2. **He worried.** He went through his day with extreme worry and doubtful feelings. His energy was not propelling him forward or engaging the law of attraction in his favor. There was no empowerment. Alignment to Wealth brings empowered action.
3. **His energy was scattered as he was on Facebook reading about others fabulous lives.**

Essentially – he did not invest himself well as he went about his actions. He had been investing, but what he did not realize is that he was actually investing in scarcity - even though he thought he was investing in success. He worried (the worst kind of investment strategy) instead of knowing the business was there for him (a great investment strategy). He got easily distracted and lost momentum (focus creates momentum).

So, the basics of the energy audit are:

1. Did I align with wealth first before taking any actions? Feeling the flow and allowing it to inspire my actions?
2. Did I check my vibration throughout the course of the day, and see if I was still aligned with the Wealthy-Flowing feeling?
3. Did I engage in some activity or interaction that put me into fear, worry or other scarcity vibration?

As we have been discussing, as you build your Wealth Consciousness and appreciate Who-You-Really-Are, you will find you are taking different actions, feeling differently as you take your actions. Powerful creators pay attention to how they are investing themselves with an energy audit. They intentionally set, monitor and adjust their vibration accordingly throughout the day.

◎ Investment Tip: Energy Investment Audit

So how have you been investing yourself of late? What has had the majority of your attention? What have you been focusing on? What have you been talking of? What have you been thinking about? How have you been feeling? Reflect on these questions in your Wealth Journal.

As you look over your day, how have you been using your time? How you invest your time is a significant view into how you have been investing your life energy. And depending on how you feel as you invest your time – you are amplifying your vibration. So many of us spend a great deal of time with social media, or watching hours of TV. This is not meant to be a judgment as much as a call to do an Audit, an energy investment audit. Noticing the energy we expend and how we feel as we expend it helps us to assess where we are building momentum. Every day, it is worth taking some time to do an energy audit and notice how you have been investing yourself. This little notion could pay great dividends.

"Pay attention to your thoughts, for they become your actions. Watch your actions for they become your habits. Watch your habits they will forge your character. Watch your character, for it will make your destiny. - Margaret Thatcher

Energy Investing: The Monopoly Example

As you are a powerful investor, I wanted to give you another example of how I invested my energy and the results I experienced. It is a simple story - but shows the impacts of investing - consciously or not.

There is a Monopoly app that lets you play monopoly against other people or against the computer. I thought it would be fun to play and see what it was like to play the game I spent many hours playing as a kid.

Now if you remember - Monopoly takes time, lots of time - unending amounts of time. So, one evening I settled down to play. I chose to play against the computer. At first it was really fun, watching the computer animation, strategizing and making deals. It was all I remembered Monopoly to be and more. I marveled at how the game really was created with real life in mind. You play; you get hit with income taxes, luxury taxes and every once in a while, you land on "chance" or free parking. You go around a board with 40 spaces (representing forty-hour work weeks) and then you can get your paycheck (pass GO and collect $200). It's scary how close to "life" this game is.

After admiring the initial novelty, I settled into making my deals and building my empire. And as you play, it is weird how you start feeling. You feel you need to make the right deals to "get ahead". You need to land on the right "properties" so you can make more money. You need to deny the computer the ability to get 3 properties so it cannot get ahead. You need to get around the board as fast as you can to get your paycheck - so you can pay for "the game". I did not notice how icky all this felt as I was playing. I was just playing the game as best I could. I was not paying attention to the *anxiety* that was building in me, as I could not pay for my properties. And when I went to jail, twice in a row and did not past GO and collect my $200, I was really mad, frustrated, annoyed and pissed. So, I continued on and on, for almost an hour, rolling and making my deals, not noticing the feeling of frustration and opportunism that was at the core of playing.

The next day, I was headed out for a vacation in Florida. I love this time because it is usually a magical journey of fun for me. But I got to the airport and my bag was overweight so I had to pay $25 (by "chance"). When I landed and went to get my rental car, my reservation had not gone through and now the cost to rent the car was $450 ("luxury tax") more than my original rental price.

I felt like I had the night before. Now, I was traveling, but it felt like I was back in the Monopoly game and paying way more than anticipated because of a couple bad rolls and opportunistic dealings.

The reason I think this story is so interesting is that I know I CREATED the experience at the airport. The night before I was investing my time (and more importantly my energy) into a game that created a *feeling* in me of frustration and opportunism. My airport experience was a manifestation of sorts of the investing I did the previous night. My experience at the airport felt just like I was feeling playing Monopoly the night before. Read that again: My experience at the airport *felt* just like I was *feeling* playing the game the night before. I attracted a *feeling* experience at the airport that matched how I was *feeling* playing Monopoly. This is the law of attraction in action.

I actually did not consciously intend to create a feeling of frustration and opportunism, but the law of attraction did not know this! Nor did I realize that that feeling was still active and because I did not realign my energy to something different, I got what I got. But I tell you what; as soon as I realized that I was attracting frustration and opportunism...I stopped, slowed down, re-aligned myself and decided to invest in feeling magical, wonderful and to have a glorious trip. I made a conscious investment decision and invested my feeling energy into what I *wanted* to experience, not what I did not.

I am always amazed at how life works according to the law of attraction and I am always amazed at how often I forget that! I have been studying and practicing energy investing for a long time now and I still make less-than-optimal investments. Sometimes I am just lazy, sometimes I forget and sometimes I don't even realize. But true to form, the law of attraction works the same all the time, every time.

Many people can relate to the idea of using their time on social media, getting lost in scrolling and clicking through pictures, and then feeling upset that they don't have time to live the life they want to live - or worse - feeling guilty about using their time that way. Seeing other people's lives on social media almost always makes us feel badly about our own because we are comparing them to ourselves and then those bad feelings become a part of our energy investment. Moreover, it distracts us from *our* desires, *our* unique approaches, *our* inner truth – Who We Really Are. The same goes for playing games. So many of us are addicted to Candy Crush and the like. These are common "energy investments" that are possibly holding you back...not just from the use of time, but also the less-than-good-feelings that can come from playing them. And remember you are a powerful investor, teaching yourself to become aware of how you are investing your precious life energy. Your creative power comes from consciously deciding how you are going to invest your energy. If you choose to play games, notice their effect on your energy system, and hone your investment approaches accordingly by limiting the time, or changing how you feel as you do them or letting them go. It is very wise to honor Who You Really Are by choosing to invest your attention, energy and focus into things that respect and honor you.

By the way, I deleted the Monopoly app—which I consider an excellent energy investment decision.

"Tell me to what you pay attention to and I will tell
you who you are." – Jose Ortega y Gassett

Awaken to You as Amazing Creator

Creating is one of the most magnificent aspects of living on earth. It is one of the reasons you came to earth. The process of creating and seeing how our creations come into being is the highest form of excitement for our Soul-Self – it is divine play. Sadly, most of us were not taught much about being a creator or tapping into our creativity. This is a shame, because understanding and utilizing our creative power, which is our souls' endowment, is one of the most exciting parts of life.

Our natural state is to create; **we are creators creating constantly**. Think about this. You are a creator creating constantly through the thoughts and feelings you chose to invest in; deliberate thoughts and feelings create outcomes that are closer to what you really want. Are you creating what you want deliberately, or are you habitually doing what you usually do to cope with your day-to-day life? Are you fixing problems or are you creating from a space of genuine abundance, prosperity, excitement and interest? Are you listening to your inner desires?

The joy of conscious creating, via energy investing, gives you the ability and excitement to realize your power. As we embrace our creative power, we become a beacon of light and a force for change. We stand at the helm of our ship and use our internal tools of conscious creation to create any kind of life we choose.

"The only person you are destined to become is the person
you decide to be." –Ralph Waldo Emerson

Sculpt Realities like Fine Clay

Over the years one of the concepts that has served me well is the idea that *I sculpt realities like fine clay*. I love the feeling of this and the empowered potentiality. Have you ever taken a pottery class where you "throw" your own pots from a lump of clay? If you have, you know the focus it takes to *center* the clay and get it ready to create the object you have in mind. If you are not centered, the clay will not center and the clay will not transform into the vase you are thinking of. And as you start to "pull" the clay up before it is centered and prepared, you usually get some blob that has to be mushed down and the clay re-centered on the wheel to begin again.

Energetically, you are the potter and the life energy you are centering and molding is the reality you are sculpting. I know we have discussed some of this before, but I wanted you to have the feeling of being a creator sculpting your life clay. I think this is such a wonderful tangible way to approach creating your realities and your here and now.

Every day, sit down and see yourself sculpting your day. Get centered by breathing or meditating and feeling aligned to the Unlimited Loving-Wealth-Energy surrounding you. See this as energy clay that you can sculpt into anything you want. See yourself creating a wonderful day filled with enjoyment, clarity, ease and satisfaction. Mold increased profits at work. Or sculpt a healthy vital body. You are the molder. You can even use your hands to actually take the energy and mold it. Feel the energy between your hands and mold it into the experiences you desire. Feel yourself molding the day clay. Once you have molded it – take the energy and bring it into your heart center – say "so it is." Know it is happening on an energetic level, soon-to be physical level. I know this sounds a bit weird – but this is a capability you have as Who You Really Are. You are a power creator that sculpts realities like fine clay and *life will show up the way you are feeling.*

I want to share with you how this molding of the clay comes into physical reality. As I mentioned, I am investor ☺ with rental properties and we own a house next door to us that we rent. Now, this was my opportunity to create my neighbors – right?! It was also a chance to figure out the kind of renters I am looking for. Over time, I have been sculpting my understanding of what I want in a renter. It is a long list of things from easily can afford the rent, to kind-heartedness, to a willingness to take care of simple things while being flexible about working with me on larger things….it culminates essentially into – a quality person/people, that I feel good about! Essentially, I pick many of my renters based on my gut and the law of attraction.

I energetically sculpt the reality that I need a renter of this caliber and usually in a week or less, someone shows up (I have had other renters recommend people to me or I get an inspiration to call someone and let them know I have a place available). And they meet all of my desires and many times more than I asked for. The renters I attracted for the house next door are brothers who are just lovely people. The one has a little son and they have lived there now over 5 years (unexpected bonus, I did not create long term renters – but I did add it to my long list.) I feel very blessed to have them next door and over the years we have become friends. I feel I sculpted a wonderful reality.

I truly believe Who You Really Are is vastly larger than the human essence you see in the mirror and that there is a larger part of you eternally connected to the Wealth-Essence-of-All-That-Is.

What if you are Something Greater than your 5 senses can detect? Each of us is made of energy, an Eternal Essence that becomes human and has human experiences. Who You Really Are is an eternal spiritual being that is connected to and a part of the Infinity of Abundance. As you expand into this greater experience and knowing of Who You Really Are (by exploring these concepts) you start to effortlessly *allow* the natural flow of well-being in. It truly is like breathing. The air is here and you breathe it in. So is Wealth. Take a deep breath in now – aha easy. Who You Really Are knows this.

> *"In one drop of water are found all the secrets of all the oceans."*
> - Kahlil Gibran

Wealth is Not Separate from You

Many of us define the things that we want as separate from us: because things that we "want" are seemingly not in our lives *now, therefore* they are separate from us. The exciting, powerful message here is that the "things" you desire are not separate from you - they are part of you - energetically.

As Kahlil Gibran said, in one drop of water is found all the secrets of all the oceans. And inside of you is found all the secrets of all the universes. **Inside, you have all you ever need – tap into it and you can have anything.** The concept of oneness, of interconnectedness and interrelatedness of everything – essentially the drop of water in the ocean - is that everything and everyone is all connected. Everything is interconnected through energy, the energy of life. We are all made of energy (with physical matter being highly condensed energy). And everything, including love, wealth, joy, the new car - anything you can imagine - is woven into this unseen but very real energy "ocean" we are all swimming in. This energy is part of you, it is flowing around you and through you - to be enjoyed by you!

Let's look at it another way: Think of a cell phone. Do you doubt that your cell phone is going to ring? No, we know if someone is calling us we will get the call. However, we cannot see the physical connection, there are no physical wires, but the energy of transmitted waves is floating in the air. The waves are there whether we believe it and see them or not. The same goes with the things we desire in life. They are in the energy-ocean matrix floating around us and through us all the time and the way we experience them in our lives is by putting our attention on them. Just because you cannot see them, does not mean they are not there. Your attention, your focus helps materialize them into your experience. Your attention on wealth (vibrating as wealth) is how you attract it to you.

Wealth is not separate from you. Wealth is not a destination - it is an agreement. It is an agreement that what you want is not something outside of you that you need to strive, fight and push to earn. Wealth is Who You Really Are; It is you...you just have not seen it as such to this point.

Just because you have not experienced wealth does not mean it is not there for you, or that wealth is not in your cards. Today is a new day, with new choices to be made. This is where the effort-lessness comes in. You do not have to effort as much as agree. You do not have to push, as much as allow, you do not have to take as much as choose.

- Agree to the wealth that is in energy form all around you – now.
- Allow the wealth to flow with grace and ease into your life – now.
- Choose to experience your wealth in all its richness – now.

"There is nothing more beautiful than the way the ocean refuses to stop kissing the shoreline, no matter how many times it is sent away."
– Sarah Kay

Wealth Journaling: Update your Wealth Agreements

> Earlier, when we were working in the Awareness chapter, you had started a list of your new wealth agreements. This is a good place to take a moment and update and add to that list.

You are infinitely respected

Have you ever just watched someone you admire, respect and believe in whole heartily? You watch them in awe and just trust what they are doing is the right thing. You know that they are strong and can figure things out. Sometimes, you are curious about what they are doing and why, but you know the outcome is going to be fine. You believe in them and know they will figure things out.

This is how the universe looks at you. You are honored greatly, known as powerful and capable. You are the master creator of your life. All of life, the Universe, Spirit, call it what you will, knows Who You Really Are: a soul that is huge and powerful. The Great-Wealth-Source honors your judgment and your process. Your life is your opportunity to create and choose whatever you want – however you want...no judgment. If you need help or support it is given without judgment. If you ask for something, you must want it or need it for your life creation. And because you are infinitely respected as the master creator of your life, the answer is always – yes, ok, as you wish!

"Our deepest fear is not that we are inadequate. Our deepest fear is that we are powerful beyond measure. It is our Light, not our Darkness, that most frightens us." – Marianne Williamson

Remember...

- You are a powerful creator who creates by investing your energy.
- You are a glorious soul having a human experience.
- Create your wealth habit by deciding to feel wealthy – anyway.
- You are a sure thing.
- You are worthy of good things.
- You are infinitely respected.
- Your life experience is your creative opportunity.
- Life is unlimited abundance, unconditional prosperity and ever-flowing everything available to you – just because - no worthiness or earning necessary.

Frequently Asked Questions

1. **Can't I skip this internal self-worth exploration?** I get it; it is not really all that fun to do the internal work. And I guess you do not have to do the exploration, if you feel you rock! And you have to be really honest because the deep-down nagging feelings of not being quite enough or not having done quite enough are what are determining wealth flow. The reason it is worth a look is so that you can see if there is an energy blockage and choose a new investment. Easy-does-it.

2. **But wealth is separate from me - I don't have it. I don't get your point.** This question is at the crux of our human agreements: that we are separate from that which we need or desire. We need to teach ourselves to think less like humans and more as the Cosmic Citizens we really are. You are a soul having a human experience and your soul knows you are not separate from that which you seek. In fact, Who You Really Are is intricately connected to and a part of the energy of it All – as is a wave is to the ocean. Your soul knows it is as easy to create wealth as it is a cookie, but our humanness has not been taught this. As you continue on this journey and play with the

concepts of the unseen energy being sculpted into physical reality your mind will see it is not all that impossible to believe Wealth is You and You are Wealth.

3. **It seems you are saying that the wealth journey is a really our spiritual journey.** YES! As we undertake our spiritual journey, or the wealth journey the way I am framing it, we look deeply at ourselves and our larger role in the Cosmic Universe. As we undertake this beyond the 5-senses journey, we become aware that there is so much more going on than our 5-senses and human minds have been taught. Whenever someone asks the question: "Is this all there is?" They are ready for their spiritual journey or their Wealth journey. Both ask us to relook at and re-decide about Who We Really Are and how we are going to live our lives based on larger principles.

Investment Strateg
I AM the Master, Power Cre

Invoke this…

I am so excited by this idea that Who I Really Am...
Creator ~ because in the past, I just felt powerless and not all the...

I am so excited to know that Who I Really Am is honored and respected as a glorious creating soul here on earth ~ because in the past I felt measly and inadequate.

I am so excited to experience myself investing energy in things that excite me, honor me, feel good and know that they are a done deal ~ because in the past, I worried that I was not doing things right and not sure that things would work out.

I am so excited to experience True Success, the feeling I am an unlimited creator with unlimited possibility, because I have the Unlimited-Wealth-Spring flowing through me, around me and with me as Who I Really Am ~ because in the past, I was not sure if I deserved it or had earned it or was heard.

I am so excited to know that I am loved, cared for, supported, magnificent and more! ~ just because.

I am so excited to know Who I Really Am is master creator, sculpting realities like fine clay, dancing possibilities into existence, using my Midas touch to create physical wealth in its many and wonderful forms ~ just because I can!

A

Awareness
Of Your Past

Alchemize
Your Beliefs

Awaken
Your Power

Align
Your Energy

Attract
Your Dreams

Allow
Your Desires

Amaze
Yourself

Chapter 6: Invest in Awakening: To the Creating Technologies

Awaken to the Creating Technologies that have been operating on earth and always have been. The Creating Technologies are comprised of the law of attraction and energy vibration that help us create anything we desire. The most exciting part of wealth creation is that you are in the driver's seat. As you consciously invest your vibration energy to engage the Law of Attraction you are using the creating technologies to create your physical reality.

The Creating Technologies

The creating technologies which include the law of attraction are what support us experiencing ourselves as creator. I am referring to the law of attraction and energy vibration as *a technology* because it is important for us to see that it is not just some "new-age" fluff, but real and tangible technology... it is the wireless (cannot see it but you know it is there) technology of creation and manifestation.

The law of attraction is engaged by your vibration and you vibrate based on how you feel. In this chapter, we will discuss your "creating tools" which are ways you can consciously choose how you feel and thus create your energy vibration.

This chapter will help clarify the symbiotic process between how you choose your energy vibration via your creating tools and the law of attraction work together to create your experience.

"You are a divine potter shaping the energy clay of the ethers with your vibrational countenance to bring your desires into physical reality."- Glorious

What specifically are the creating technologies?

I am using the word "technology" because it is important for us to realize that there is a "wireless-system" in place for us to use to experience ourselves as creators. The concept of *technology* elevates our understanding that we are applying scientific knowledge for practical purposes. We use the law of attraction (science) for the practical purpose of creating our experience. The law of attraction is a powerful technology.

You have already been using the law of attraction your whole life... every moment really to create your experience. But most of us engage with it unconsciously and thus we are not sure how we attract what we do.

The law of attraction is based on magnetic attraction - a.k.a. like attracts like. It is simple and powerful. The law of attraction enables us to create by magnetizing experiences to us based on how we are vibrating. Similar vibratory experiences are thus attracted to us. Vibrate scarcity, attract scarcity. (I know this sounds crazy but if we were only taught this in school, like as a part of science class it would make better sense – I believe.)

I am describing it in an extremely simplistic way but I want you to see that the fundamentals of creating are not just made up ideas and niceties people wish to be true. But a real and tangible system that we engage and use every moment of every day.

Our *creating tools* create our energetic vibration and are the way we *engage* the law of attraction to create our life experiences. These tools move energy in the form of vibration and thus stimulate the law of attraction. Your creating tools are the way you choose to think, speak, act, and feel. *Because these create your vibration. What you put your thoughts, feelings, emotions, words and actions toward, attracts similar vibrations to you.* Be clear that you have an energy vibration you are emitting right now and it is engaging the law of attraction to attract similar energy vibration experiences and people to you.

"You are that creator creating every moment with every thought." – Writings of the Mystery of the Universes – Book 2 by Beverly J. Thompson

Invest in understanding the Law of Attraction

One of the most beneficial investments you can make is to deeply understand the law of attraction because it is the foundation of creating.

The law of attraction is at the center of your entire wealth creating experience because the **law of attraction is always in action** – always. It is a universal law that is a constant of life and a constant of our day-to-day creating reality. **The law of attraction is your friend, working with you to bring you what you put your attention on**. It makes possible the unconditional power we have to create, as we wish. Understand the law of attraction and you understand how things happen on earth. As you understand how your vibration engages the law of attraction, you will understand the mechanics of manifestation.

Let's take the example of a car to show how you and the law of attraction work together. *The car does what you direct.* Through your intention you steer the car. With your vibration you are either putting on the gas or the break. The car never says, "Hey, I don't want to drive there." Or "You don't deserve to go there." Or "You have not done enough to go here." It just does what it is designed to do—take you where you say you want to go. The law of attraction and your vibration work hand-in-hand to *unquestioningly* take you where you say you want to go, unconditionally and non-judgmentally. The law of attraction responds immediately to your vibration and starts movement in that direction. The more clearly and eagerly you vibrate the more gas is applied and the faster you go. And the brake pedal is fear, worry, judgment, lack of self-worth, scarcity thinking and all vibrations (feelings) that are resistance and are slowing you way down.

There are many great books out there that discuss the law of attraction. I suggest reading those written by Ester and Jerry Hicks and their work with Abraham. I have been a student of Abraham for years and listen to them on Youtube.com every day. In my opinion, there is no clearer instruction regarding Law of Attraction than that shared over and over by Abraham. Please avail yourself to these teachings. Please invest your life energy into understanding the law of attraction - as this understanding will be the bedrock upon which your Wealth Foundation and Power Creation will be built.

Law of Attraction Basics:

- The law of attraction is always in action.
- It works based on the magnetism: like vibration attracts like.
- Your vibration energy is what the law of attraction responds to.
- The stronger the vibration the more momentum is building.
- Much of what is being attracted cannot be seen with the naked eye, as the eye cannot see energy, just the physical result of energy applied. But your body feels your vibration and knows way before your eyes.

> *"Once something has manifested into physical reality it is old news. The majority of work was done in the energy realms unseen by the naked eye."* – Abraham-Hicks

The Creating Technologies are Impersonal

As we have discussed, the law of attraction is always operating (like the law of gravity). There is no judgment or assessment on what you want. And this makes the creating technology system profound and clear:

What you feel (vibrate), what you say (and how you feel behind what you say), what you think (and what you feel while you think it), what you do (and how you really feel as you do it) attract more of that to you.

So, if you say, "I am going to send my resume to this company" but *feel* (think/believe) there is no way they are going to hire you because you feel you are not what they are looking for...you can be assured that you had a hand in them not calling you. The same goes with money. Many people say they want and need more money but then end up attracting the exact opposite experience. Because they *feel* bad about money, or they feel *lackful* and insufficient, they *talk* about how they do not have enough and they *think* there is not enough in the bank account. This is essentially *vibrating not having enough* and the law of attraction is engaged to bring the experience of not enough. We are honored as powerful creators and not questioned about what we are putting our attention, energy and focus upon.

So, what to do instead?

I do some version of the alchemizing process. Because, I too can get caught in this lackful, not enough vibration. Usually I notice I am feeling heavy. For me, when I feel heavy or sad or lethargic – something is not right in my vibration. So, then I check in and notice what I have been thinking about, talking about, and giving my attention to. It does not take much for me to notice what changed my vibration. This is a version of the acknowledge and accept steps of the alchemizing process.

After I notice my energy has shifted and what I am feeling, I spend a few moments releasing the lackful vibration. I just sit with it, breath and let the energy go bit by bit. I surrender. Then, I make a conscious choice to think something, say something or do something that makes me feel better. I might go for a walk, or listen to 80's dance music, or pet my pup. I try to do some vibration shifting. And I try not to go back to that subject until I am fresh and in a Wealthier mood. Then, I take a few breaths and ask my Big-Laurie-Greater-Wisdom, *got any ideas?* (reach for something greater) And then wait. I usually feel something that gives me clarity, and I let that be enough. Thank you!

Create consciously by directing your vibrational energy

Every day we are provided with thousands of decisions about how we are going to use, direct and manage (a.k.a. invest) our vibration energy. Energy invested, whether consciously or reactively, is still energy applied at creation.

Your creating tools are those that direct and move energy through your body thus creating your vibration. The most powerful are those that move lots of energy through your body, like emotions and beliefs which create a strong vibration. From our mind, we can direct energy through what we focus on, what we pay attention to and what we choose. Energy investment is the skill of a Conscious Creator and *choice* is the most important investment tool we use to direct that energy and create our vibration.

Energy is directed through our bodies by the following creating tools...

- *Your beliefs:* what you choose to believe - what you choose to agree to (free-flowing wealth or hard-to-come-by wealth);
- *Your emotions:* how you choose to vibrate, or feel (feeling eager and excited or worried and doubtful);
- *Your thoughts:* what you choose to think about (thinking lack or abundance);
- *Your words:* what you choose to say (thoughts expressed) (talking about what is not going well or what is working well);
- *Your actions:* what you choose to do; thoughts acted upon (shlumping down the street or skipping down the street);
- *Your heart:* where you choose to come from (open-hearted and generous or closed-hearted and tight-fisted).

"Wealth is largely the result of habit." – John Jacob Astor

Your Choices Create

Choice is a most powerful investment tool. It is our main tool for crafting the life we want. What we choose to focus on and how we feel about it creates our vibration and therefore how we engage the law of attraction. And as we have been discussing, we can consciously choose or habitually react – either way we are making a choice, it is just that many times we are not aware or conscious of what we are choosing.

From a wealth perspective, you have the choice to notice the wealth that *is* around you or notice what is missing. You have a choice to live in prosperity-consciousness or scarcity-consciousness. You can choose to see the glass half-empty or half-full or over-flowing!

"The remarkable this is that we have a choice everyday regarding the attitude we will embrace for that day." – Charles R Swindoll

◉ Investment Tip...Choose Wealth

It is hard to imagine but most people do not choose wealth or to be wealthy. Many don't "want to go there"; others feel it is wrong or selfish to choose wealth; and many more just think wealth is not available to them and leave it at that. But the first rule of creation is to decide what you want—and it is ok to want wealth. Choose to have it, choose to agree to it, choose to feel good about it. Play with Choosing Wealth now.

Wealth Journaling:

- What does choosing wealth mean to me?
- If I were to choose wealth, what would that **feel** like to me now?

Your Beliefs Create

Many see beliefs as thoughts, which is partly true, but beliefs have an emotional component lodged in the body as well. Beliefs are deeply held agreements (usually made early on in life and repeatedly thought and felt over time) as we discussed in the Awareness Chapter. This is why beliefs are so powerful with respect to wealth creating. They are the *original thoughts* and associated emotions connected to an agreement that re-attracts our current experiences. Our beliefs are the paradigms and assumptions we were taught about how the world works. We see the world through these lenses and take action based on them. Beliefs tend to be unconscious because they are so ingrained after years of living from that perspective. They become the way *we agree* life works and thus attract what we experience.

If you believe the world is dangerous, you are going to live (make choices) from that perspective. If you believe money is scarce you are going to attract based on that perspective. If you believe you are a sinner, born in original sin...You get the point...

> "What's keeping you from being rich? In most cases it's simply a lack of belief. In order to become rich, <u>you must believe you can do it</u>, and you must take the actions necessary to achieve your goal." —Suze Orman

◎ Investment Tip: Believe in Your Wealth

You cannot undo a belief overnight. You have come to believe what you have based on good reason. So now, we are creating new ideas for new agreements. As you notice and focus on wealth, you will see evidence of it. Then you will start to agree to wealth in a new way—and then you will develop new beliefs. One of my teachers says he asks his students if *he can believe for them until they are ready to believe* and most are ok with this, as they trust him as their teacher. So I ask you, can I believe for you until you are ready to believe that there is great wealth flowing around you always and in all ways? Play with believing your wealth is around you *now*.

Wealth Journaling:

- What new wealth agreement(s) feel like ones you can adopt and incorporate into your belief system?

Your Emotions Create

Emotions are feeling energy in motion...your vibration, essentially. Emotion is our body vibrating with our thoughts. It cannot be underestimated the importance of understanding the mind/body impact on creation. Many want to say it is only the mind that creates (e.g. thoughts create), but our bodies and the corresponding energy (feeling vibration) that moves through them is what stimulates the law of attraction. Your emotions turn you into a whole-body radio tower beaming out a vibratory signal.

How you feel matters a great deal. Our emotions, feelings and beliefs push energy through our bodies. Respecting the role they play in creating our experience is vital.

From a wealth perspective, if you feel scared, worried and/or limited, you will vibrate in a way that creates an energy vortex around you that pulls more of that vibration in.

> *"Empty pockets never held anyone back, only empty heads and empty hearts can do that."* – Norman Vincent Peale

◎ Investment Tip: Feel Wealthy

Play with feeling wealthy now. Allowing yourself the gift of feeling what you want before you actually see it is how you manifest. Feel wealthy now, just because. Feel wealthy now because it feels good. Feeling wealthy now is fun. Play with feeling wealthy now in whatever way you can.

Your Thoughts Create

We all have a choice about what we think. Let's do an experiment: find something on your desk and just focus on it and only it for 2 minutes. Try it now.

Afterward ask yourself, did you just focus on the object and nothing else? (Two minutes can be a long time.) Did you start to think of anything else besides the object, like what is for dinner or your to-do-list? The point is, so many of our thoughts are random and not mindfully chosen. This is too bad, because our thoughts are creative and what we put our attention and focus on grows and becomes our reality.

But a jumpy mind is not nearly as troublesome as a mind that dwells on negative scarcity thoughts. When we think a thought repetitively is when we start to create reality. Become aware of how you use your mind, because your mind and what you choose to think are powerful, creating investments.

From a wealth perspective, you choose what you think over and over - what you dwell on. For many of us, the unconscious thing we think over and over is "I cannot afford that", or "that is too expensive." And then that becomes or continues to be our reality.

"I dwell in possibility." – Emily Dickinson

◎ Investment Tip: Think Wealthy

"Change your mind, change your world" is a line from a popular song—and it is right on. Better to dwell on" I could if I wanted to. I could afford that if I wanted to." This little change of thought will change your world. Play with thinking, "I could if I wanted to" or "things always seem to work out for me." Pick a thought that works for you and think about it. Play with dwelling on something fresh and wealthy *now*.

Your Words Create

Eagles soar, but vultures circle. A bumblebee gathers, but a spider ensnares. There is energy in the language we use. Take time to reflect on what you say and *how you say it*. Feel into the word energy of scarcity. Now feel into the word energy of abundance and plenty. Feel the difference? There is energy in words, so choose words of inspiration and positive action because not only are others listening but so are you. You are listening to you and sending messages to your subconscious mind. Pay attention and speak only supportive constructive thoughts that move you toward your creations.

From a wealth perspective, you can choose words that enhance your wealth-essence or words that create lack and uncertainty in yourself.

"Words are containers for power,
you choose what kind of power they carry." - Joyce Meyer

◉ Investment Tip: Talk Wealthy

Given there is power in words; here is a list of words that feel wealthy. As you go about your day, see if you can incorporate these into your day-to-day conversations and see how the energy changes as you use and feel into wealth-based words like: unlimited, satisfied, abundant, flowy, joyful, certain, well-cared for, loved, healthy, creative, vital, cradled, honored, capable, eternal, fulfilled, free, pleased, effortless, peaceful, magnificent, glorious, magical, powerful, enlivened, successful. Play with using these today.

Your Actions Create

We love to take action. For most of us, life is all about what we are doing, more than how we are feeling when we are doing what we are doing. Actions are dense energy movement. Physical actions move lots of energy, more than words and thoughts. That is why many counsel, that we "act as if…" Act as if you are successful. Act as if you are beautiful. Act as if you already have your creation. But most of us act while feeling less than successful, not so beautiful, and doubting ourselves the whole way. When we do this, the results are mediocre because our energy vibration is conflicted. It is like driving with the gas and the break on at the same time. Taking an action and feeling its success is gas baby – gas all the way.

You have the choice to take actions that come from a place of knowing your connection to your wealth. Changing our feelings as we take the action directly affects the power of our actions. If you call a prospective client but feel you will not get the job – you will project that. But if you feel you are a great fit for the client – you will convey confidence and positive energy that is more likely to get you the gig. The point is that you may very well take the same action, like making a phone call to a new client, or purchasing what you need but how you feel and what you really believe is going to affect your actions and thus the outcome. Invest in taking actions while feeling good, satisfied, empowered and expanded makes them even more powerful and likely to yield more success.

> *We all have tremendous potential, and we all are blessed with gifts. Yet, the one thing that holds all of us back is some degree of self-doubt. It is not so much the lack of technical information that holds us back, but more the lack of self-confidence."* – Robert Kiyosaki

◉ Investment Tip: Align to Wealth – then Act

They say actions speak louder than words. So, what if we took every action from the place of knowing that all is well and wealth is all around us, available to us? Play with taking an action; from drinking your cup of coffee to brushing your teeth knowing wealth is all around you now.

Your Heart Could Create

The heart-center is a most wonderful creating tool that many of us are afraid to use because we see it as a point of vulnerability. When we open our hearts to something or someone it feels risky, so we do it very sparingly and cautiously. But the heart is one of the most underutilized creation tools in our world. If we went into our hearts before we made decisions, we would often choose differently and we would begin to create a different kind of world.

Our souls speak most clearly to us through our heart. If you want to "hear/feel" what your desires are for your life, move to your heart. When you are meditating and asking for guidance on what decisions to make, go through your heart. Most of us don't 'honor our hearts'. It seems like a luxury, something only a few can do at very limited times.

For me to feel my heart, I start by focusing on that area in the center of my chest and I say to myself, *"all is well and all will be well."* I let that seep in for a bit. I then find something that makes me feel in my heart, like my pup Hercules, he is just the cutest! Or I watch a movie that makes my heart happy like The Princess Bride or listen to music--usually anything Celine Dion or Barbra Streisand awakens my heart center. Going for a walk in nature and noticing the birds opens my heart. Or just crossing my hands over my heart can make me feel comforted. I feel in that heart-center for a bit and then ask my question and feel into options that feel like I do when I think of Herc and I am in my heart center. ☺

My guess you have things in your life and in your memory that bring you quickly into your heart. It could be a sweet thing your child said, or a moment when a butterfly drifted by. There are so many things in life that stop and make you say "awe"! That is your heart popping open. And once you are in that space you are vibrating differently, you are ready to create differently.

If we only committed to our heart-felt urges (like the ones that feel like peace, or excitement, or fulfillment) and pursued them with as much energy and action as the things that we think we "should" do, we would create a very different life experience.

And I want to acknowledge that it is not possible to only follow our heart-felt urges. But I know for sure when I ask my heart how it feels about a certain person that drives me crazy or how I feel about a certain aspect of the business that is not making money, my heart always shows me how to have compassion – and then I say, *"and please show me a way through, so I can honor my heart."* The key is to remember back to your higher intentions and not get lost in the minutia to the point you feel like you have no choice and become powerless. Remember even a holocaust survivor chose to see life as beautiful in the concentration camp. When we choose to move to our bigger intentions and larger wealth visions for our life, annoyances become less of a big deal.

You have a choice to know there is always an unlimited, unconditional sharing of the plenty of life. Generosity, sharing, compassion, fulfillment, and joy are emotions of the heart and they are wealth-promoting. As you move through the easy-does-it-process, remember: as you open your heart, you open to welcoming in the Wealth of life.

"Everyone should carefully observe which way their heart draws them, and then choose that way with all their strength." – Hasidic saying

⊚ Investment Tip: Engage your Heart

When I decide to come from my heart, I feel my internal environment change. I feel generous and expansive. When I am in my heart, I am not trying to attract wealth; I feel *I am the source of wealth.* Through being in touch with your heart you can move from trying to get wealth to being the ultimate Generator of Wealth – you are the "wealth-spring". And really this is the key point of this whole book. **You are the source of wealth. You are the creator, the radiator**...Play with moving into your heart and feel the power of expanded love now.

"I love, I love, I love, I am open to receiving more and more love." Amazing Heart Center Meditation by Christie Sheldon on Youtube.com

The Story of Maggie Using her Creating Tools

Maggie *did not want* to be in Chicago for the winter. *What her heart wanted* was to be somewhere warm and sunny *because* it just made her feel happy and care-free. So, Maggie decided to engage the creative technologies on her behalf.

First, she started doing research feeding her mind with ideas and *possibility thoughts.* She spent a great deal of time in the library reading all kinds of books—not on Florida ☺, but on the law of attraction and creating your reality. She was very *excited* by what she was reading and feeling. (And that feeling of excitement is an indicator that you are in your heart vibrating in a way that will be fulfilling). She became so excited about spending the winter somewhere warm, she inspired to create a job for herself in the warn location. The prospect of being somewhere warm and having a means of income was very *exciting*.

She looked around the Internet for different options. And as the law of attraction would have it, she found a job ad for a marketing director in the Bahamas! She sent in her resume and had an initial interview. They liked what they heard as Maggie is a very open-hearted, capable marketing professional, and they brought her out for an interview.

She got the job and moved to the Bahamas in October – right before the Chicago winter hit.

Maggie used the creating technologies powerfully – mostly by vibrating (investing) excitement and empowerment as she created this new possibility for herself. She also got her thoughts aligned as she researched and read about the law of attraction. She spoke enthusiastically about moving somewhere warm and she believed she had what it took to find a job. It was not a matter of "if" she was going to find a great option, it was a matter of "when" and "what".

The creating technologies are in place, always at the ready, always engaged – so use them to create anything and everything your heart desires.

"If you can accept that everything you need for the fulfillment of what you want is already in place and working for you. Your singular work is to accomplish an atmosphere around you that allows the realization to show up when it does."
- Abraham-Hicks

Create Wealth by <u>Vibrating</u> Wealth – It's about Harmony of Vibration

You attract what you vibrate. If you want to experience the Wealth that is already here you need to vibrate wealth. *You need to be in **harmony** with the wealth experience you seek and be a vibrational energetic match to what you want to experience. Harmony, harmony, harmony!* So, if you want to create wealth in your life, spend time vibrating wealthy feelings and putting your attention on *the wealth experience* you desire (not on the lack of it now). Harmonize your energy vibration to WUW – wealth unlimited wealth.

This concept is most clearly seen when we look at the desire to create more money in our lives. We say we want more money. We affirm we want more money. But deep inside we do not believe we can have more money, or we do not feel we are worthy of more money, or we just notice not enough money in our bank account, or we don't think we are doing what it takes to get more money. **Essentially, we are vibrating *not-wealth* and *we are not in vibrational harmony* with our money desire.** In the case of Maggie, she put herself in vibrational harmony with her heart's desire.

Vibrational harmony:

- If you do not believe you can have more money... you are vibrating limitation and thus in harmony with experiences of limitation and not having more money.
- If you do not feel worthy of money... you vibrate inadequacy and thus attract experiences that are a vibrational match to not feeling worthy.
- If you are vibrating scarcity of resources you are in harmony with scarcity experiences.

Can you feel what a downer these vibrations are? Can you feel in your body how low vibrating these statements make you feel? Do you feel in harmony with the experience you desire? Does any of this feel good? I bet not. *This is your internal compass telling you, you are out of alignment with what you want.* You are not in harmony and your vibration is a miss-match. When you do not feel good about what you are thinking, saying or doing you can be sure something is out of sync. And the exciting thing is, once you are conscious of how you feel, you can realign yourself to thoughts and feelings that feel better and more wealth attracting.

Don't get down on yourself. Just say, "That does not feel so good, what small thoughts can I take to move myself towards feeling better?" What would bring me more internal harmony? We will explore more tools for shifting your energy as we go on. For now, just notice and become aware.

Or you might want to alchemize these feelings using the process in Chapter 4. Because as we discussed in the Alchemizing chapter – *acknowledging* our limiting beliefs is the first and most helpful step to productively using the downer vibrations to shift our energy to a new vibration in harmony with wealth.

"You miss 100% of the shots you don't take." –Wayne Gretzky

Leverage the Power of the Universe

As you practice vibrating and watching how your vibration attracts, you are learning to use the law of attraction to leverage the power of the Universe. As you leverage your attracting power you will experience the wealth and vitality you desire. You have all the resources you need. The universe, in its unlimitedness, is backing you up...flowing what you vibrate - to you. As you practice using your creating tools you are leveraging your power by choosing your vibration and investing your energy in the direction of wealth. As you invest your energy through your creating tools and your emotional vibrations in the excitement of what you want to experience (e.g. by speaking about wealth, feeling wealthy, taking actions that make you feel wealthy, opening your heart to Wealth etc.) and let the law of attraction do the work of pulling it to you. You are leveraging the Wealth producing power of the universe to engage the flow to you.

◎ Investment Tip: Energy is the real currency

Most of us think the thing we invest is money. But energy is the real currency because energy is vibrating. Our energy is what we really invest. Our thought energy, our word energy, our feeling energy and our action energy are ultimately our investment currency. And these choices create our vibration that interacts with the law of attraction. So notice how you feel and how you are vibrating. Because those investments lay the groundwork for experiencing more of those vibrational matches.

Now we know better

As Maya Angelo said, "When we know better, we do better." Now you know better. Now you know that you can use the Creating technology system to engage the law of attraction via your creating tools to create your vibration and therefore your wealth experience.

You can now invest with your creating tools to *choose* to focus on wealth. Now you can *speak* eagerly of the wealth that you have and are going to have. Now you can *feel* wealthier and wealthier every day. Now, you can *think* about wealth and how you are on the clear path to it. Now, you are choosing a harmonious vibration to engage the law of attraction to attract Wealth in all its forms. Now, you can start to believe in the wealth that is flowing continuously to all (including you) unconditionally. You can allow yourself the joy of wealth filling your heart and enjoy the playful, effortless nature that comes from your internal Wealth-Spring. No more are you a victim of the system. The creating technologies are yours to use as you choose – invest wisely.

"If you had one goal and that was to feel good, you would never again need to hear another word from anyone. You would live successfully and happily and in a way of fulfilling your life's purpose ever after." - Abraham-Hicks

Remember…

- There is a creating technology system (based on the laws of magnetics) in place for us to experience creative fulfillment.
- The creating technologies are always at work, impartially bringing like experiences to you based on your vibration's interaction with the Law of Attraction.
- Your creating tools of choice, thought, word, feeling/emotion, belief, and heart create your vibration.
- You create/attract experiences to you via your vibration, which engages the law of attraction.
- Choose to invest in wealth by being in vibrational harmony with wealth.
- Feel Wealthy
- Talk Wealthy
- Think Wealthy
- Vibrate Wealthy

Frequently Asked Questions

1. **Why do you call them technologies?** Because I wish for you to realize there is a powerful system in place for you to concretely use to create. It is based on science and it is practical and impartial - not hairy-fairy. Again, the definition of *technology* is the application of scientific knowledge for practical purposes. The vibration we choose, engages the law of attraction and this is the use of scientific knowledge for the practical purpose of creating.

2. **For someone who is very practical-minded, I don't feel there is enough proof to make the argument that the law of attraction is based in science. How can you make this claim that it is science?** Much of our "science" has yet to catch up with physical truths we experience. Much of the "technology" we experience today was considered crazy impossible Star-Trek fantasy some 30

years ago. Now it is considered daily-reality. So too is what I am discussing about the creating technologies. In the future, the use and understanding of these concepts will be considered elementary.

3. **Why don't we learn this stuff in school?** Because these are still considered new age ideas. But yoga and meditation were not taught in schools just a few years ago – things are changing.

4. **How do I know if I am using the law of attraction? How do I know if I am using it correctly?** We are always using the law of attraction…we cannot not use it. So, notice what is showing up in your life. This is what you attracted. Ask yourself, "How was I feeling as I was doing that?" How do the different areas of your life *feel*? These manifestations are harmonic matches and the energetic equivalent of your past vibration around that creation.

5. **This sounds too simple – how is my wealth entirely in my control?** Because our vibration is in our control – thus what we attract is also.

6. **How do I know if I am vibrating wealth?** Do you feel good, satisfied, excited, contented, at peace grace-filled, expectant, empowered, valued and valuable? These are the feelings of vibrating wealth.

7. **To be clear, the law of attraction and our vibration energy are the creating technologies?** Yes, actually, the law of attraction and our creating tools are part of the larger creating technology *system* in place for our creating fulfillment. Our vibration energy is how we engage the law of attraction.

"Wealth is not a result – it is an approach."

Investment Strategy:
I am awake to my creating tools

Invoke This...

Now, I have an important piece of my education: an understanding of the creating technology system. I understand how the law of attraction and my energy vibration work in concert to create my reality. I am ready to enjoy using the creating technology system to invest in what I want to experience.

Now, I understand the law of attraction and how I am vibrating is what attracts a similar vibration – so I am using my creating tools to invest more deliberately. I am an empowered investor.

Now, I see that how I feel and vibrate is the basis for my experiences. My vibration matters. And how I feel as I take my actions in the world is what is really creating my reality. I am willing to mindfully choose my vibration and take actions that feel higher vibrating.

Now, I am awake to my power creating tools – YAHOO! Now, I can think wealthy! I can speak wealthy! I can feel wealthy! I can believe in my unlimited connection to the Wealth-Source!

I am Wealthy!

A

Awareness
Of Your Past

Alchemize
Your Beliefs

Awaken
Your Power

Align
Your Energy

Attract
Your Dreams

Allow
Your Desires

Amaze
Yourself

Chapter 7: Invest in Awakening: To the Wealth Inherent in Life

The third aspect of Awakening is investing in seeing the Wealth inherent in life. Life is an opportunity to tangibly experience the Wealth that is always flowing to you and through you. As you awaken to some new ways to view life's possibilities, you will see the Earth was meant to be your creative playground to experience life in any way you choose.

Life is Wealth and Wealth is Life

One of my favorite quotes is a question, actually: *"What would you do if you knew you would succeed?"* Success, love, wealth and health are the natural way of life; the natural way your life was meant to be experienced. Well-being, love, and abundance are woven into the fabric of life; this energy is intertwined in everything; it is everything. We can enjoy more and more of it by allowing ourselves to feel it. Life has tremendous support to help you experience fulfillment in its many forms.

Most of us really do not agree with this. Life is considered hard and limited. But after these Awakening chapters, I hope you feel, remember, and moreover, embrace that life was meant to be a satisfying creating experience. And you allow wealth and success into your life more and more...effort-lessly.

Throughout this exploration, I hope you are awakening to a new wealth of possibilities, seeing life as a constant process of prosperity and creation... and knowing that you are the genesis of the creative urge. You are at the helm of the ship, navigating your ship to whatever shores you decide. And as we are discussing, you are a powerful wealth creator who already has all of the tools of wealth creation naturally within you and it is because of your energy investments that you land where you do.

In this Awakening chapter, we will continue to build your Wealth Consciousness foundation by exploring new awarenesses on how life was set up for your creative fulfillment. This is important because if you cannot see life was set up for your creative fulfillment, you cannot give yourself permission to really enjoy Who You Really Are and what you are really up to.

"What if gravity was a form of love and from her very core, the Earth was holding you to her, whispering in your ear, 'I'll never let you go. We are in this together.'"
- Quote On a bottle of Synergy Kombucha from Mary Rose

What will I be awakening to?

We will be awakening to seeing life on earth in a new, prospering way. So many of us were brought up in the school of hard knocks, with messages of scarcity, inadequacy and limitation. But these messages are so far from the way the world and the universe were created to operate. Awakening is about waking up to the truth of how life was really set up for us to play here on earth — that we are energy masters making physical that which is energy. As we make this journey, it is my hope that you:

1. See the wealth that was and is meant for you,
2. Feel how lovingly and respectfully this world and life are set up for you to create and enjoy the creating process,
3. Experience life as a magical playground.

As you see and feel this new way, effortlessness will seem less like a crazy notion and more like the way things were meant to be: ask and it is given, seek and you will find, knock and the door will be opened for you; simple, effortless and tons of fun.

"Be the instrument you have incarnated for, the life that brings you in contact with You. All knowingness shall return to you when your receptors are open." - Sananda

◉ Investment Tip: Go Back to Eden

We have all heard the story of Adam and Eve, who lived in paradise. Paradise! Through a few bad choices they ended up losing touch with this paradise. But did the Garden of Eden go away? No. In fact, Eden is here in this very moment, waiting for us to notice it and adventure back. This magical capability to create is ours, always has been and always will be. It is our opportunity to create heaven on earth for ourselves. Go back to Eden by slowing down, taking a moment to notice something beautiful in your immediate surrounding or open the palm of your hand and appreciate its complexity. Eden is appreciation. Let yourself go back to Eden where all things are possible and available, and let that energy come forth to create heaven on earth...your little piece of paradise.

"Life is much greater and extends into multitudes of experiences. It is always alive with new creations ever-expanding." – Writings of the Mystery of the Universes by Beverly J. Thompson

Invest in Awakening to Life as a Wealth Experience

Our journey to wealth consciousness asks us to look at life from a new vantage point; one in which you and the unlimited, unconditional wealth of life are intricately, completely connected and eternally unified. The questions (and opportunities) presented in this chapter are: Will you remember the truth of your Essence? Will you give yourself permission to remember Life as it was granted to you by yourself before you were born? Will you open to the idea that life was meant to be experienced from a Wealth perspective?

What follows is a list of "Rememberings" that I have come to learn over the course of my wealth journey. I call them rememerings because our soul knows these fundamentals prior to embodying…and the rememberings are meant remind you of what you knew before you were born into your body about how "life", your life, is meant to be experienced from a Wealth Consciousness perspective. You might want to get your Wealth Journal out and write on the questions at the end of each remembering. Minimally, stop for a moment and reflect on them – there is gold in any realizations you might have.

> *"The desire of monks and mystics is not unlike that of artists: to perceive the extraordinary within the ordinary by changing not the world but the eyes that look. To form the intention of new awareness is already to transform and be transformed."* – Jane Hirshfield

Remember…Life is Abundance

Abundance is the essence of life. Life is teaming with abundance. Everything we could possibly need is all around us. Everything we could imagine, we can create. There are countless grains of sand in the beaches of the world, millions of different species of animals, plants and bugs. There are billions of trees, trillions of blades of grass, millions of leaves in your backyard, billions of neurons in your brain, thousands of hairs on your one head, trillions of cells in your body…abundance is the way of life. And life wants for you to live abundantly, wealthy, the way the rest of life lives.

What if life is abundant?
How would that change how you feel and act?

◉

Remember...Life is friendly

Have you ever asked yourself if you believe *the universe is a friendly place or not?* Take a moment and really contemplate that question and the wisdom behind it. Many of us believe that life is dangerous or threatening. And this belief makes us approach life in a way that is fearful or security-seeking.

What do you believe? I have spent a great deal of my life in search of my answer. I realized that it was a fundamentally important question for me to ponder because I constantly struggled with wondering whether life was a deck stacked against me.

What I have come to learn, feel and believe is that the Universe is incredibly friendly. In fact, it is unbounded in its love and abundance. It is unconditional in its care for us. But quite a bit of searching led me to this understanding! And I believe it is important for you to contemplate your own answer to this question. Because it is the center point of your ability to experience Wealth and the creation of effort-less wealth.

What if life is friendly?
How would that change how you feel and act?

◉

Remember...Life is on your side

I love the book *Pronoia Is the Antidote for Paranoia* by Rob Brezsny. The book makes the case that life loves you greatly and it is on your side and that there is no reason to be paranoid that life is going to come and whack you on the side of the head. Instead, be proniod. Agree that life is set up to help you out and has been in every way. And if you felt that, it would even more.

You might be thinking that if life is on your side then it must be against another. No, this is human thinking. All-That-Is is powerful, creative and imaginative beyond our wildest understanding. All-That-Is works to help each of us out, in wonderful and unique ways that are not about win/lose, but win/win/win and more win. It is only our human minds that keep creating, attracting and assuming win/lose.

What if life is on your side? What if All-That-Is has your back?
What if you believed things are always working out for you?
How would that change how you feel and act?

◉

Remember...Life wants what you want

Life is set up as a fulfillment machine. The energetic grid of the earth uses the law of attraction as an unbiased fulfillment mechanism for you to experience what you vibrate - unconditionally. Therefore, what you desire is what life desires for you...and moreover as soon as you desire it sets about a chain of events to fulfill that desire.

What would you do if you knew that life wanted what you wanted? What if you
knew you would succeed? How would you act and be?
What would you change if you knew that you are
supported and helped out in every way?

◉

Remember...Life is a YES Machine

Life agrees with you always. It is like a YES Machine, always saying yes to whatever you feel. Through the law of attraction, life brings to you a vibrational match to whatever you have been feeling. It does not argue with you, or judge if what you desire is appropriate, it just says - Yes! And goes about bringing you whatever you are dwelling on. So, if you say, "I really want to increase my wealth" the answer is YES! And if you then vibrationally say, "But I don't have the right education," the answer is YES! If you say, "I don't know what to do to make more money," the answer is Yes! And it will continue to be YES until you change your vibration by changing the messages you are saying to yourself. Say things like, "I want to increase my wealth." - YES! "I will find ways that support this." YES! "Every day, I make progress toward allowing my wealth to flow to me." YES! "I notice and enjoy all the wealth I have right now!" YES! "This is getting easier and easier." YES! "It's all happening." YES!

> *What if life is always saying yes to you? What if you asked and*
> *it was given - period? How would this impact your day?*

@

Remember...The essence of life is Well-Being and you are surrounded by well-being at all times

Well-being is woven into the fabric of life and well-being is all around us, always. There is so much life set up to support us. The sun comes up without us telling it to. Trees produce oxygen; plants produce food. So much is happening that we do not have to manage or direct. A friend of mine once said, "What if Starbucks was created just in case one day you wanted a cup of coffee while you were out? WOW did that floor me. Could it be that all of life is facilitating me? YES! Well-being is your essence, it is the energy that flows through you and it is there for you to enjoy, freely and effortlessly, just like you enjoy the air you breathe.

> *What if at the essence of your life is well-being; unlimited, unconditional*
> *well-being? How would this change how you feel and act today?*

@

Remember...Wealth IS and it is experiencing itself AS you

One of my favorite teachers says that two of the most important words we need to revisit and understand are IS and AS. He goes on to explain that Wealth IS and there is nowhere in the universe that the Wealth-Source-Energy is not. It has always been and It always will be. *Wealth is already here.* It just IS. So much so that we take it for granted that it IS always here, always flowing, prospering, loving, supporting and nurturing, like the air we breathe. *Wealth is always wealthing.*

And this Wealth-Source-Energy has physicalized into life to experience itself AS you. You are the essence of wealth, love and magicalness with all the creative power of this Essence.

> *What if Wealth IS already here: always flowing, always available and Unlimited? What if you are Wealth experiencing itself AS you? How would that change the way you look at yourself and your life?*

◎

Remember...Life is Always Evolving

We are growth-seeking beings because life is meant to be an expansion experience. As such, we are in a constant state of evolution. It is the essence of life to grow, change and prosper. Even in the ending of something there are the seeds of new beginning. Things end so something new can begin. The definition of prosper is to grow, to flourish. And it is the essence of your life to constantly prosper. You are leading-edge creator ever evolving.

> *What if you are always prospering what you put your felt-sense attention on? How would that change the way you invest your attention, energy and focus?*

◎

Remember...The Nature of Life is to Flow

According to the ancient philosopher Aristotle, "Nature abhors a vacuum." Aristotle based his conclusion on the observation that nature requires every space to be filled with something and that empty or unfilled spaces are unnatural. Wherever there is a void, the universe seeks to fill it... meaning life is constantly in flow to us, through us and around us. But many of us have a big bubble around us that the wealth just bounces off of. Over and over again, I have seen people put a *resistance bubble* around themselves.

The resistance bubble is where life shows up to move us in the direction of our desires and we actively push what we desire away.

For years, a friend of mine said she wished she had more money so she could do all the things she always wanted to do – like travel and do nice things for her friends. Well as life flows, she was left an inheritance of over $1 million dollars; which to be honest freaked my friend out. She just could not see herself with that much money – for so many reasons. You could feel her resistance to the money, it totally felt like she put a huge resistance bubble around herself to undo the good that was coming to her. And you know what, ultimately, she created losing the money through a bizarre accident. Please don't resist the wealth that is flowing to you – it just is not a good investment.

What if life is flowing good to you right now? Have you put a resistance bubble around you blocking what it is bringing?

◎

Remember...Life has *all the resources you need*

Have you ever made a meal when you had everything you needed on hand? Doesn't it just make cooking so much more fun when you know you have everything you need and you can relax into the preparation process? Well, life is like a giant pantry with everything you need already in stock and just waiting for you to decide what you are going to cook. We have at our access the ultimate stock of every ingredient needed to create the things we desire. The Universe is backing you up and can supply all you need on time with abundance. The law of Attraction is the ultimate Just-In-Time delivery system that is always at the ready and always delivering.

What if you have universal access to all the resources you need? How would that change your day-to-day living?

◎

◎ Investment Tip: Just know it

How many of us have launched a prayer with real clarity about what we wanted? And then that little voice jumps in with our habitual doubts… those little nagging thoughts that say, *I wonder if I was heard? I wonder if I asked right? I wonder if this can happen?* …and on and on. Next time you launch a desire, make a prayer, initiate a creation (all the same thing by the way), let the thought move into the creative ethers *without* all the doubts and scarcity thoughts.

How would you feel if you just knew that you were heard and that all of the creation has your back? What if you just knew that Wealth (with a capital "W") was flowing continuously to you, unlimitedly? What if you just felt honored? What if you just felt taken care of? What if you just could be at ease about it all? Just know it is in the works and be excited about experiencing it. What if…play with this for a bit and see how you feel.

"The prayer's purpose is to draw you to a felt gratitude, which in turn leads to the silence in which you feel that the prayer is praying you, not the other way around."
– Roger Housden from *for lovers of god everywhere*

What if…

What if we looked at life from the vantage point of these rememberings? What if we saw life as a source of inspiration – helping us clarify our desires and understand our power? As we reflect on these new ways to see life, we might allow ourselves to release our resistance, take down our defensive walls and move into a new empowered understanding of ourselves - not as victim but as magic makers! Hum what a concept.

Invest in Awakening to the Earth as your Creative Playground

I believe our souls come to earth to experience tangible reality. The fun of seeing thought materialize into physical form is great fun to us souls. The earth is set up for you and me to have fun molding the energy clay of our lives into a unique expression of what we would like to experience. Time creates a space between our thoughts and the manifestation of the thoughts into physical reality. Time is one of the things that makes the earth experience different for us souls because it slows manifestation down and gives us space to get clear about what we really want.

◎ Investment Tip: I matter

We souls are powerful creators able to mold energy clay into whatever physical forms and life experiences we desire. The process of us creating is mattering – that is, turning energy to physical matter. Spend some time thinking about this interesting concept that *you matter*! 1. That you matter by turning energy to physical matter. 2. That you matter because you are needed and an important part of life experiencing itself!

The earth was designed for you to experience the fulfillment of your desires.

The earth really is a magical place, where we can tangibly taste, feel, touch, smell and see our creations in 3D. This is a very cool experience for a soul, which is pure light energy and does not experience all of the nuances of physical creation the way we do in human form. And earth has been designed specifically for us to experience the results of our thoughts and actions played out in physical form.

As we live, we make decisions and *feel the results* of those decisions play out through the process of time and physicalizing (energy turning to matter). On this magical playground of earth, we get the opportunity for this experience. And what we decide to create (through our thoughts, beliefs, actions and choices) is manifested. If the result is what we hoped for, great;

if not, there is an opportunity to choose a new thought, a new action and a new belief. That is it. There is no judgment or punishment for thinking "wrongly" or acting mistakenly. There is an opportunity to choose again. That is what is meant by "today is a new day". Every moment we can choose again.

◉ Investment Tip...Keep your Feeling Energy on the North Star of your Desire

When we take a trip, we head in the direction of our intended destination. We use a compass to help us navigate there. We chart the course and keep checking in with the compass to see if we are still headed in the right direction. If not, we make subtle changes to our path, to keep us on course.

The same is true for our desire of wealth. We chart our course, we determine what we desire (how we want to feel) and then along the journey, we check in with our internal compass. How are we feeling? Are we putting our attention on what we desire? Are we excited about it coming into our lives? Are we getting closer and closer? As we journey, we make subtle changes to our course, recalibrating it (finding a vibration that feels good and shows progress) all the while we are on the journey to the north star of our desire...all the while knowing we are headed to a wonderful place and it can feel good on the journey as well as at the destination.

All outcomes are already possible in the infinite field of possibility.

Think of a life as a magnificent video game. As you play (have desires) the law of attraction starts to work on those desires – instantly and a variety of options to fulfill the desire starts to coalesce. Every possible outcome and means to get to that outcome are available and possible. It is really beyond our imaginings! Every ending and every twist and turn producing that ending is possible because of your energy and the law of attraction working together. It is just part of the creating technology system. This does not mean there is pre-determination, it means that all possibilities are a possibility and come into physical manifestation by our feeling and thinking about them - by what we focus on and how we choose to feel moment by moment.

What if you did not have to effort as much as choose what you wanted to experience – like in a video game? What game would you play today? What outcome would you focus on?

⑥

⑥ Investment Tip...Notice

Many of us ask why haven't I experience wealth to this point if it is always flowing? You have, you are – but you are not really *noticing* it as such. Much of what we are discussing is a change in perspective. "Seek and *notice* you have found, knock and *notice* the door is opened, ask and *notice* you have been answered" is how the old saying should go.

The Law of Attraction is the foundation of the Creative Playground

The law of attraction is always in action. I know we have already discussed this, but it is important to note the role the law of attraction plays in facilitating your creating experience here on earth. It is the force that makes the playground possible. How you play with molding the energy of your life and what experiences you choose is up to you. The law of attraction will keep reproducing your thoughts, words, beliefs and feelings – like a Xerox machine. It *does not judge or select what creations to support and which to ignore.* All creations (choices) are honored. This is why we are discussing conscious investing. Become conscious of the investing you are doing on a day-to-day basis so you can use the law of attraction effectively.

What if you and only you, are the creator of your experience? How would that change how you see yourself right now?

⑥

◎ Investment Tip: Feel enough

Enoughness is a feeling we can give ourselves to allow a felt-sense of completeness and contentment. This is the feeling that all is well. If we keep pushing ourselves and never feel we have done enough, how are we going to appreciate the good that does happen? How are we going to be aware of what wealth we do have? Give yourself permission to enjoy what you do have…give yourself blue sky moments of release from doing and let yourself enjoy just being.

Lay on the ground and watch the birds float by. See the clouds and just appreciate them as they are. Life is around us calling us to see its wonder and glory…and a flower will keep flowering and keep sharing its beauty, even if we do not notice. Slow down to feel and enjoy it. Life is constantly giving to us and it is not fair to say life is not. And as we feel enough, we open to the bounty.

> *"My conscious awareness of the Divine Presence*
> *as my supply is my supply. I am now consciously aware*
> *of the indwelling fountain of overflowing abundance."*
> – John Randolph Price, *Nothing is too Good to be True*

Effortlessness is the way fulfillment was meant to happen

The excitement of wealth creation, from the vantage point of effortlessness, comes in knowing wealth is yours and you are moving towards it with grace and ease, which is the way the playground was meant to be experienced.

I know this sounds cray-cray, but we were not meant to struggle…life is supposed to be fun and flowy. This is one of the things that tripped me up in my journey toward effortless wealth; my resistance to effortlessness. Many times, I fall into difficult-effort mode. It's a habit, a learned practice of pushing myself hard, demanding I do more and forever moving my own cheese so I always feel behind. But this is not the life experience that was meant for us – play-filled effortless fulfillment was.

I want to make the distinction between difficult-effort and joy-filled-effort because there is a difference. Joy-filled action is the exertion of effort on something with excitement and enthusiasm – it feels like play. It is energy put forth from a different vibration, with a very different intention. Even a task like washing dishes can be joy-filled, just add some bubbles and use a good sponge and you are off. As we invest our thought, word and deed energy, we don't need to add the judgment that it needs be difficult or requires difficult effort.

Many times, I am just in a satisfied place and then I am *inspired* to an action or idea. One day, I was making the bed and I thought it would be fun to put a message to myself on my pillow for when I go to bed at night. I was so excited by this idea I made *pillow-top inspiration cards* and then sent them out as Christmas card gifts…it was so fun!

Another example, with this book. I felt inspired to write it. I wanted to write it and I enjoyed it so much! But sometimes when it felt like effort, I decided not to write. I just did not do anything until I felt called to it or inspired to work on it. In fact, I took 2 years off before moving it forward to the final edits. I was tired and busy, and I wanted this to be an uplifting experience for you the readers. I wanted it to have high vibrating energy infused into it – at every step of the way.

My writing teacher once told us, *"If you do not feel like writing, just walk around and hug your manuscript! "* I loved that. Sometimes I would hug it and most of the time, I had the manuscript on my blessing table with crystals and the Goddess Lakshmi looking over it. That felt good, really good! And feeling really good is how you know you are enjoying the playground.

And of course, there are times we *have* to do things that we really don't want to do. Sometimes we can't just put our obligations aside, such as an assignment at work, or even mowing the lawn. How can we bring ourselves to do these things with joy-filled effort?

Can you feel the energy of the word obligation? Pretty dense, right? Getting at the core of why you are doing what you are doing really can make the effort more uplifting. I mow the lawn because I love the look and smell of fresh mowed grass. I complete the project at work because I enjoy having a paycheck that affords me to live my life. Remember, we have the ability to choose what we think and how we vibrate ultimately creating the resulting experiences flowing to us.

◎ Investment Tip: Enjoy Skipping

It is time to go out and skip for a bit...on your next walk skip for a few moments. Feel your body float along as you skip. There is something so wonderful about skipping. It is effort, but really very fun. No difficult efforting, just gliding along like a little kid enjoying their body. Notice how people look at you - a grown adult skipping. You will look crazy but feel wonderful! Play with the feeling of skipping and notice the enthusiastic effort of doing something you want to do.

> *"The best and most beautiful things in the world*
> *cannot be seen or even touched - they must be felt with the heart."*
> - Helen Keller

You are Dearly Loved

"You are dearly loved" is how Kryon, the metaphysician, closes every letter and conversation. There is only love in the universe for us...only divine love. And this love is truly unconditional and non-judgmental. We as humans have imbued human expectations, demands and limitation on the Love-Wealth Source. It is kind of crazy to see how we have come to misunderstand the Love Source. We have substituted judgment for compassion, expectation for understanding and assessment for freedom. But the Love Source, the unseen energy at the core of life, is always wisdom, understanding and freedom. We are love personified!

In *Conversations with God*, it is said that the 5 essential aspects of the Love Source (life) are that it is always blessing, always loving, always joyful, always grateful and always accepting - always - in all ways. And what we choose to create is honored and respected unconditionally by the Love Source – with the addition that the Love Source would love for you to experience the bliss of your creations. Therefore, if we are choosing to create a wonderful business that brings us joy and prosperity we will be helped to learn all we need to create such an experience. Our internal wisdom will be guided to just what we need, just when we need it on our journey to our creation.

Don't think like a human and don't let old messages about how others have decided the world and life should work dissuade you from feeling *the truth*. You are a part of the Great-Creator-Of-All and you have magnificent creative capabilities within a fulfillment playground of infinite possibilities for you to experience the inherent wealth of life.

⊚ Investment Tip: Remember you are most precious

Hold out your hands and cup them like you were going to dip your hands in a pool of water to drink. Now look in your hands and imagine a perfect little child cradled right there in the center of your hands. Your heart opens because the child is so precious and you are feeling very nurturing of this little one. Feel your love for it grow and notice how you would do anything for this one.

This feeling is the feeling the Love Source has for *you*. It does anything for you - unconditionally - nurturing you on your life journey and making way for your greatest joys to be fulfilled! You are dearly loved - please open to it and enjoy!

"To change the conditions of our outer world, we are invited to actually become the conditions of our desire from within. When we do so the new conditions of health or peace or wealth are mirrored in the world around us."
– Gregg Braden from The Isaiah Effect

Remember...

- WUW - Unlimited wealth is inherent in Life
- Life is abundance
- Life is friendly
- Life is on your side
- Life wants what you want
- Life is a YES Machine
- The essence of life is Well-Being and you are surrounded by well-being at all times.
- Wealth IS and it is experiencing itself AS you
- Life is always evolving
- The nature of life is flow
- Life has all the resources you need
- The earth is your creative playground designed for you to experience the fulfillment of your desires.
- All outcomes are already in the infinite field of possibility
- The Law of Attraction is the foundation of the Creative Playground
- Effortlessness is the way fulfillment was meant to happen
- You are dearly loved

Frequently Asked Questions

1. **How do you know all this stuff is true?** Experience.
2. **Why don't we hear about people who use the Effort-less approach?** Mostly because effort-less-ness does not make sexy news, the School of Hard Knocks does. When something happens easily, like no one overcoming adversity, fighting the bad-guy and all that drama we love, we are not that intrigued. But effortlessness is happening more and more, as people are choosing it. These effortless wealth creators are out there...seek and you shall find.
3. **I don't agree that outside forces are not impacting my wealth.** Don't give your power away. Try not to blame the stock market, the

greedy CEOs, the thoughtless boss, the real estate bubble, whoever or whatever. I have done this too. Some part of me likes the drama of blaming another and feeling self-righteous or victimized. It is much easier to put the responsibility on someone or something else.

But the downside of the blame game is we give our power away to that which we blame. We disempower ourselves when we give in to the idea that outside forces are what are causing our situation.

One of my greatest wishes for you is that you know how amazing you are, that you remember what incredible creative power you have and what internal strength you possess. You are *the* force that impacts your wealth.

"What is meant to be will find a way."

Investment Strategy:
I AM playing with creating my life

Invoke this:

I can feel how the energy of life is supporting me in my creative endeavors. I can see how the earth experience is a creative playground set up for me to realize my creating power and support my creating urges

...how AWESOME is that!

Right here, right now, I feel powerful! I allow the flow of the abundance of life into my daily experience. I allow the wealth-energy of life to flow through me. I feel my power to shape energy into physical reality and this is exciting stuff. As I enthusiastically focus my energy in a particular direction, my ideas, desires and dreams are moving into reality easily and effort-lessly.

...that is AWESOME!

This is so exciting to know that my life is meant to be a magical experience of expansion, growth and love! It feels so good to know I don't have to struggle or feel lacking. It is wonderful to feel tremendous well-being around me always and as I play with creating my life – I can have my cake and eat it too.

...this is AWESOME!

Awareness
Of Your Past

Alchemize
Your Beliefs

Awaken
Your Power

Align
Your Energy

Attract
Your Dreams

Allow
Your Desires

Amaze
Yourself

Chapter 8: Invest in Aligning!

When we invest in Aligning we're developing our ability to vibrate in harmony to the never-ending flow of prosperity that is around us always. By feeling wealthy, we align to the ever-present Great-Ocean-of-Wealth allowing the wealth to flow freely through us with no resistance.

Align to the Wealth-Energy

This Easy-Does-It investing process is meant to help you realize your true Wealth. To that end, a key skill we develop is our ability to align to the never-ending flow of prosperity that is around us always and in all ways. **Alignment is, in essence, a sense in your body of feeling grace, ease and satisfaction.** These good feelings can range from flow, tranquility, and harmony to joy, exhilaration, love, unlimitedness and peace. And the good news is you can learn how to cultivate these feelings within yourself at will. It takes a bit of practice – investment – and once you get the hang of it you will find that you are making choices that ultimately align you to the life experience you desire. *This ability to choose how you feel is your ticket to prosperity.*

In this part of the process we get clear about what makes us feel joyful, fulfilled, prosperous and generally wonderful (aligned). We will also spend time understanding what takes us out of alignment and throws us into the felt-sense of fear, worry, doubt and general anxiety/scarcity (out-of-alignment). Then we will learn how to journey back from scarcity to prosperity.

As a part of your prosperity journey to effortless wealth you can make conscious energy choices that put you in your natural state of wealth attraction and enjoyment. Remember, your feeling choices (investments) have an impact - a feeling result – that can either put you more or less in alignment with the prosperity experience you desire.

The Legend of Bagger Vance

The Legend of Bagger Vance is a wonderful movie that to me exemplifies the idea of aligning. It is the story of a golfer with great promise, Juno (played by Matt Damon), who is sent to Vietnam and comes back pretty emotionally damaged. He has lost his mojo. As happens, there is a great golf tournament in Juno's hometown, Savannah, Georgia, where Juno is going to play an epic 3 rounds against two legendary golfers of the time.

During the tournament Juno is 12 strokes back at the end of the first round - basically taking him out of the running. It is at this point, his caddy, Bagger Vance, played beautifully by Will Smith, stops Juno and says, "It's time."

"Time for what?" Juno asks.

"For you to see the field," Bagger says.

"What field?" Juno retorts, annoyed.

"The field, where every possible shot is already available. But you got to see it. You got to stop hacking at the ball and feel the game, feel the breeze and wonder of all of life going on around you. And for each of us there is a perfect shot, one that is just for us and all you got to do is get out of the way, so it can find us."

BAM. That is aligning. There is a perfect shot, your perfect shot - that *wants you* - and is just for you, but we've got to get out of the way, so it can find us. There is unlimited abundance, wealth and wonder - especially for you. All we need to do is get out of the way with our old habits and align to it. Quiet the chattering little mind so we can feel the field of Unlimitedness, Gloriousness, Joy – essentially, Wealth.

What am I aligning to?

In short, what you are aligning to is the ever-present, unconditional Wealth that is inherent in life. Alignment allows the wealth to flow and virtually takes the kinks out of your energetic hose. Alignment is not meant to be complex or require effort. At its most simplistic, alignment is feeling good.

You may not be feeling aligned right now, but that is ok, that what this chapter is about and will try to help you accomplish.

One of my teachers says this ever-present Wealth is Perfection; another calls it the Vortex; another Well-Being; another calls it Allness; and some call it "God". Whatever you want to call it, the key is that we are making ourselves available to merge with this ever-present Well-Being that is a constant as we discussed in the awakening chapters.

I think one of the best comparisons of this ideal state is the connection between a wave and the ocean. There is an ocean of energy, a vast, powerful, unlimited energy of Possibility, Love and Wealth that we (the wave) can choose to consciously re-connect with. We, as the wave, have access to and are a part of the same power and unlimited possibility that is the essence of the Ocean.

There is no separation between you (the wave) and this magnificent ocean of unlimited Wealth-Possibility. You are an energy wave, in the energy ocean. You are part of it, always have been and always will be...you cannot be separated from it. It can seem you ran up on shore and cannot get back - but that is just not true. Wealth is. It is the nature of the Ocean and you as the wave are just agreeing to the wealth that is already you and yours. This is Alignment.

"You are not a drop in the ocean,
you are the entire ocean in a drop." – Rumi

Alignment Feels Good

I want to tell you a story of a woman who was out of alignment and then was in:

I was giving a workshop to a group of 15 or so women in a battered woman's shelter who were trying to get themselves on their feet. We were discussing the concept of the power they have to create and make different investments to create different outcomes. To be honest, it was not going well.

Many in the group just felt frustrated and powerless (out of alignment). My ideas were too far away from where these women found themselves. They were deep in poverty, literally, and I was talking about investing. I was not helping and really moving them farther from alignment. I was speaking about creative empowerment and they were in a more practical place of trying to get a house to live in.

So, I switched gears. I lead the group through a guided meditation where I asked them to think and feel back to a time of their lives when they felt they created something—anything—and to re-experience that, re-feel it as if it was happening right then. After the meditation was over, one of the ladies shared her creation. She said she remembered a time when she got to swim with the dolphins. As she swam with them she felt so loved and so at peace. You could tell she went back and swam with them again. If you could have seen her face - it still gives me goose bumps. In that moment, she had found an experience of her past and re-felt it to the point that it allowed her to move into alignment. She was beaming and everyone in the room felt it! I encouraged her to come back to that aligned feeling every time she was feeling alone. I am not sure what happened with her, but on the road to life change these aligned moments help us construct our new wealth perspective over time.

Align First

The key to Effortless Wealth is that we need to align first! Take time in the morning and during the day to re-connect to the ever-present ocean of wealth and feel it flowing through you. Take a moment in traffic or in line at the grocery store and allow the peace and ease to permeate your being.

Many of us don't really want to bother with this alignment thing. People feel it is an "extra step." We think, *why can't I just take some action (like research a stock) and that will bring me the money I desire?* Well you could, but you'd be missing something. When you take action when you are scarce, worried and desperate (basically out of alignment) the likelihood that you will have a prosperous outcome is mitigated, a.k.a. the likelihood that you will find a great stock that has good prospects is diminished. Feel aligned to wealth and it is more likely you will be attracted to and interested in better stock options in which to invest.

When you are aligned, you just feel different, you see the world differently, you attract opportunities, people and help that out-of-alignment people don't. Alignment is the magic in this process, really. And alignment makes it so much more fun, adventurous and truly magical.

If you can really get good at Aligning - you probably don't even need the rest of the process. Because alignment inspires you, moves you and motivates you like nothing else and you become your own best powerhouse wealth creator. You are in the field and your perfect shots are finding you and you are enjoying taking them.

If I could give you a gift, it would be that you Align to the Wealth that is - right now, here for you. That you would allow yourself to enjoy the magical wealth that is flowing around you, through you and as a part of you, right now and every moment of every day. Spend time in that magical feeling of well-being and you have created the spark that will ignite all manner of good things to flow into your life...that's true wealth.

◎ Investment Tip: Realizing I AM

It is interesting to notice how you feel when you are presented with something. Most of us make a quick judgment whether we agree with it or not, almost habitually. It is one thing to read the words in this book; it is another to take them into your mind and body and see if you agree with them. So I would like you to get out a piece of paper and write down a few sentences. Please do use paper and pen, as it becomes more of a full mind-body experience when you hand write.

Here are 30 powerful words: Wealthy, Beautiful, Glorious, Love, Harmony, Peace, Rich, Fulfilled, Unlimited, Amazing, Gracious, Powerful, Joy, Clarity, Abundant, Awake, Playful, Fulfilled, Limitless, Creative, Creating, Healthy, Free, Well-Being, Empowered, Effortless, Worthy, Accomplished, Successful, Prosperous.

Write each of these words into a short sentence beginning with the words: I AM [insert word]. Go through the list of words and write, "I am" in front of each one. For example, write "I am Wealth". You should have

30 sentences, all starting with *I am*. Write slowly, breathe and feel each statement as truth.

As you write, check in with *how each sentence makes you feel*. If you do this with the intent to feel each sentence, you will notice some sentences are easier to write than others. Some will "ping" you (i.e. make you feel uncomfortable). It will be interesting to note which ones do and to what degree. Actually, it does not matter so much why some ping you more than others - just that they do...and inside of those pings is an opportunity to get comfortable with that sentence.

If you really want to benefit from this experience, write whatever sentences "pinged" you as many times as you need to until it feels true. There is much wisdom to teachers having us write 100 times on the black board, "I am Wealth." Give it a try and see the powerful transformation. Play with this and see what you feel.

Invest in Learning What Alignment Feels like - *for you*

Masters and teachers share many stories of alignment experiences. These stories are meant to give us a road map - a feeling guide - of what alignment feels like. But words cannot teach you what alignment feels like - *for you*. I can tell you what alignment feels like for me, but that might not give you the felt-sense of it. Someone can tell you how amazing a sunset is, but you need to be there and experience it - *for yourself*. I can tell you what a lemon tastes like, but your experience of the juice and flavor is *unique* to you.

So here we are, talking about investing in aligning to wealth, but I cannot give you a felt sense of it. You need to intend to experience alignment and then consciously understand it so you can re-create it, or feel something like it, for yourself - like the woman who swam with the dolphins. She had a unique-to-her felt sense of that experience and you need to find *your* unique felt sense of alignment. As you intend to feel aligned, you will, more and more. As you intend to know what alignment feels like, you will, more and more. And as you intend to understand what takes you out of alignment, you will get better at moving from out-of-alignment back into-alignment more easily.

Alignment is one of the most powerful investments you can make that will yield dividends in every aspect of your life. You have an internal investment guide that will tell you "this feels like a good investment" or "this is not going to be a good use of my life energy." You already have all the investment guidance you need, right inside of you. It is how you feel. Honor this guidance and your life wealth will increase.

Sometimes you might just ignore that great investment advice you get – you might just ignore how you feel (we've all done it). But no worries, there is always a steady stream of great opportunities to invest in, every day. So don't get bummed; get excited that you are becoming a very powerful investor of the highest order.

Invest in Understanding What Puts you IN Alignment

The feeling of alignment is as different for each of us, as the things that bring us into the feeling-state of Alignment. I'm going to help you get a bit of clarity on what *you* have noticed puts you into the state of feeling that "all is well", that life is good; that feeling of peace or contentment. This is a short list of things I have noticed can bring people into alignment.

- For many, **meditation** is the way into Alignment. The process of quieting the mind, slowing down, setting aside free time to just be, helps us feel at peace, relaxed and refreshed. Maybe listen to soothing music that puts you into a state of being that feels wonderful. That is alignment, that wonderful feeling!

  In my entrepreneurship classes, I always begin the session with a short-guided meditation. I guide the students into becoming present and letting go of the day's activities so they can be fully present. I talk them through a breathing technique and ask them to relax and allow themselves to become open, available and ready to hear new things, make new connections and learn freely. By the end of this short meditation, most are in a different state ready to make the most of class.

- For others, just being with their **family, friends** or **children** allows them to relax to the point they feel at peace and have moments of alignment.

- One of my friends told me that at breakfast one morning, she and all six kids were eating pancakes, talking and joking. She said it was so wonderful to have them all home and enjoying each other. And she had this wave of contentment come over her. She said she felt so wonderful – that is alignment.

- For some, listening to **wise teachers**, like Eckart Tolle as he speaks of the power of Now, or Adjashanti as he speaks of everything being all right - right now as it is, or Abraham-Hicks as they share the Art of Allowing. Wisdom teachers can transport you into an aligned space. Great teachers, which I am sure you are aware, can help you feel a certain way that just shifts you into Alignment.

  Every day, I watch lectures on YouTube from the teachers that inspire me. A 15-minute clip from Abraham-Hicks as they share their understanding of the Vortex brings me into alignment almost every time. Or check out Mooji, Christie Sheldon's Releasing Abundance Blocks, or the Deepak Chopra Center.

- For many of us being in **nature**, whether in our gardens, walking along the ocean, or swimming with the dolphins, helps shift us into that place of grace. Nature is always in alignment and when we are available to it, we can feel the magic that is already around us, tapping us on the shoulder saying, "Hello, dear one, we are here waiting."

  One of my favorite sayings from the Talmud is that every flower has an angel standing over it saying "Grow. Grow". There is magic in your garden, or anywhere outside. As you enjoy the magic of a rose, tree or bird doing their thing, you can easily slip into alignment.

- The process of **creating** something can bring you into one-ment with the Creative Allness (alignment). In fact, the act of creating something is one of the best ways to experience yourself being yourself...time flies, your energy rises, the creation has your undivided attention, it is exhilarating and this is Alignment.

I love to bedazzle stuff. I paint, glitter-glue and put crystals on pedestals and turn them into coffee tables. I love to be in that space where I am playing with the paint, bobbles and fringe and just go for it. Creating these little tables makes me very satisfied. As added benefit, I listen to inspiring music or lectures from my teachers and I am aligned.

- Doing something you **love** is Wealth in action. Running a business, selling a product, blogging, writing, being a great carpenter, it does not matter. If you love it, Love loves it and that is effortless Wealth.

  Every year at Christmas, my next-door neighbor decks out their entire yard with all manner of Christmas décor, from flying Santas to candy-cane paths. Cars stop and people jump out just to take a look. I asked my neighbor what got her started and she said," I just love all things Christmas." She was inspired to do something she loves and that brings cheer to so many of us who get to enjoy what she enjoys...that is alignment squared.

- **Yoga** brings people into alignment. At the beginning of class everyone is jittery and scattered. By the end of class, everyone floats around and looks almost beatific. In fact, I believe so strongly in the power of yoga to bring people into alignment, I have co-created a conscious creating program developed with yoga at the core of the process.

  One day after my entrepreneurship class, a student came up to me and said she was having a hard time figuring out what to write for one of the papers I assigned. She had mentioned earlier that she did yoga. So, I said why not go to yoga and then try to write the paper. The next week she came to me and said, she went to yoga and then after she was able to write the paper in less than an hour... she was thrilled. This is the power of alignment.

- We cannot leave out our **pets and animals.** Animals in general are always in alignment. They are at peace with what they are, how they are and they do not use their minds to push themselves out of alignment. Our pets are perfect as they are. We love them unconditionally and when we choose, we can focus on this perfection and how wonderful they make us feel and how much we love them and—boop—into alignment we go.

  In Alaska, a whole zoo was created out of the love of an Elephant. Through a weird set of circumstances an Alaskan woman came to own a baby elephant. As the elephant grew, she knew it would need space and room to roam. So she started raising money for a space for the elephant. Because of her alignment via the love for the elephant, support grew and land became available. Now this zoo is a home for hurt animals that cannot be returned to the wild. There are eagles, wolves, bison and all manner of creatures...happily cared for because of the love for an elephant.

- **Feeling good** about you; feeling empowered and capable. One of the reasons we are investing is because it feels very empowering. You decide where to invest and what to invest in. And this empowerment feels good.

  Over the past few months my parents have been redoing a house down the street from them as an investment. What has been quite beautiful to watch is my mom exerting her preferences about what she wants to see happen. Because, for most of their 50+ years of marriage my dad called the shots...especially with investing. But with this project, my mom has really been standing up for her perspective. I feel her empowerment and every time I go over to visit, she takes me on a tour of the house to proudly show the progress. She is going through a later in life renaissance of sorts with this project. It is allowing her to feel empowered. You can tell she feels really good about what she is creating and it is fun to witness.

- **Money** can bring you into alignment. I know this sounds crazy, but I really love money and what it can do. I love to be generous with it, I love to create with it and I love all the possibility it allows me to imagine. Money can be great fun! And it is very worth investing in coming to peace with it and letting it be another source of joy in your life. Please see the "Making Peace with Money" chapter later in the book for some investing ideas around money. But for now, we all have a story about how money made our heart happy. It might have been when you helped someone out or someone helped you... or when you felt lucky when you found a $5 on the ground – my guess is that in that moment you felt pretty great!

As I was walking out of the grocery store a Girl Scout was selling cookies. I was not going to purchase (as I don't need cookies around the house:) but I really like supporting young entrepreneurs so I purchased $20 worth. The little Girl Scout was thrilled. When I got back to the condo, I put the boxes out in the general area and offered them for free. They were gobbled up. I felt so good! Money is so fun to play with.

- **Exercise & Working Out** can really make you feel good. Sometimes you need a real sweat session and other times a little walk is just enough to get the endorphins going and — tada — you are in the zone and feeling aligned. I use exercise to burn off frustration, anger and general low energy. Try to get in the habit of using exercise to help you feel better and bonus, get aligned!

- **Other things that can put you into alignment:** All kinds of music from calm meditation music, to Hawaiian luau music, to hip hop; taking a good nap, or just going to bed and resting; eating a good meal; preparing a good meal; entertaining guests; doing something you don't usually do; taking a car ride somewhere new; sitting in the sun; sitting in the shade under a tree; enjoying a rain storm; a good deep breath; looking for seashells on the beach; watching a cloud formation; blessing your food; driving down the expressway, daydreaming, making love, laughing, a good joke, flowers, a good book, uplifting movies, bubble baths, basically any experience that puts you in your heart and you feel connected with the prosperous energy around you is aligning.

- **Appreciating**. If you notice the list above, at the heart of each is appreciation! Appreciation of nature, loved ones, creating, love, exercise, pets, you. At the core of the experience is genuine appreciation...and appreciation is one of the best ways to get aligned and stay aligned because what you appreciate appreciates (grows).

I could go on and on, but I am hoping you can feel how these things just feel good. There is no "ick" energy in any of these (well maybe family - haha). But that is a point - if there is *ick* that one is not for you. And just because I did not list your aligning experiences, does not mean you do not have them. We all have had times when we just felt wonderful, powerful, amazing, or alive in a way that just felt good! This is what we are becoming aware of, that is what we are noticing. Once you understand what alignment feels like and what puts you in alignment, you can invest more in those thoughts and activities - so you spend more time aligned. ***This is energy investing 101: do more of what works and do less of what does not.*** Don't worry about constantly being in alignment as that is not necessary. The key is to know when you are in and when you are not and *gently* move yourself closer to feeling good by choosing something that helps you feel a bit better and moves you closer to that aligned feeling.

◉ Investment Tip: Invest when you are "In Between"

Usually the best time to feel aligned is after you have done what you were supposed to get done. You have worked out - check - it is off your to-do list and you have a moment of down time. You have just dropped the kids off and you feel you have completed a task. You come home from work and feel that part of your day is done. In these moments when we are feeling spaciousness after completing something we can enjoy the feeling of aligning. So take advantage of it. Next time you find yourself in-between "tasks", sit for a moment with the intention of enjoying the moment, relaxing and letting the resistance drip out of your body. Feel any tension or stress just dribble out of your body and let yourself steep in the wonder of nothing...in the comfort of the moment. It is right here, in-between to-dos, in-between breaths that the felt sense of alignment can be noticed. Play with this...and see what you feel.

Wealth Journaling:

In your wealth journal write down the things in your life that you feel make you feel aligned to grace, ease and satisfaction. These might be things, people, experiences, or moments that give you that sense of non-resistance and open-heartedness.

"You may say that I am a dreamer, but I am not the only one. I hope someday you will join us and the world will live as one."
- Lyrics from *Imagine* by John Lennon

Invest in Understanding What Takes You OUT of Alignment

I hate to say this, but many of us are usually investing in *things that keep us out of alignment* with the richness of life – essentially, scarcity. Bummer, I know. But as we become aware of this, we can choose to make different investments. It's really just that easy.

When we are out of alignment, our energy feels blocked. We feel insecure, unclear, worried, resistant, small, heavy, doubtful, disempowered, weakened, conditional, and frustrated. Above all, we feel limited and scarce. When I am out-of-alignment I have my scarcity hat on and I feel I need to defend and make my way in the world because if I don't I won't succeed.

The interesting thing about the stuff that takes us out of alignment is that it is usually pretty juicy and almost addictive...at least that is what I have found. Who does not love a good drama or intrigue? How many of us can leave a conversation that is negative? How many of us can turn off the news or not listen all together? And what about a good fight, where you know you are right?! Juicy - yes; engaging - you bet; alignment fostering - nope, not at all.

Sometimes it is hard to tell if these things are taking you out of alignment because we get so much energy from them (and they seem to feel good – in the moment). But really, this is ill-gotten energy-booty. Energy gotten from negativity, "being right", winning, or even arguing is scarcity energy. And, we are looking for prosperity energy, like the things we were exploring previously. No one has to feel less than for us to feel better. No one needs to lose for us to feel like a winner. There is plenty of wonder to go around.

Again, the things that take me out of alignment might not be the things that take you out of alignment, so it is important for you to do a *feeling assessment* and notice what does not feel so good and/or throws you for a loop. Here are some biggies to consider:

- **Trying to get the "right answer"** or do the right thing or be right. One of my friends says, *"It feels good to be right."* For many of us being right is mandatory; it is almost a moral issue. But when we are engaged in being right or trying to find the right thing to do, we are putting a lot of pressure on ourselves - searching and analyzing to the point where we usually get out of alignment. Finding the right answer can lead to a win/lose (scarcity) mindset. And for the purposes of our work together, alignment is what we are going for.

   The better investment would be asking your inner wise one, "What would be a way to handle this so I can honor me while honoring them so I can stay aligned?" Determine what works for you and be ok with that – and let others decide what works for them and be ok with that too.

- **Feeling like we are not good enough,** have not done enough, am not enough, don't have enough. Inadequacy and not-enoughness in any form is non-aligned. For most of us this is at the heart of much of life's problems. Agreeing to inadequacy is scarcity thinking and scarcity thinking is nowhere near the abundance life is trying to flow to us.

   The better investment is seeing the prosperity potential in the moment, in the person, in the experience and moving from inadequacy to something that feels better. If you find yourself stuck with feelings of inadequacy try going back to Chapter 5: Awakening to Who You Really Are for a reminder that you *are* enough.

- **Striving** can take us out of alignment when we feel we need to do more, be more, get more – which is a form of inadequacy hiding inside of the socially acceptable drive for success. For over a year, I had a daily reminder set on my phone with the message, *"I am happy where I am and eager for more."* When I created it, I wanted to remind myself to be satisfied where I am and *then* realize there is more wonder to come. But what ended up happening – unconsciously - is that when I saw the reminder I just focused on the "eager for more" part. Then one day I noticed I was feeling out of alignment when I saw that reminder and checked in with myself. I realized I was striving for more and feeling inadequate, which was taking me away from the magic in *this moment* and the contentment intent of being satisfied where I am.

The better investment is to find contentment in the now moment and know that striving, or pushing, is not needed nearly as much as knowing, glowing and flowing. Knowing you are on your way, glowing with the gratitude of this now moment, and flowing with your inspirations.

- **Arguing, fighting,** talking politics, or anything where you are on opposing sides usually takes us out of alignment. Again, it is the need to feel right that blows us out and really can pollute the whole energetic environment, making it uncomfortable for everyone in the vicinity. There is a reason polite society says not to discuss politics or religion at the dinner table...it messes with the taste of the food.

The better investment is to know what your hot buttons are and choose not to invest in making them stronger by focusing on them.

- **Worrying** about money, health, or relationships. Any time we worry, we are cutting ourselves off from the natural flow of the

Goodness of Life. Worry is a result of looking at what "is" and thinking it is inadequate in some way, that there will not be enough, etc. Notice how insidious worry is; once you are in its grasp, pulling out can be difficult.

The better investment is to remember the Wealth of Life (as we discussed in Chapter 6). Remembering the Well-Being that has us safely cared for may help the worry begin to subside. It is also helpful to look around and notice what is going ok... focus on what is working. If you can appreciate something for just 17 seconds you start the momentum in a new direction and if you can keep focusing for a minute you will feel the energy shift.

- **Money** is one of the best ways to throw you out of the wealth vortex. Actually, it is *worry* about money and all the corresponding thoughts, feelings and emotions that feel crappy when you think about money, your checking account, bills, etc. Money worries is one of the reasons I went on my prosperity journey. I was sick of feeling bad about myself and my life as a result of money problems.

The better investment is to focus on wealth and to put yourself on the journey of understanding the truth of Who You Really Are and the power you have as an investor who is a conscious creator! Remember 60 seconds of that kind of investment and you are going to start some real momentum in a new wealthy direction.

- **Poor health** or health issues make us not feel good, period. And not feeling good is the opposite of alignment. Nothing stimulates our desire to feel good faster than the flu, toothache or some other issue that knocks us on our butt.

The better investment is to focus on improving your health. And, with that said, like me you might have something that is not all that healthy going on for you right now. One of my yoga buddies was sick with cancer. So, during her chemo treatments she would do *Yoga Nidra*. Yoga nidra is this wonderful yoga practice of total relaxation which can help you to allow the natural health of life to flow through you. After she got well, the nurses asked her to teach them about the yoga nidra so they could share it with the other patients.

I also heard tell of a man in the hospital with cancer. So, he had his son bring him lots of comedy movies and shows that would make him laugh. He decided to laugh himself well. He only watched things that made him laugh and feel good – no news and no visitors – only comedies. Both of these examples show how we can choose alignment even in the face of health issues.

- **Judging, comparing, assessing,** evaluating are all things where our minds are pitting one thing against another and this can put many of us out of alignment. If I get out of alignment, I have found it is because I am unconsciously agreeing to scarcity somewhere in the mix - that there is not enough to go around, so I need to compare, judge and find the way to "get mine" or protect mine. This is where you need to be very in touch with how you feel. Does the thing you are looking at feel good to you - if not, why not? Don't label it as bad. Just say it does not feel good and look for a different option, without the judgment and labeling.

The better investment is to feel into the options and pick the one that feels best to move closer into alignment.

- **Guilt** is not an aligned emotion. Guilt is a bad feeling caused by knowing or thinking that you have done something wrong. Many of us carry guilt around with us, feeling bad about most everything from the way we look, to the way we think we have hurt someone. Guilt is a very expensive feeling because it eats up tons of energy, leaves us feeling low, heavy depleted and poor; which is the opposite of aligned.

The better investment is to free yourself of the demands of perfection and not be so hard on yourself. If you have hurt someone, find a way to make amends as best you can and move on (forgive yourself) so, you can move back into alignment and feel frisky, satisfied and free.

- **Being hard on yourself.** Nothing takes you out of alignment faster than being hard on yourself and trying to fix yourself. This is because your inner essence knows you are magnificent and does not agree with any of the negative stuff you are agreeing to.

  A better investment would be to stop when you are in the middle of beating yourself up and give yourself a break. Say things like, "I know I am getting better and better." "I know wealth is all around me." "I will figure this out too." "I might not be perfect, but I am pretty good." "I am not going to let the fear of the impossible, stop the flow of the possible." Or engage in some other feelings that give you some *relief* from your current mind-beating.

- **Fixing and problem solving.** For many of us, fixing and problem-solving is very fun; finding a solution to an issue can really put you into alignment actually, because it feels good to resolve something. It feels good to relieve us of "the problem". Here is the rub: many of us know that the "fix" will put us into alignment, so we become great problem seekers. We end up living in the problem, or problem-fixing mode, way longer than we would like. But feeling stuck in a problem or frustrated by a situation does not make us feel empowered or aligned.

  The better investment would be to realize you are in a problem-solving situation and get aligned! Then a solution will arise from the aligned state of awareness...and problem solved. Then move on and let it go.

- **Clutter.** Interestingly enough, our physical spaces can throw us out of alignment. For some clutter does it because uncompleted tasks make us feel bad. It is wise to invest in creating your physical space into something that makes you feel the way you want to feel...be it peaceful, energized, comforted, secure. Whatever you desire, invest in creating your physical space so you feel aligned. This is worth the time and effort.

• Other things that *can* throw you out of alignment (in no particular order): traffic jams, news shows, some talk radio, waiting in line, your email not working, not having milk, running out of coffee, too many people in yoga class, not getting the gift you wanted, running out of gas, haters, losing at Wii, fashion magazines, seeing/hearing of someone who has lost weight and makes you feel guilty, politics, dehydration, demands, over-scheduling, no food in the refrigerator, aggressive music, Facebook, Instagram where everyone looks like they are living way better than you, violent movies, make-you-feel-inadequate commercials, too many commercials. I hope you are getting the point; there are little things everyday things that can throw you out of alignment because you feel frustration, anger, worry and many of the things we have already discussed. *It is the feelings that result from the above things that are important.* Because the resulting feelings are misaligned with the prosperous energy around you. Learn what these are - for you - and decide to limit the presence of these in your life or find a way to feel neutral about them, or decide to feel good anyway (like in a traffic jam).

What I have noticed with the above list is that a lot of mind yapping and judgment create a feeling of *resistance and heaviness.* I think this is why so many of the great teachers discuss meditation (taking a break from thinking) as a part of the awakening process. How can you awaken/align/feel your gloriousness, if you are so distracted by so much thinking?

When you notice you feel heavy, sad, frustrated, or low by any of the above – take a break. Change what you are doing, change what you are thinking or take a nap. Even the process of noticing "worry" can free you from its grip and let you slip back into alignment. You may need to consciously use some of the things that put you in alignment to help you get back in alignment.

Wealth Journaling:

- In your wealth journal write down the things in your life that take you out of alignment with the flow of wealth energy? Are there things, people, experiences, or moments that exhaust you? Frustrate you? Make you feel guilty? Worried?
- What things from the list resonate with you (be specific as to how they show up in your life and why you feel out of alignment)?
- What can you choose instead?

◎ Investment Tip: Be an Independent

Henry Maslow created the *Hierarchy of Needs* pyramid, which is a description of the needs that motivate human behavior. Mr. Maslow said, "The highest quality that a human **being** can reach is to **be independent of** the good opinion of others." How freeing this would be not to worry about what another expects of us, not to consider what another believes about a situation, or not modify our behavior to please another...all of which could take us out of alignment.

Our wealth journey needs us to be independent of the good opinions, beliefs and expectations of others because many believe in scarcity, limitation and the school-of-hard-knocks. This might sound kind of harsh and self-centered. That is the point; we are on our journey, our prosperity journey - one that requires us to be centered on self; making choices that help us stay aligned to our wealth intentions.

Stay independent of others by remembering and understanding what you are up to: effort-less wealth. Creating wealth consciousness asks you to know when something takes you out of alignment and makes you feel uncomfortable, fearful, annoyed, scarce, resistant, etc. Be independent of anything that takes you from the feeling of unlimited freedom. Play with this and see how your alignment stabilizes.

"There is much more than "money" when you think of a wealthy person. A person who is really rich is one who has wonderful friendships, harmonious

family relations, sympathy and understanding in business relationships and inner harmony which bring peace of mind." - Napoleon Hill

Choose to Align

Aligning is a choice. More often than not, we need to consciously choose better-feeling thoughts to move our way into alignment. Sometimes alignment can happen quickly, like my friend having breakfast with her kids. I can be walking along and see something beautiful and bam, I shift into an aligned space. I can be listening to my teachers and all of a sudden they say something and bang, I shift. Or I will be meditating (OOMMing) and bingo, there I go.

But to be honest, this is more of a rarity for me. Most of the time, I need to walk myself up the prosperity ladder (more on this in Chapter 14) to get relief from feeling heavy and limited. I have to choose thoughts that move me to a better energy state until I am closer to that sense of alignment where I feel dearly loved, supported and connected to my unconditional Wealth-Spring. I created the prosperity ladder, which is based on the emotional ladder that Abraham-Hicks created. It is meant to help you move from a place of feeling worried about money and wealth to feeling better and more prosperous. Please see Chapter 14.

◎ Investment Tip: Wanting, Happening, Done

This is a tool to help you quickly move from the vibration of wanting, to having - literally in a few seconds. It is aligning your energy from possibility, to probability to certainty. The key is to practice shifting the energy in your body as you move through the steps. I will talk you through it here:

1. Have you ever heard yourself desire something? You usually say, *"I want this to happen."* And this is the first step - wanting. Can you feel this *wanting* in your body? It usually feels like, "I want this...*but* it is not here" or "I want it...*but* it is not possible." Basically, I want it and I am not experiencing it. It is important you feel the *wanting* aspect of this first.

2. Next, you are going to tell yourself: *It is happening!* Feel the relief you have when you tell yourself the thing you want is happening. It is in progress; your desire is on its way and you can relax a bit. You are moving your vibration from *wanting* the desire, to feeling the desire *happening*. Notice the change in your body; notice the feeling of relief as you let yourself feel it is happening. Again, *feel it happening*.

3. Finally, you are going to tell yourself it is *done!* Move from that feeling of it happening to it being done, a done deal! Yahoo! Now notice how you feel. If you let yourself agree it is done, you will now probably feel excitement, contentment, ease, peace, success, completion: all of the feelings of wanting something and then experiencing it come to fruition. That is the feeling we are looking for, knowing *it is done*. Spend as much time milking this *done* feeling as you can, because it is in this vibration you want to engage the law of attraction.

Do you notice how you can change your vibration pretty quickly as you walk yourself through these three steps? You have just shifted yourself from the vibration of wanting (and not really feeling all that good), to it happening (which feels better), to it being done (and feeling even better).

Play with this, with the many desires you feel yourself *"want, but..."*. Invest in moving from wanting the desire, to it happening and then to the feeling of it being done...and stay in the feeling of *done*. Get good at this and you are becoming a power investor.

Aligning is Easy

Aligning is easy! Remember this is the Easy-Does-It Investing process. Don't over work this or over think it. Just notice how you are feeling and agree it is easy to be aligned. It's Easy! And if you feel out of whack, agree it is easy for you to move yourself back into feeling good and flowy. Alignment is easy; ease and flow is the way to go! Just play with all of this alignment stuff. ☺

Alignment leads to inspired action

You will notice that as you are aligned more and more, you will feel inspired and want to take action! And this is where the real fun kicks in. Because your alignment will inspire you to things you might not have thought of before which will lead you to the ideas, people, places and things you need to move ever closer to your wealth desires. And as we discussed in the last chapter, enthusiastic action is so much more productive than difficult-have-to action.

With alignment, we are consciously putting ourselves in that flowy, consciously-connected to Wealth-Energy place where our actions become inspired. And to be honest it feels like magic. The flow, the inspiration, the fun you are having creates a momentum for more of the same. Alignment is the place to start and from it stems the effortless feeling of inspired actions. To quote Dr. Seuss, "Oh, the places you'll go!"

Practice Aligning!

*"Within the depths of authenticity lives integrity; waiting for our
return. When we arrive, we are met with effortless joy, abundant
living, peace and wholeness—nothing lacking, nothing broken.
This is soul equanimity, the state of pure alignment with will of
Source and will of self."* — LaShaun Middlebrooks Collier

This is a simple practice you can do when you want some one-on-one
time with your True-Wealth. It helps to set aside some time to practice
aligning. The time set aside helps your mind quiet and it helps your body
relax so you can be fully present and peaceful at some point during this
process. You might even what to schedule it on your calendar. Sometimes
you might need to do some yoga or other physical energy exertion (like run,
jump or dance around a bit) so that you can relax. This will enable you to
release resistance and allow the Ever-Present Wealth to seep in.

1. Prepare your physical space

> Create a physical space that feels "sacred". It should be set apart or
> devoted to the intent to create and align. You can create a sense
> of sacredness by lighting a candle, burning some incense, sitting
> on the same cushion and playing music you love. Even tidying up
> or clearing the tabletop will be symbolic of this special time. It is
> really up to you, but the key is to create a symbolic habit that tells
> your subconscious and your conscious mind that you are here to
> align and create. The physical space helps invoke a sense of peace,
> harmony and empowerment.

2. Do some breath-work to come into the present moment

> Usually when I sit down to align, I am still groggy from waking up
> or focused on the last thing that happened prior to this alignment

session. So, I need to do something that will bring me into the present. A yoga breathing technique called Kumbhaka helps me become quiet, relaxed and in the present moment. Begin by deep breathing and focusing on your in-breath and then the out-breath: simply enjoy the breathing and allow yourself to start to relax. As you breathe in slowly, to a count of 3 to 5, hold your breath at the top of the inhale for 3 to 5 seconds, then slowly exhale (to a count of 5), then hold your breath out for a count of 3 to 5. Play with this and notice how you feel. Notice how your body responds, notice how your head feels and notice what happens to your thoughts. Intend to slow down and relax. Intend to become present and relax.

3. Raise your energy vibration by moving into your heart

When we create from our hearts, we create from a place of grace. And from there, no matter what we create, it will be aligned to the highest and best good for all. Our hearts are the home of inspiration and love and this is an excellent place to align to. So now, find something that makes you feel in your heart...it could be inspiring poetry or a book, it could be listening to music or hugging your cat, there are so many things that can put you in your heart where you feel joy, love, peace, comfort or whatever your heart's desire. Go through your list of things that put you in alignment and think about those. Appreciate. ☺

4. Allow the Wealth In

Slowly feel your True Nature, your True Wealth seep into your being; feel it permeate your skin. Marinate in liquid love. Let love-light seep into your cells and the space between your cells. Relax and feel released of tension. Feel yourself expand. Feel present, at peace and connected to the Unlimited Energy of Life. Invite wonder into your space and release the notion that you are "less than" or separate from your wealth. Agree to the prosperity and abundance that is around you NOW always and in all ways! Feel it, let it in, marinate in the luxurious feeling of WUW unlimited wealth.

5. Enjoy

Feel into your heart and enjoy. Enjoy the heart-felt feeling of unconditional Wealth that is all around you. Enjoy the well-being that is flowing, right now. **Bask** in the wonder of the ease and effortless flow. **Steep** in the expanded feeling, **stew** in the wealth juiciness and **enjoy**! **Steep, Stew, Enjoy** – now that is a wealth recipe for success. WOWWEE!

Remember...

- Easy does it
- Your perfect shot wants to find you as much as you want to find it.
- You are a wave in the great Ocean-of-Wealth
- Do more of the things that help you feel aligned like dancing, petting your pup, etc.
- Do less of the things that move you out of alignment like judging, worrying and watching crap TV.
- Choose to Align
- Aligning is Easy!

Frequently Asked Questions:

1. **Can I be somewhat in alignment?** Yes, there are many shades of alignment, from feeling at ease to feeling all out exhilaration, joy and many feelings in between. All are alignment, because basically you feel good. But they do feel different. This is why we invest in understanding what it feels like to be in alignment. So when you are there in different feeling states, you can enjoy the unique feeling of being aligned. Use the prosperity ladder (see page X) to get a sense of where you are on the alignment continuum and then use your energy to move to better and better feeling places.

2. **How long will this take?** As we discussed, alignment can happen in a holy instant, or it could take an hour of yoga. Or if you have experienced some kind of big emotional whack - like your lover left you, it might take a while to get back in alignment. It is well worth the investment to practice when you are feeling pretty good, so you have a felt sense of it. So when something comes up that throws you for a loop, you have the alignment memory to go to.

3. **How much work is this going to be?** Aligning is not meant to be efforting. It seems we effort even when we don't mean to. We make a project out of things and we can even make aligning into "work"...

something we need to do and do *right* to move in the directions we say we want to go. Even as I was writing this, I found myself efforting to "get in alignment" so I could share effectively with you what I wanted to say. Efforting is such an unconscious habit and the beauty of alignment is that effort is not needed. Present moment awareness or a good deep breath might be all you need. Allowing or resisting-less is usually enough to let you enjoy the feeling of enjoying. Yes, I did say that - you can enjoy enjoying, love loving. This usually happens when you are relaxed, at peace and contented. So don't try so hard, don't push or wrangle yourself into this. Ease and flow is the way.

4. **Is there an easier way than meditating?** For many, the notion of meditating is about sitting and trying to stop our minds from doing what they do naturally — think. It was frustrating for me at first and really did not feel all that good. Then I realized I could use guided meditations, where someone speaks and helps me work through relaxing and then speaks powerful thoughts. Consider using guided meditations where the messages are of love, empowerment and upliftment and see if that does not feel better and helps move you to alignment. Check out the Oprah & Deepak meditations.

5. **What if I don't know what alignment feels like for me?** Sometimes we are not in touch with how we really feel. We feel, but we do not have much conscious awareness of it. That's ok, this is a journey. Taking the feeling journey and making the investment to become aware is so vitally important to this process and to living as a conscious creator. One thing to note is that every day, at least once, you are in alignment, whether it is just as you wake, before your mind starts up, or right before bed, or at a stoplight (in between events). There is a moment, a peace place, where you get pulled in, even for a split second. Intend to become aware of this moment and then one day you will notice it and you will be on your way!

6. **I don't get the connection between alignment and wealth?** Alignment is like turning on the faucet of Wealth. The wealth is always flowing, like water is always awaiting us when we turn on the faucet, but we need to turn the knob. So too is Wealth always

flowing to us. Through aligning, we are turning on our faucet to allow Wealth to flow into our lives.

7. **Is aligning just feeling good?** In some ways yes, and in some ways no. Feeling good is the crux of alignment and the start but not the whole thing. Alignment also has an aspect of being in your heart and feeling the flow of the wealth of life through you. Alignment feels good and feels like flow together.

"When I don't resist – I am in grace."

Investment Strategy:
I AM Aligned

Invoke this…

I AM aligned to the Wealth is always flowing around me and I let it flow to me. I turn on the free-flow of Wealth-Energy through my own faucet. In fact, I AM a great wave in the great ocean, floating in oneness with the huge expanse of Wealth. I AM It and It is me. Boy this feels good, boy I feel good.

I AM aligned to the perfection is always here. My nature is Wealth's nature and I AM unlimited. I am unlimited. What I do with my power is my free will and this aligned state of being leads me to inspired action. I always have a choice to align to the amazing perfection of All-Ness and I choose alignment now.

I AM aligned with the nature of Wealth that allows the details of my life to take care of themselves. I am supported as I move my desires forward. I align with Wealth and flow with my heart and I bring myself into accord with my Wealth-Power. I enjoy the wonder and magic I create in my life. I feel so wealthy!

A

Awareness
Of Your Past

Alchemize
Your Beliefs

Awaken
Your Power

Align
Your Energy

Attract
Your Dreams

Allow
Your Desires

Amaze
Yourself

Chapter 9: Invest in Attracting... Focus on the Wealth You Desire

Investing your attention, energy and focus is how you engage the law of attraction. The key is to invest your energy into what you desire—really desire—and reduce the amount of attention energy you put on what you don't want.

Attract Intentionally

Attracting is an intentional focus on the wealth experience we want, in a conscious mindful way. In this *Attracting* module of the Easy-Does-It Process, we learn to invest both quality and quantity energy into vibrating wealth to create a momentum of energy that pulls the experiences to us. We will make intentional energy deposits into our wealth bank account by engaging our felt sense of wealth and applying two basic aspects of attracting: identifying what we want and vibrating *as* it.

Attracting energy is magnetizing energy. As we focus on what we want, we are drawing it to us (and sorry to say, as we focus on what we don't want we are drawing that to us also). And in this attracting chapter, we will magnetize or activate experiences we want to us through a 2-part process:

- Part 1: Identifying WHAT we want to invest our attention energy on (e.g. what we will choose to think, what we will choose to speak about and what we will choose to act on).

- Part 2: Focusing HOW we invest our energy (e.g. how we feel and vibrate as we do what we do).

The key is to consciously create by intentionally choosing our vibration to be wealth welcoming. You are always attracting as you are always emanating a vibration. This chapter's process is about making our vibration, the felt-sense, a *conscious* body-mind choice instead of our usual unconscious day-to-day vibrating habit.

Energy investments build momentum. As we focus on our wealth desires in our mind and feel them in our body, we pull them to us.

Let us take a simple example from work. How do you feel at work much of the time? As you speak to customers and fellow employees how do you feel?

We of course want to experience success at work, but it is really easy to talk about how bad things are in the economy or around the office. It is easy to think things are not going to work out. And it feels mandatory to act on stuff that dumps into our email. I get it – I totally get it. These are the WHAT investments we make at work. Then there is the HOW investment we make. How you are feeling as you talk, think and act creates a vibration that attracts more of that vibration to you.

"Just whistle while you work… it won't take long when there's a song to help you set the pace. " - Snow White and the Seven Dwarfs

◎ Investment Tip: Don't Wallow

Be careful not to invest your valuable energy in low-rate-of-return experiences such as bemoaning a difficult situation, judging the situation, playing it over and over in your head, or talking incessantly about it to whoever will listen. Don't be a drama king/queen. This is not a beneficial use of your energy. Just use what you learned from a difficult situation and say, "I do not want to experience that again." **And this is IMPORTANT:** Decide what you want instead! Then focus your attention on what you want. Move forward, let this old stuff go (Alchemize it) and be free.

"Whether you think you can or think you can't you are right."
– Henry Ford

Engage the Law of Attraction Intentionally

As we have been discussing, the Law of Attraction is always in action and works in the *present moment.* How we feel and what we agree to creates an attractive vibration *in this moment,* which attracts similar vibrations. The Law of Attraction does not take into consideration the past (sunk costs) or future scenarios, it reflects *only what we are vibrating now* and connects a perfect match to what we are vibrating now - thus attracting that feeling experience to us. Repetitive thinking of the same thoughts and feeling is a vibration that creates a magnetic vortex of momentum for a match to that vibration – and that vibration gains more momentum. Once it gets going, it follows the basic laws of physics - energy in motion tends to stay in motion. So, it's as simple as it seems: feel satisfied, attract more feeling satisfied. Feel wealthy, attract more feeling wealthy. Then as you vibrate wealth you are molding the energy clay of life that helps it materialize physically into your reality - welcome to becoming a divine alchemist. ☺

"Thoughts which are mixed with any of the feelings or emotions constitute a "magnetic" force which attracts from the vibrations of the ether other similar or related thoughts."
- Napoleon Hill circa 1937 *Think and Grow Rich*

Part 1: WHAT - Get Clear on What You Want

When you ask people why they want to be wealthy, they often tell you about how it is so hard to pay their bills, why they are frustrated about not having enough money to do the things they want to do. In general, they speak of the *money they don't have* (which is actually talking more about scarcity then wealth). We want to be disciplined investors who know how to focus on wealth; who know how to shift back to focusing on wealth when we forgetfully fall into an old scarcity habit. This takes a bit of attention at first to refocus (and invest differently) but the shift in approach will shift the results dramatically!

Sometimes it is hard for us to know what we want because we have been focused on what we don't – so let's start there. Let's begin by clarifying what you don't want.

Experience is a teacher, giving us information as to what feels good and satisfying (what we want more of) and what does not feel good - unsatisfying (what we don't want to experience again) …both very valuable and important information…so use it as such.

Wealth Journaling:

>In your wealth journal copy the CLARITY chart on the next
>page and fill it in.

The **CLARITY** chart will help you get clear.

Spend some time answering the following questions:

1. What don't I want to experience anymore?
2. Now that I know what I don't want, what do I want instead? (Flip the previous statement into a want statement and add any additional wants to this chart.)

THE CLARITY CHART

What I don't want to experience any more	What I do want (flip the previous statement into a want statement)

You may want to do this with a friend. Have them ask you each question and then fill in your response for you in each column (so you can just talk freely). Allow them to clarify any questions they have as they listen to you.

Wealth Journaling:

> Reflect on WHY you want what you want. Make statements like "I want this because___" or "When I have this then I will feel___"

For example:

1. *What don't I want?* To feel poor, to feel lackful. To not be able to do the things I want to do. I don't want to feel poor anymore.
2. *Now I know what I don't want - what do I want?* I want to feel good; I want to feel powerful and rich. I want to be aligned with wealth, so I can feel the flow and magic of life. I want to feel empowered.
3. *Why do I want this?* I want this **because** it feels good and satisfying. When I have this, then I will feel loved and honored. When I have this, I will feel connected to my Wealth-Stream and I will feel at peace and beautiful. I want it because I want to feel powerful and capable, magical and resistance free. AND I do not want to rationalize or defend what I want! I want to just let it flow - let it flow- let it flow. Guilt Free!

> *"There will come a time when you believe everything is finished. That will be the beginning."* —Louis L'Amour

Wealth Journaling ... Attract Wealth

Before you start writing, spend a few moments to align and re-awaken to the veritable fortune that is all around you, waiting for you. Take a few deep breaths and feel yourself open and become available to and aligned with the Wealth-energy that is flowing to you and around you. Notice how rich it is, how powerful it is, how available it is to you. Take a few deeper breaths. If you don't feel aligned yet, take a few deeper, long slow breaths, relax, and intend to allow the wealth in. It wants you!

Now, begin to describe the wealth you feel and the wealth you see for yourself. Describe how your Wealth experience *feels*, physically, mentally, emotionally and spiritually. What are you doing? Talk about the enjoyment you ARE having. Talk about **what** you want and **why** you want it. What beliefs do you hold going forward? What wealth assumptions will you now make? What experiences are you having? How are you speaking? What are you saying? What thoughts are you holding? Take your time with this.

If you get overwhelmed, take a break. Let this be a joyful exploration in investing in the wealth experience you really want. You might even want to walk away for a bit or come back to this later...as you get more inspiration and ideas. Let this be really fun!

If you are tempted to talk about what you don't want, or your frustrations, fears, worries and experiences to this point, Stop. Notice and try to refocus by flipping these to *what you really want* and get back to the business of talking really wealthy!

> *"In the place of stillness, rises potential. From the place of potential, emerges possibility. Where there is possibility, there is choice. And where there is choice, there is freedom!"* —Gabrielle Goddard

Part 2: Vibrate AS what you want - Already fulfilled

Gandhi said, "Be the change you seek". Be peaceful if you seek peace. Be joyful if you seek joy. **Be wealthy if you seek wealth**. In this amazing statement based on the law of attraction, Gandhi nailed the power behind conscious creating, being/feeling that which you choose to experience. Feel what it feels like to be living AS you are in the middle of your wealth desires.

One of my great teachers said, "Do not meditate ON the desire, meditate AS the desire." What he is saying is that the power of the investment comes as we are able to **agree to the desire in our lives *now*, not someday, but in the present moment, right now, by feeling it, seeing it, being it.** I call this *Feelizing*...feeling yourself as wealth and visualizing yourself wealthy **now**. Vibrate AS wealth and the law of attraction will match more of that to you.

Feelizing is a very effective way to mold the energy clay of life by using your creating tools of mind (thought) and body (feeling) focus.

Get passionate; give yourself permission to have this desire - free and clear. The more strongly you feel about it, the more emotion (energy in motion investment) that is generated and felt, the more attractive power you are directing. This is powerful. There is an amplification of energy - a momentum - that creates an activation vortex that pulls your desire to you and you to it.

⑥ Investment Tip: Ok, Done Deal!

This is a very fun tool because you are going to say all the things you want to have happen and the answer is going to be OK – Done Deal. It goes like this: You say, *"I want to lose 10 lbs,"* and the answer is **OK, Done Deal!** You say, *"I want to sell my house as soon as heavenly possible,"* and the response is **Ok, Done Deal**! *"I want my 401K to be at one million dollars* (remember to put your pinky up to your lip like Dr. Evil when you say that). And the response is **OK, Done Deal!**

Make a list of all the things you want to have happen. Write them in your Wealth Journal. Then write – OK DONE DEAL next to each. Every now and again, come back to that list and see how life helps you tick them off one by one. DONE DEAL - How fun! Side note: if you come back and it is not done – remind yourself it is *still in progress*, it is not done – *yet.*

Pray Rain

There is a great story told in the book *The Isaiah Principle* by Greg Brandon. Greg tells of how he and his American Indian friend David are going to pray for rain, as there was a drought in the area. David and Greg ventured into the desert and found a sacred spot where David's ancestors said, "the skin was thin between worlds". Meaning it was an aligned physical and emotional place to create. David removed his shoes (as a symbol of respect), focused for a while and then said, "OK, let's go".

Greg said, "I thought we were going to pray *for* rain?"

David said, "No, we would never pray *for* rain, that is like saying we agree to the current reality of no rain."

David then said, "We **pray rain**... feel yourself in the middle of your new choice, **as** it is happening."

Went David focused, he feelized (felt and visualized) himself walking in the mud during the rain, enjoying the mud between his toes. He enjoyed seeing the villagers with the produce that came as a result of the rain. He enjoyed the rain and being in the rain, AS it was happening – he really experienced it and felt it (in his mind and body).

> He then said, "I gave thanks - not for the rain, but for the opportunity to choose a new "medicine" (a.k.a. new experience)."

David prayed rain by vibrating the reality of enjoying the rain. He did not come from a place of lack, *there is no rain and we need some*, as that would create/attract/activate more "no rain".

I love this example because it highlights the important aspects of investing in what you want, not what you don't. And it also shows how to powerfully and effectively engage the Creating Technologies...not just by thinking about what you want or wishing for something outside of you to provide it, but by whole body actively vibrating the experience in the now moment = living it AS it is a DONE DEAL.

For many of us, it is difficult to take our attention from current reality and how things are showing up right now. By giving our agreement to them we continue to invest in creating more of the same. But as the powerful creators we are, we can choose to invest our energy by powerfully feelizing our new wealth experiences in the now.

◎ Investment Tip: Pray Money

Take a moment and go to a place that you feel is "sacred" or where the "skin is thin between worlds" (it might be your backyard or your meditation space – you decide). It actually is just a "place" where you feel at ease and where you can allow yourself to *pray money*. Take a few breaths and align with the grand wealth that is always flowing. Take a few more breaths and become present and excited for this *opportunity to choose a new medicine*. Then, pray money. Feel the money flowing to you with grace and ease. Feel checks showing up in your mailbox and money just being deposited into your bank account. Enjoy yourself opening your bank statement and feeling excited and relieved at the numbers you see. You are enjoying this new reality, not giving thought to the how or why...just that it is. The natural wealth that is flowing constantly is easily showing up in your life and you are enjoying the experience of it, *right now*. Enjoy the money, enjoy playing with it, enjoy spending it, enjoy seeing it be deposited and growing in your account. Enjoy, enjoy, enjoy the money. Enjoy, enjoy, enjoy playing with the money. *Give thanks for the opportunity to choose a new medicine.* Play with this and see how you feel.

Wealth Journaling:

- In your wealth journal write about your experience praying money.

Feelize Wealth

Feelizing is visualizing and feeling together - seeing our desire in our mind as well as feeling it and getting excited about it in our body (like jumping for joy) as it happens in our life. What we are doing here is creating a felt sense of wealth. Feelizing is a great way to engage both the mind and the body at the same time. David feelized rain. He did not wish for rain or just think about rain, he danced in the rain in his mind and body. We engage our creative mind when we visualize and see our desire happening. We engage our body when we emote and feel our desire.

Many of us visualize the experience (see it) but counteract the energies by feeling that it cannot happen or feeling it will happen *someday* (when we become better, different, richer). We focus on it happening someday, versus feeling it happening now. *Slight shift in perspective - huge shift in experience!*

◉ Investment Tip: Practice Feelizing

To do this tip, it you might need 10 minutes or so, as we are going to feelize a time you felt wonderful.

Take a few moments and just breathe. Breathe in the wealth of the moment. Feel how there is an abundance of air, it is just here, what you need when you need it. Breathe in and out.

Now, think of a time when you felt wonderful - just go with the first thing that pops into your mind. It can be a split second or a longer moment in time, it does not matter; all that we are looking for is a moment when you felt great, or free or peaceful...recreate that *feeling* in your mind and body. (Remember the example of the woman who swam with the dolphins – she totally re-experienced that event.) Reconnect with your experience and re-live it and re-feel it. How did you feel? What were you doing? Who was with you? What were you wearing? What was the lighting like? What was on the radio? What sounds and smells were you experiencing? What were you thinking? How did you act? Breath it all in again, feelize it now. It is amazing how much pleasure you can get from reliving a happy moment over and over again in your mind.

Play with this for a bit and see how you feel...and see if you can re-feel the experience in the Now moment.

Wealth Journaling:

In your wealth journal write about your feelizing experience and any insights you had about your wealth moment.

Notice the wealth you do experience

Noticing is attracting, because it is where you are putting your attention. AS you notice the richness in your life, your attention goes to it and you attract more of it. **We live in a world of inclusion; what you notice (wanted or not) is attracted**. Over time, we train ourselves to notice certain things. Like when you are in the market for a new car, you start to notice it more and more on the road. This is the law of attraction at work.

As you might be noticing, we are talking a lot about wealth. My hope is that you are getting a feel for how to *consciously* create wealth (we are putting a lot of attention on it). And noticing the wealth, abundance, prosperity and joy that is already around you is a wonderful way to enjoy more of it. This is why teachers talk about the power of appreciation. **Appreciation is really noticing. And *what you appreciate appreciates*.** What you notice and put your attention on grows. Thus, noticing and appreciating is your investment growth strategy!

◉ Investment Tip: Notice the Wealth That Is - Right now

It is powerful to set your intention to feel wealthy - today - and then **notice and appreciate** the wealth that comes. And as we have been discussing, wealth shows up in a huge variety of ways – but it is usually a moment that makes you stop and go "wow, thank you, that is great!" At the end of the day, capture those moments in your wealth journal...because what we put our attention on grows and you want to notice and appreciate - so you can have more of them. As you intend to feel wealthy, it is powerful to notice wealth experiences as they happen to you - every day; and write them down. Then you see how much wealth you are experiencing and the momentum you are building and agree that you are wealthy!

Wealth Journaling:

- In your wealth journal write...What made you feel wealthy today... and note the things that made you feel wealthy a.k.a. joy-filled, inspired, loved, touched, open hearted, fulfilled, cared for, peace-filled, generous, empowered...you know wealthy.☺

What you put in your journal is up to you, as what makes you feel wealthy is very personal. Give yourself permission to notice all kinds of wealth from a bird singing while you are having your coffee, to a person letting you in as you are driving in heavy traffic. Putting your attention on wealthy moments attracts more wealthy moments. Noticing the wealth you are experiencing, right here right now, is a great way to enjoy more wealth going forward. Play with this...and see how it makes you feel.

Do things that make you feel wealthy

Part of attracting wealth is noticing things that make us feel wealthy and *doing more of those*. I think many of us discount the little wealth things that actually make us feel really rich, in the moment, right here today. So, it is powerful to notice the things that make you feel wealthy on a daily basis - and schedule them in - **make them a priority**.

Here is a very short list of things that make me feel wealthy. I wanted to give you an idea of what I am talking about so you can start your own list of wealth-producing experiences.

- Having breakfast with Marc makes me feel rich, so we have breakfast together a lot.
- Dressing nicely makes me feel wealthy - so I invest (make time to "shop") and find things that feel good, so I look good.
- Hanging out with my friends and laughing together makes me feel crazy wealthy - so I schedule lunches and dinner with them every chance I get.
- Watching my dogs sleep in the sun (or doing pretty much anything) makes me feel wealthy - so I hang out with my dogs a lot. I take them to work, enjoy giving them treats and take them for walks so we can be together and enjoy each other.
- The greenness of the garden makes me feel wealthy - so I invest in my garden and find plants that are colorful and smell wonderful. Watching the peony bloom is an amazingly rich experience.
- Fake bling is so sparkly and glittery, it makes me feel wealthy. So, I go on "bling-a-thons" where I purchase inexpensive, but expensive-looking bling that makes me feel fabulous.
- My bedazzled tables make me feel wealthy - so I spend time bedazzling...time where I put on inspiring music, get out my paints, glitter and rhinestones and bedazzle just for the fun of it.
- Pants that actually fit make me feel wealthy - so I invest in finding pants that are made of comfortable fabric and then I have them tailored to fit. So, when I go in my closet, I feel good about what is in there.
- Being generous makes me feel prosperous - so I buy coffee for my friends, share my good fortune when I can and in general I try to be generous with my time and money...as it feels good, I give from surplus, not from lack.

- Being healthy makes me feel wealthy. So I work out every day. I go to the health club, take walks, lift weights and dance around the house to club music.
- Writing makes me feel rich, as sharing wisdom feels good to me. So I am making time to write this book and blog about wealth!
- Hanging out with my Cosmic Financial Team and Book Success Team makes me feel wealthy - so I have meetings with them regularly.
- Marinating feels very wealthy to me - so I sit and marinate in love for 15 minutes or more each day.
- Listening to the recordings of Abraham-Hicks always makes me feel wealthy - so I listen to them every day on youtube.com

I hope what you notice in this list is that it is an odd smattering of experiences and things that speak *to my heart and me*. Wealth is very personal, as is success or any other word we try to put to that amazing feeling of loving life. So, please take the time to identify those experiences that speak to you and that are unique to you and do more of them.

Wealth Journaling:

In your journal write things that make you feel wealthy...

Hmm, did you notice that there is a similarity between the things that make you feel wealthy and the things that put you in alignment...interesting, huh?

◎ Investment Tip: Stay in Character

Sometimes it is easier for us to imagine wealth for someone else. We can see it for them, but not for us. So what we are going to do here is create a wealthy character - your wealth persona, if you will - that is all of the things that you desire to be, do and have. Take out your wealth journal and start to create a character that has all the qualities, capabilities and experiences of Big-*Wealthy-You*, the wealthy person you envision, then practice getting into the feeling-place of that character. You will become the part in your mind and feel it in your body, so you can play it with believability. The power of this is you get to write the character; you get to create the character and be the character you want. To really bring your character to life you need to practice staying in character, feeling yourself as this character you want to be and really becoming it.

My character is Laurie, The Miami Millionaire. She is Big-Wealthy-Me. She has it going on in so many ways and she is wealthy in so many ways. She has the Fabulocity of Kimora, the grace, beauty and hotness of Beyonce and the investment wisdom of Warren Buffet. Hey, why not create a character that is *all that?!* I am not going to say much more, as I don't want to bias your character. But you might want to consider adding characteristics of your wealth role models, add experiences of people you think are having the time of their lives. Most of all have fun with this. Let yourself playfully create. I know when I leave the house as Miami-Millionaire-Laurie the world is my oyster and I have a great time everywhere I go.

The great thing about this is it will allow you to approach wealth with less resistance, versus trying to "make wealth happen"... Play with this and see how you feel.

Wealth Journaling:

> In your journal write Your Big-Wealthy-You Character Description...

Employ Infinite Intelligence: Create a Cosmic Financial Team

I found this wonderful book, *Hiring the Heavens* by Jean Slatter. Jean says just as there are many humans here on earth that have special talents and skills, so too is **there a bevy of talent and wisdom in the non-physical world, call them Infinite Intelligence, just waiting for us to call on them** and ask for their wisdom and help. There are cosmic gardeners, negotiators, counselors, mathematicians, and there are financial wizards, masters in their field, all available for us to ask for their help...and employ them.

What she suggests and I have found to work too, is to get clear about the help you need, go to the "cosmic yellow pages" and say who or what kind of help you need. And then *ask* for what you want!

I have found that having a team that is working with you helps you vibrate more aligned with what you want – because you need to be clear about what the team is helping you with, and clarity aligns our vibration.

Even Napoleon Hill had a team of Infinite Intelligence working with him. In his seminal book, *Think and Grow Rich*, Napoleon notes that plans are inert and useless without sufficient *power* to translate them into action. He assembled a Master Mind group of Infinite Intelligence to tap into their collective wisdom and power to move his plans into action.

So of course, I have a Master Mind group. My Infinite Intelligence Cosmic Financial Team has a money manager / accumulator, growth fund manager, passive income portfolio expander and a graciousness facilitator. You can put your team together, as you need. I also ask for anyone else I need that I don't know I need and they show up.

How I work with them is by first aligning to the unlimited flow of wealth by meditating, doing some breath work or going for a walk. I clear and prepare my space, light a candle, etc. Then I ask them to join me in a conscious creating session (more on this later) and know they are there. Then I ask for them to work with me on the project or plan I am intent on.

You can also hire the heavens for all manner of help. I have a cosmic book success team and a cosmic sales team for our company. Remember your asking is thanks enough and your appreciation of their help is a bonus!

Wealth Journaling:

>Create a list of cosmic infinite intelligence team members and what you wish for assistance and power with. Have fun and tap into their infinite capabilities and strengths... Remember Life is friendly and wants what you want.

Say yes to wealth!

One day as I meditated, I was feeling how abundant and wonderful life is. And then I felt that the only thing I needed to do was to *say yes to it...and* to let it in. That wealth is mine for the enjoying, but I need to give *myself permission* to have it. I need to agree to it and allow it in, in the many and wonderful ways it can flow into my life. **I realized I was the gatekeeper; I was the one deciding if and when it could come.**

This is where the effortless part really comes in. If we can let ourselves say yes to wealth, we can relax. We know that we are giving permission for the well-being and wealth of life to flow though us naturally – as it is always doing anyway; as it does whether we notice it or not.

Please stop for a moment and check in with yourself. **Can you give yourself permission to have wealth and be wealthy?** What happened in your body when you checked in? You might want to journal about this and capture any wisdom that is showing up with that question at this point in the process.

As we have been discussing, for many of us inherent in the notion that you must effort to have wealth is the unquestioned assumption that wealth is not yours and that *some condition outside of you is deciding whether or not you can have it.* Many people believe this and so it has become part of the collective consciousness. But we are awakening to our creating power to attract what we invest our energy in. As we do this, we realize it is within our power to engage the law of attraction and it is up to us to agree to what we want. It is up to us to say, "Yes, I give myself permission to have my heart's desires."

"The more you recognize the immense good within you,
the more you magnetize immense good around you." —Alan Cohen

◎ Investment Tip: Practice Saying YES!

In the spirit of feelizing and engaging the law of attraction, let's practice saying yes. I am going to give you a bunch of statements and I want you to agree with them. (We did a similar exercise in earlier chapters, but we have more understanding under our belt now, so it is worth repeating to deepen our experience.)

What I wish for you to do is say yes and agree to the statements! You do not have to justify them or show how you are deserving of them. Give yourself permission to *feel* that they are true...unconditionally. Feel the ok-ness of them and feel the love for you that is inherent in them. And please,

no "Yes, but." You are going to say YES! Sweet! Yowza! OK! Sounds Good...
and really mean it - OK!

- I am dearly loved. Your response - *Oh YES!*
- I am a powerful creator - your response - *Yes, I am.*
- There is WUW unlimited wealth flowing around me always and in all ways. - *Yes, there is.*
- I am magical, glorious and in every way ready to experience my wealth - *Yes, I am.*
- I feel rich more and more. *Yes, I do*
- Right now, I allow myself to enjoy the wealth that I desire. *Yes, I do. Yahoo for me!*
- The wealth that I desire, desires me. *Oh yes - that feels good.*
- The angels of the universe have my back. *Yes, they do. Thank you.*
- I can relax in knowing all is well. *Yes, I can.*
- I am surrounded by wealth and abundance...it is everywhere really. Life is abundance. *Yes, I am and yes life is. Sweet!*
- I am wealthy. *Yes, indeed!*

Play with this a bit more. Say the statement out loud and repeat it over and over again until you can feel your energy shift to agreeing with the statement and see how you feel!

Wealth Journaling:

In your wealth journal write this list and add some of your own.

"A little strike each day can chop down big trees. Give it a try!"
— Israelmore Ayivor, The Great Hand Book of Quotes

Attract by Telling Your New Wealth Story

A couple of years ago I was at a bookstore and found a book called *The Lottery Heiress* by Angelia Assanti and of course I had to buy it! It was about a woman who inherited a huge amount of money from her parents who had not told her they had won the lottery when she was very young. It is a very fun book of love and the joys and perils of money.

As I read the book, one of the things I felt was that the author was feelizing herself as a millionaire heiress. She was telling her story the way she wanted it to be. I felt like the whole book was an exploration in what it would feel like to be a millionaire – it was a feelizing experience for the author. And to be honest it was a wonderful feelizing experience for me. I still feel the vibration that book ignited in me – and it is powerful. The author of the book had the focus and feeling I am talking about. The kind where you want to write a whole book about your millionaire experiences.

Engaging the law of attraction is great fun! It is writing your story your way and then feelizing it and thus molding the energy clay into reality. So, what if you write your own millionaire story? Be the author of your millionaire story.

◉ Investment Tip: Tell your <u>new</u> wealth story

We all have a wealth story we tell about ourselves to ourselves…usually it is more of a scarcity story. Your usual story might be a funny story you tell to your friends (for entertainment) about a tough time, or your family, or something you tried and did not feel went the way you wanted. Most scarcity stories involve experiences of loss, disappointment, or inadequacy. But this is your opportunity to **write the story the way you want it**…and then of course feelize it! Here you are giving yourself permission to write your story; the way you want it, from a no limitation, all things are possible place. Let this be a free flow of ideas, desires and won't-it-be-great-when. This will plant the seeds of the wealth consciousness you are creating. Play with this and see what comes out.

Wealth Journaling:

Write your <u>new</u> wealth story.

Don't Effort To Attract

In this chapter, we have discussed a variety of ways you can invest yourself to *attract* your wealth, essentially putting your attention on wealth and wealthy ways. And you might be feeling there is much "work to be done to attract what you desire." But please, these ideas are not about efforting more. Remember easy-does-it. They are just about helping you focus your vibration on wealth and prosperity. They are meant to give you back your innate wealth consciousness through simple conscious focusing of your attention.

A story about effortless attracting: I remember when I was walking down the beach in Miami. I saw this girl with a huge conch shell…I had never seen one on the beach, as the beach in Miami does not have shells really. I was just taking my walk and felt very at ease and satisfied to be hanging out… and I thought fleetingly, *boy it would be fun to find one of those*…but I totally forgot about it. A few days later, I was out taking my usual sunrise walk (I was staying on South Beach in January when winters are brutal in Chicago) and there right in front of me was a huge conch shell! Just sitting right in my path. There was nothing around but it! I was like WOWOWOWOW! I brought it home with me and it is sitting in our TV room to remind me about the love that is all around constantly sharing!

When there is wealth in our consciousness, everything around us becomes wealth prospering and so exciting you will want to go out and take inspired action. Attracting wealth is natural, like breathing, when we feel our wealth at our essence. *So easy does it.* **Ease and flow is the way to go.** Have fun noticing, enjoying and playing with life in a wealthy way and you too will experience your life unfolding in magical ways.

"When there is love in your heart,
everything outside of you also becomes lovable." —Veeresh

Practice Attracting!

"The mind has been likened to a piece of paper that has been folded. Ever afterwards it has a tendency to fold in the same crease–unless we make a new crease or fold, then it will follow the last lines."
– William Walker Atkinson

Have Conscious Creation Sessions

I wish to encourage you to put quality time and energy into wealth creation. This is why there are so many "play with" investment tools scattered about in the book. These will help you align and create a wealth consciousness that I hope will become a way of looking at life. *Another way to invest quality energy is by having conscious creating sessions.* In these sessions, you will set aside around 15 minutes to feelize your wealth. You can do this to create something specific like a new house, new car, a different job, whatever you would like to have. A conscious creation session will intensify your attractive power, helping you feel you have invested in what you want. Having a conscious creation session with your Infinite Intelligence Cosmic Team is even more fun, so invite them in if you like.

A Conscious Creation Session goes something like this:

1. *Make an appointment with yourself to create wealth.* Put this creation session on your calendar, so you see it as a priority and as your time to invest your energy into the wealth experience you desire. At the appointed time, turn off your cell phone and close yourself off from the world as best you can, so you can really focus. Sometimes I go for a walk, sometimes I sit and write (it can be really beneficial to write your desires, but that is not necessary). Sometimes I go to a coffee shop. Whatever feels good.

2. *Next, invite in your cosmic team to join you* and ask them to work with you in aligning you with the wealth you seek (and that is already

waiting for you). Then just sit for a moment aligning with Wealth and feeling the love of your team and the excitement with which you all will be creating. This step is so fun, because you do not have to feel alone in your desires for wealth. When you take this step, you acknowledge the love and support, the unconditional love and support that is available to you. So, engage it!

3. *Now feelizing being wealthy.* Enjoy the freedoms of being wealthy. Enjoy the play and fun you are having as a part of being wealthy. The opportunity here is to become in mind and body the wealthy person you see. Ready your wealth story you wrote or talk like the wealthy character you created earlier in the chapter. I like to get the energy going by speaking out loud the experience I am having. Enjoying the moment. Conscious creation sessions are fun and powerful. And don't underestimate the impact these sessions have. Many people say they want wealth but feel lack-full much of the time. In these sessions, you are only going to feel abundant, playful, enthusiastic, excited, glorious and free. In your conscious creation sessions, you really got it going on and the more engaged you can get in the experience the more attractive the result.

   Note: If your mind jumps in and starts to say things (like this is just fantasy or other not-so-helpful-things), just say, "thank you for sharing but I am in the middle of a conscious creation session!"

4. Notice any insights you have or ideas that flow from this – you might want to get them down in your wealth journal. Many times, in these sessions, ideas will come out, but if not that is ok – the energy is out there molding the clay.

5. At the end of the session, say a quick thank you to your team for joining you and then go about your day, knowing that you have just invested quality energy into your creation. This is you investing very wisely and the dividends will be far reaching.

Play with having some conscious creating sessions and see what you notice.

Wealth Journaling:

> In your wealth journal write...Insights, ideas, feelings from your session. Also come back and note any ideas or insights you might have had later in the day or any dreams that happen.

Just a quick story: I did a conscious creating session where I was saying how much I wanted to share with people about all the abundance of life. I got really into it – so much so I was weeping at the idea of sharing. A couple of days later, totally out of the blue I got a call from the department chair at DePaul University. I had never gotten a call from him (nor have I since). He said a Women's leadership conference needed a speaker (in Dubai) and had contacted DePaul to see if anyone was interested and thought of me! That is the power of conscious creating sessions – and you never know how the law of attraction will fulfill your desires – it is usually beyond any ideas you currently have. BTW, I really wanted to go and do the talk but my schedule at the time was not facilitative. No worries and no guilt - many other opportunities are always flowing!

Remember:

- Attracting wealth gets easier and easier.
- Feelize it – Create your vibration by feeling in your body and visualizing in your minds-eye.
- Be the wealth you seek. Don't meditate on wealth, meditate AS wealth.
- Put your attention on wealth and what it feels like to be wealthy
- Do things that make you feel wealthy
- Notice the Wealth you do experience
- Feel wealthy today
- Attract wealthy
- Employ Infinite Intelligence via your cosmic wealth team
- Say yes! to your wealth
- Tell your new wealth story
- Easy-Does-It: don't effort to attract.

Frequently Asked Questions

1. **How long to I have to do this?** Everything you desire is already in the infinite field of possibility – so technically the answer is as long as it takes for you to allow yourself to have it. Another way to look at it is the way Abraham gives: Everything we desire, we desire because we think that in the having of it we will feel better. We will feel happier, joyful, wealthy - amazing really. So, what we are doing here is creating a wealth vibration habit, one that is not necessarily about "manifesting money" or getting something tangible (which will all happen too), but **we are getting something very valuable in the process: the ability to feel satisfied, feel wealthy, as a way of being, as a state of feeling**. The effects are cumulative. And the results in how we feel, how we act and how we walk in the world are noticed and felt. Invest in wealth, consistently enough and the dividends will be there and will keep paying off more and more.

Because the better it gets, the better it gets. So don't be concerned with how long you have to do this - like you are on a money diet, waiting for it to be over. Shift to feeling like a powerful, wealth investor and reap the enjoyment dividends every day, starting today.

2. **Isn't feelizing just creative visualization?** There is something to keep in mind about visualization. It is a powerful tool for *seeing* what you choose to create. However, visualizing might become limiting if you become attached to the visualization happening *exactly* as you see it. Additionally, many of us stay in our minds when we visualize and the key is to get in your body and feel it to. This is why we *feelize*. We focus on feeling as much or more than seeing. The feeling is what is vibrating and attracting the essence of what you desire without limitation.

3. **Creating wealth feels a bit greedy. Shouldn't I attract something more appropriate?** The Law of Attraction does not judge what we want to create (attract)...neither should we. As one of my teachers says, "The Law of Attraction does not judge if 7 Rolls Royce's is too many! We do, but It does not." So here is a good place to dig in and look at your beliefs about what is greedy, what is worthy, about what is worthwhile and about deservedness, etc. There are many unspoken assumptions in this question...dig in and look at what you really feel and believe.

4. **Where is this wealth coming from?** As we have been discussing, Wealth is in energy form until we physicalize it. It is the essence of the energy of life. Life energy is unlimited, unbounded and available to everyone in every way. You, as the master artisan that you are, are shaping this energy into the life experience you desire. Remember, you matter and what you focus on physicalizes the energy...makes the energy become tangible. You are the creator of your experience and you are the one molding the life energy clay into tangible wealth.

5. **What about all those lottery winners?** *They created wealth and look, many of them are worse off than before they won the lottery.* I am not sure about that, to be honest. First, I do not know what they were creating – what was the intent energy behind their creation? Nor

do I know what they were feeling as they were doing it. (Two very important aspects of conscious creating.) Also, there are thousands of lottery winners a day and there have been millions over the last 20 years. The TV shows only highlight a handful of people...the most sadly sensational. Be careful to invest wisely here. Invest in your wealth consciousness, invest in knowing that wealth is available for you and trust that as you become more and more aligned with your internal guidance system, you will know what feels "good" and what feels "not so good". Invest now in feelizing that when you win the lottery you will have a glorious experience of joy, freedom, growth and contentment.

6. **I am not sure I know what wealth is?** You know the great thing about deciding to invest in your wealth consciousness is that as you invest, you will get more and more information about what wealth is - *for you* - and about the wealth experience you want to have. You can even ask for more clarity about the wealth you want - and the clarity will come. As we have discussed, wealth is personal and sometimes we think we want one thing, usually money, and then we realize we really want something else. That is totally fine. Keep adding to your wealth portfolios. Add experiences, wealth wishes and joys - modify freely, play with your feelizations often, expand as you wish...it's all good.

7. **What if I don't know what I want to create (invest in)?** This is an important question, because many of us have not thought of ourselves as wealthy nor do we feel we have the power to create wealth for ourselves. We also have preconceived notions of who can be wealthy, what is appropriate, what is adequate, what is all right to desire. All of these things may be swirling around in your mind about experiencing your own wealth. I do wish for you to expand your wealth definition and maybe ask yourself: "What do I need right now?" "What is wealth to me at this moment?" Interestingly enough, you might start to realize you don't need a million dollars as much as you need more time, or more time for yourself, or you need adventure or play. As we have been discussing, the Law of Attraction is not limited by money. Money is only one way in an infinite field of

possibilities to help you experience the life you desire. Most people think money is the only way they can get those things. But the Law of Attraction is powerful; if you need more play and fun and time (which are all aspects of wealth to me), then feelize that. And in a holy instant you will be amazed at how quickly someone will call you to pick your kid up for a play date, or someone will send you a youtube.com clip that is rip-roaring hilarious, or whoever you are meeting is 15 minutes late and you have 15 minutes of free time.

8. **You talk of the law of attraction like it is a person. Is it?** The law of attraction is not a person or an entity – it is not benevolent or critical…it does not have a personality. It is neutral. It is a building block of the universe, a technology – it is a physical, energetic law that supports the creative engine of the earth. Vibrate and receive more of that vibration. Again, the law of attraction's characteristics are magnetic and ubiquitous like the law of gravity. Learn the principles about how it operates and then you can consciously use it.

9. **So what price do I have to pay to have this wealth?** Sacrifice is not necessary! We can create the wealth our hearts desire - free and clear. There is no price you must pay, there is no appropriate or inappropriate desire and there is no transaction necessary (e.g. "if I get this, then I must give/do/sacrifice that.") This is hard for us to imagine! But whom would you pay? The Law of Attraction? What would you pay? What does the Law of Attraction need? You are tapping into a magnetic force, an energy system, which operates universally, equally and freely, like the law of gravity. You do not have to pay to use the law of gravity, it just is…freely, effortlessly accessible.

10. **Why have I not experienced my wealth to this point?** If you do not have the wealth experience you desire, ask yourself some energy (vibration) questions.

    • Have I been investing in **Awakening** to a new understanding of wealth and how life was really meant to be experienced?

    • Have I been **Aligning** to Wealth/Well-Being around me always and in all ways? And feeling it flow NOW to me, effortlessly?

- Have I been **Attracting** (feelizing) the wealth in my life NOW? Not "praying for it" but "vibrating AS it".
- Have I **Alchemized** my doubts, worries and fears?
- Have I been distracted? Have I changed my mind? Are other things more important?
- Do I doubt I can have it?
- Have I let fear, worry, limitation, disbelief, etc. creep in?
- Did I say I want it, but then focus on its exact opposite? (E.g. I say I want more money but focus on how little is in my bank account?)
- Have I been **Allowing** my desires to get to me by reducing my resistance and going with the flow of life?
- Am I enjoying (appreciating) the wealth that I have now?

11. **Don't I have to create something with a higher purpose, or betterment for all, or something spiritually more appropriate?** No, no and no. Say this a thousand time, "I can invest in whatever I want, I can invest in whatever wealth I want. Free and clear. No judgment." It is interesting though, as you get more comfortable and successful at investing your energy, you will feel fulfilled, satisfied and great-full. It is the coolest feeling and this fullness swells in your heart and you do end up wanting to share, to help, to contribute (usually for the betterment of all). But notice this is a result, not a mandatory pre-condition. The desire to contribute comes from "your cup overflowing". Try not to limit yourself by agreeing to rules that don't apply. The only rule, if there is one, is to learn how to invest your energy consciously.

12. **Can I use the conscious creating session for more than just wealth?** Yes you can use it for anything and everything from creating great eyesight to attracting an unexpected surprise.

13. **If all we have to do is vibrate wealth, why don't we just do it?** A couple of points here: First, vibrating wealth is a huge part of the equation but not the only part. As we vibrate wealth, we feel more empowered and excited to engage with life in a different way, which is attractive. And it is in the engagement and action that things really take off. As I mentioned in the first chapter – Wealth first – then

money (the actions that make money). Our wealth vibration is the precursor. And secondly, as discussed in the awareness chapter, there are all kinds of "agreements" we have made that keep us from feeling wealthy and thus acting wealthy. And these are just old scarcity agreements. As we let go of them, our wealth vibration will become stronger and clearer and our interactions with life we be greatly enhanced.

14. **If I don't have to do anything for it to come, how am I going to get it? This sounds like crap.** I feel ya – really I do. And I am not saying you will not be doing anything for it to come. But the first thing you are *doing* is developing your wealth consciousness, so you vibrate wealthy. This vibration engages the law of attraction – so you are doing something – something very powerful. *And then you will be taking actions that arise from a different vibrational vantage point;* it is the difference between inspiration and perspiration. Can you feel how differently you approach something when you feel excited and inspired versus fearful and worried? Worried how you are going to *get it* is exactly what keeps wealth at bay – **worry is like a force field the wealth bounces off of.** Inspired action from a place of knowing all is well, allows it to flow to you and you to flow to it. This attractive flow is what we are up to here.

"The only limitation is that which one sets up in one's own mind." - Napoleon Hill, Think and Grow Rich

Investment Strategy:
I Attract Wealth

Invoke this...

- I am wealth – therefore I attract wealth. It's funny...because in the past I was not clear about that. But now I am.
- I am attracting wealth and it gets easier and easier. It's funny... because in the past I thought it was hard. But now I feel the ease and flow of how it works.
- I am putting my attention on wealth and what it feels like to be wealthy. It's funny...because in the past I thought I was doing that but really, I was focusing on the wealth I was not experiencing. But now I invest differently.
- I radiate a wealthy glow, I vibrate AS wealth...and the law of attraction responds in like kind. Now I see the power of my investing.
- I think wealthy thoughts, I talk about the wonder of how things go well around me and I feel so comfortable in the abundance of life that I have plenty to share and to spare.
- I am attracting opportunities, experiences and people in my life that feel aligned with my desires.
- I am noticing all the prosperity around me and I feel so great-full. I notice my wonderful friends and family, my loving relationships and the things that bring me joy and know that all is well. Aaaaaahhhhh.
- I am living my wealth story!
- I say yes to my wealth experience. I say yes! Please! Thank you! And wealth responds – YES dear one! Yes. Let's play some more together.

A

Awareness
Of Your Past

Alchemize
Your Beliefs

Awaken
Your Power

Align
Your Energy

Attract
Your Dreams

Allow
Your Desires

Amaze
Yourself

Chapter 10: Invest in Allowing!

Allowing is cultivating a felt-sense of receptivity to the ever-present Wealth-Energy. It is when we develop our ability to receive and to enjoy this energy in grace and ease. We allow what we desire to flow to us and we allow others to be who they are, as they are. Allowing is a state of being where our mental, emotional and physical resistance is lowered so the Wealth-Energy flows freely through us, as it naturally does - and we get to experience it.

Learn What Allowing Feels Like

We live in a world of "make it happen", which is great—wonderful, actually. However, this "make it happen" energy often ends up feeling like we have to constantly struggle, push, force and endure. In the Easy-Does-it-Process, the energy of managing and efforting is replaced with the energy of possibility and play; life was not meant to be a struggle and wealth creating is not meant to be difficult – quite the contrary. When we learn to focus and invest our energy, creating wealth becomes simple and smooth. Allowing feels like ease, flow and receptivity.

Allowing is often the step that is most difficult for many of us to grasp because it asks us to believe, trust and know. Allowing is about *believing* **in** the wealth of the universe, *trusting* that it is there for us unconditionally and *knowing* that when we call on it, we have it, so we can be excited and enthusiastic for it to show up.

Interestingly enough, investing in allowing is not about doing more. It is investing in enthusiastic expectation and learning to go with the flow, allowing that which you desire to flow to you in grace and ease. "Doing more" is not necessary.

I want to tell you a story of a friend, "Marjorie". She is a wonderful woman and one of the most generous mothers I know. She is a caretaker at her essence and she is glorious. We have been working together for a while practicing the law of attraction and creating all kinds of wonderful things. A year ago, her husband lost his job and it has been scary for her family. During this time, she and her husband have been trying to create a job, income, anything that can keep them financially solvent.

One day as I was discussing Attracting (feelizing) with Marjorie, I realized she is amazing at attracting, but not so good at allowing. Her natural mothering (caring for) capabilities are always at work, so much so, it is almost not in her cosmology to receive, to allow. I think this is an issue for most of us: most mothers, most fathers and most grown-ups. We become responsible adults; we learn that we need to take care of ourselves and be self-reliant if we want to make it in this world. And this adulthood-thing, taking care of children, family and friends becomes so habitual that "allowing", being cared for, becomes less emotionally and energetically available to us.

However, allowing is such an important piece of the Easy-Does-It process. **If you ask but cannot receive, if you create but cannot allow yourself to have your creation, if you seek but do not allow yourself to find, you are only experiencing part of the fulfillment process.** You are missing out on a big piece of why you came to earth in the first place; which I believe is to not only want, but to *experience* the things you want. It is not only to create wealth, but also to enjoy and *experience tangibly* that which you have said you desire.

> *"I want to be able to leave $100 bills under peoples' pillows...*
> *like the tooth fairy. Yes, great and will you allow $100 bills to*
> *be left under your pillow?" Conversations with Wealth*

As I talked to Marjorie of this she said, "Yes, absolutely I am not good at allowing because I want to be in *control,* I want it to show up the way I want." I can so relate to this. We are not sure life has our backs, so we feel we need to control everything. And as household managers, or parents, we get so used to managing and controlling, we forget how to be taken care of and go with the flow. We are so in the driver's seat, we lose touch with the ability to be amazed, delighted and cared for by the well-being that is around us. But as powerful wealth investors, we are learning to allow (i.e., experience the return on our investment) the good/wealth/joy etc. that we have said we want.

One reason I love yoga is that at the end of practice the last pose is shivasana (corpse pose or final relaxation), which many say is the most important pose. This is where you just lay flat on the ground and let the practice and everything else go. You get to just relax and *be* for a few minutes without any distractions. The asanas (the actual yoga poses) get all that control energy - the resistance and "do" energy out – and helps us align so we can "be". **Because when the mind is quiet and the body is relaxed... allowing happens**. Let me say that again: *when the mind is quiet and the body relaxed...allowing happens*. We allow the natural well-being of life to penetrate in and flow freely through us, as it naturally *wants* to do, when we are not resisting it...through control, worry, managing, pushing and in general, over-doing. You would be amazed at how many people pack up and leave before shivasana or squirm and fidget during the pose. Allowing ourselves to receive and relax is difficult for us. But we need to learn; we need to give ourselves permission to give ourselves permission to receive and relax.

*"What makes allowing abundance difficult? Awareness of not enough abundance! You can't have it both ways. You cannot focus upon the absence of money and let money in. It cannot be! You have to start finding moments that feel like you think you want to feel...and **savoring** them!"* – Abraham-Hicks

◉ Investment Tip: Learn the language of allowing

How we speak to ourselves, our self-talk, is an indication of how *kind* we are being to ourselves and if we are vibrating in scarcity mode or wealth mode. Many of us use internal language that is not all that kind or wealth-ful. As we learn the language of allowing, we take the pressure off, giving us permission to be on our unique wealth journey, enjoying as opposed to demanding perfection. As you go through your day and you are not feeling at ease, speak some of these ideas to yourself:

- There is no rush. I have plenty of time.
- It's a done deal! So, relax.
- Things are always working out for me.
- Easy-Does-It.
- Relax, it is all good.
- Chill! Ease and flow is the way to go.
- I don't have to figure all of this out right now.
- It's natural for things to work out for me.
- Things are getting easier and easier.
- I am getting pretty good at this.
- Financial well-being is flowing to me more and more every day; I feel so excited.
- Things are getting better and better every day.
- Wealth is always available to me.
- I love loving.
- I am in the right place at the right time.
- I am blessed and fortunate.
- I have the leverage of the universe flowing to me.
- I like what is coming.
- I know I am on the right track.
- I am excited to see what comes.
- I trust myself.
- I believe in the law of attraction and I believe it is consistently reflecting my vibration
- I like focusing on what I want.
- I look forward to getting there.
- Wealth is eternally flowing without restriction.
- All my dreams are completely underwritten.
- I have the perfect pattern for abundance.
- I love, I love, I love.
- The universe is on my side.

- I can let the law of attraction do its job and orchestrate the circumstances for my wealth fulfillment!
- Look how easily my desires are fullfilled. Look how easily solutions come to my questions.

Play with these and add some of your own. As you focus on finding allowing language that relieves you of self-pressure, your vibration will rise. Play with giving yourself a break and practicing kindness with yourself and others. Then notice how your wealth consciousness and experience shift.

Allowing feels like ease, flow and non-resistance

There is a part of me that knows the word *investment* is an action word. Invest means to "do" something, take action, which is very appealing to us humans. Allowing almost feels like the antithesis of investing. But most investors are in search of the holy grail of returns, *passive income*. This is where the money you have invested pays you back without you having to do any work. You have income even though you are passive (not efforting). **Think of allowing as enjoying your passive income.** It is the time when you enjoy the ease and flow of knowing you have the "cash flow" even though you are not "doing" anything - because you have already done lots of great investing (via consciously investing your energy daily). *Now you are investing in relaxing, enjoyment, positive expectation and ease.* I wish for you to train yourself to be able to allow the wealth and well-being to flow to you.

As I mentioned earlier, for most of us responsible adults, allowing feels too passive, too lazy, and this is what makes allowing seem so hard. Hard work, suffering, no pain-no gain...all these messages are the opposite of what I am talking of here. I want to help you understand how trying too hard, efforting too much, actually might be keeping your wealth from you.

This is because of the unquestioned assumption behind hard work and efforting, which is that *you have to do something* (and it going to be hard) to make wealth happen. This attracts the need for more "difficult effort". The law of attraction reads our vibration as "I am not doing enough" and "I don't have what I want, so work harder." Which, in essence, is like moving our own cheese.

One of great things about allowing is that you attract ease and flow, with the feeling of ease and flow and that all is well. What if you spent a few moments every day in the feeling that all was well and that your wealth was already yours?! You would feel and act differently moment-to-moment, I guarantee you. *Invest in vibrating ease and flow to experience ease and flow.*

Allowing is inherent in the idea we have discussed before, *what would you do if you knew you would not fail?* The implications behind this notion are plentiful:

1. Success is guaranteed
2. Things will work out
3. I will have what I need when I need it
4. Life is working with me
5. I don't have to fear or worry

....so many great allowing statements are behind this quote. It is in our best interest to cultivate an inner knowing, an inner feeling that everything is available to us – so we can relax. The energy of what we desire is here *now* and it is in the process of becoming physical, tangible and available to us in a way we can experience.

> *"Through allowing, you become what you are; vast, spacious. You become whole. You are not a fragment anymore, which is how the ego perceives itself. Your true nature emerges, which is one with the nature of God."* - Eckhart Tolle

◎ Investment Tip: Play with Flowing

Flow is the feeling that things are moving along as smooth as buttah – with no resistance, fears, doubts or worries. Flow is shifting our energy from one of pushing and difficult effort, to following synchronicity - acting on our inspirations, honoring unexpected coincidences and paying attention to opportunities that present themselves. Flow is the experience of things coming to us in grace and simple ease; where things that seemed difficult become a magical smooth fulfillment.

A wonderful way to get into that "flowing feeling" is to imagine yourself soaring like an eagle above the clouds - gliding effortlessly through the sky. This might sound odd, but if we want to flow, it is helpful to feel flowy.

Other ways to get that flowing feeling is to drive your car down the expressway later at night when there is no traffic and just enjoy gliding along the highway. Or feel yourself skiing down a hill or roller-skating, swimming in warm water, gliding down a hill on your bike, or floating down a gentle river in a raft. Whatever method you use, give yourself permission to engage your whole self in a flowy experience; let your mind be free and your body float...that is ease and flow. Play with this and see if you can cultivate ease in your body.

*Live in **ease** and ease will live in you.*
*Live in **joy** and joy will live in you.*
*Live in **peace** and peace will live in you.*
*Live in **wealth** and wealth will live in you.*

Know your wealth is here...and what you desire, desires you

This is an amazing concept to me, because I always thought that what I desired was wrong or selfish – that to desire was bad or evil. But once again, on the journey to effortless wealth, we are faced with deciding anew about what we are going to choose to believe. *To believe that what I desire desires me can be an amazing new revelation.*

Throughout time, we have been given countless words of wisdom that agree with this concept. Probably the most widespread is from Matthew 7:7-8 in the King James Bible, "[7] Ask, and it shall be given you; seek, and ye shall find; knock, and it shall be opened unto you:[8] For every one that asketh receiveth; and he that seeketh findeth; and to him that knocketh it shall be opened."

The thing is that, over time, we have put all kinds of criteria, conditions and assessment upon the "and you shall receive". It has become transactional— you shall receive *if...if* you deserve it, *if* you have earned it,..if... if...if But there is no *if* unless we agree to it.

I cannot stress how important this aspect of investing is. Knowing it is already yours, that what you desire desires you. Isn't that the basis for beginner's luck? People who don't know they shouldn't make it, make it. People who do not know the obstacles, or don't know to worry about how difficult it is to make it, get what they intend. It is because they come at it with openness, enthusiasm and childlike excitement. Children understand flow...let's learn from them.

"Worthiness, in very simple terms, means I have found a way to let the Energy reach me, the Energy that is natural, reach me. Worthiness, or unworthiness, is something that is pronounced upon you by you. You are the only one that can deem yourself worthy or unworthy. You are the only one who can love yourself into a state of allowing or hate yourself in a state of disallowing. There is not something wrong with you. You are all, in the moment, practicing the art of allowing or the art of resisting." – Abraham-Hicks

◉ Investment Tip...Know it is yours

"Before they call, I have already answered and while you are yet speaking, I will hear." Isaiah 65:24 in the King James Bible notes the unlimited universe of possibility and every potential outcome to every desire is already in the infinite field - ready for us, when we are ready for it! The physical fulfillment is just waiting for us to put our attention on what we want. We do this by vibrating AS what we desire and by putting our attention and focus on it, thus we attract it to us. Play with the feeling of relief that comes with knowing it is available and it is yours – effortlessly.

Invest in learning to receive

As we learn to allow, we are naturally learning to lower our resistance and receive the wealth of life to flow to us and through us. One of the best examples of the give and take process of life is breathing. We breath in, we receive, we breathe out, we share and give of ourselves. Each moment, we are in this wonderful effortless giving and receiving dance with life. But many of us have a hard time with the idea of receiving and allowing ourselves the pleasure of experiencing free and clear. And isn't this one of the reasons we are not so comfortable with receiving? Many things given are not always given free and clear. But when we are talking about Wealth-Energy it is always available free and clear - with no strings attached.

ⓢ Investment Tip: Play with Yes, Please, Thank You

One of my favorite ways to receive is by saying *yes, please, thank you*. And if you really want to get fancy you can say *"Oh Yes, Oh Please and Oh Thank you!"* *Yes* allows you to have what is being offered, or what you have asked for. *Please* helps us to soften to it. And *thank you* is a statement of appreciation. So the next time you find yourself saying, "No, thanks - that's ok" or resisting a compliment or help - stop for a moment and allow yourself to receive and just say, "Yes, please, thank you!"

Let the Universe Handle the Details

This might seem hard for many of us who have been taught that we need to manage things and make them happen. Yes, we need to take action to attract our creation, **but many of us get so caught up in the details and dictating the how, when, where and who that we can get in our own way.** Take this from an expert who gets in her own way all the time! I don't mean to, but all of that old programming comes in and soon I forget to trust the process and to trust that it is already here in the infinite field of potentiality.

It is time to start trusting in our beyond-logic and the beyond-5-senses world we live in and start remembering we are Spirit-Beings, amazing Spirit-Beings. We have tremendous love, support and creative-helping-hands surrounding us every moment of every day! Handling the details, orchestrating an infinity of events, people, places and things to help our creation get to us. Nothing is impossible for the universe! Nothing. And when we start dictating, expecting and pushing *our* way, we take all of magic right out of the equation.

ⓢ Investment Tip: I will keep my valve open ANYWAY

Wealth is flowing always and in all ways. We humans have a choice if we are going to allow the wealth to flow through us. We have free will to choose whether *we* are going to resist the wealth and close ourselves off to it, or to allow it to flow by being open to it. It is as if we are a faucet that is in charge of how much water (wealth) flows to us by whether or not we open the valve.

There is a brief moment when we can decide what we will choose, what we will feel next...it might be a split second, but it is there. The opportunity is to allow prosperity to flow through us or not. The choice we have is to keep the Wealth flowing, the Health flowing through us - *anyway*. We do this by choosing to keep our alignment (we keep the valve to our Wealth open) even when we feel like shutting down. A bill comes in the mail and you have a choice—right then. The choice is: "I will feel wealthy - *anyway*. I *will* stay aligned - *anyway*. I will keep my valve open - *anyway*." Play with this and see how you get to be in charge of your feeling vibration.

Let go of expectations and feel the lightness

Expectation trips me up over and over. Lately, the message has been coming in loud and clear – usually accompanied by a bout of the flu! The expectations put tremendous pressure on me and those around me. I start to push and grind to make the creation happen. I notice what is not happening and work harder and feel I am doing something wrong. I exhaust myself and then I am susceptible to ailments and illness. It is the over-achiever in me, the one who wants to excel and I ignore my health and body. I am not happy to be writing this, but I often get caught in my old ways and miss out on the fun ways to creation fulfillment! This is my plea to you, to learn from me and be free. Free yourself of demanding and pushing.

For me, when I catch myself in expectations and pushing hard, I use one of my alignment techniques (from Chapter 8) like yoga to change things up and then engage the wonder and magic of dancing with life or I schedule a conscious creating session or call a bestie. You can realign yourself in any way you choose. And flowing is much more fun than difficult effort. At first, it might seem like you are cheating (*I don't have to struggle to get what I want*), but you are not. You are learning a new way that facilitates your achieving what you desire, *effort-lessly*. Allowing is more life enhancing and joyful... and who could not use more joy, fun and play in their life?!

"May what I do flow from me like a river, no forcing and no holding back, the way it is with children." ~ Rainer Maria Rilke

◉ Investment Tip: Expend yourself and then just be

Do you know the feeling of relaxation and peace after you have accomplished something you needed or wanted to do? It is the peaceful feeling of getting the driveway shoveled, or the release after putting all the groceries away, or one of my favorites, sitting on the deck after I have mowed the lawn and enjoying the beauty of the freshly mowed landscape.

That is what we are after here, expending yourself and then stopping for just a bit to "be" and enjoy that moment of peace, accomplishment or ease. All you need is to do something that makes you feel accomplished - exercise, use up your physical energy, run, dance, clean one bathroom, clean out a cabinet, mow the lawn, dust the living room (pick only one). After you are finished, sit and breathe in ease and flow with the intention of enjoying the moment.

"Accepting, allowing and interacting with your life as though it is exactly as it should be, without making yourself wrong (or right) for what you discover is the way to Self-Realization."
~ Ariel Kane

Act before your logical brain kicks in with old beliefs, expectations and habits

Allowing can feel uncomfortable to our logical brain. Sometimes we get an inspiration, an idea and then almost instantly our logical mind jumps in to give us the 50 reasons why it is not possible. Flow asks us to honor the inspiration and act before our logical brain kicks in with old beliefs, expectations and mental habits.

This reminds me of Tina, who recently lost her job and has always wanted to pursue a career as a freelance graphic designer. But she's always been too scared to pursue independent work. She feels she needs the security of a "real job." Sometimes she gets so excited by the prospect of completely stopping sending out resumes and going on job interviews. Instead, she'd like to put all her energy into pursuing freelance clients and getting her business off the ground. But her logical brain kicks in with all the reasons why it won't work. The need for a steady paycheck, health insurance, etc., etc. Sound familiar?

How amazing it would be if she honored her internal desires and inspiration, *believed* that wealth is already hers, and pursued her graphic design business as if it is already succeeding?! The clients and money want her to find them as much as she wants to find them! How awesome would that be!

This is why we have done so much preparation work. We are opening to the power we have to create by investing in our wealth consciousness and therefore trusting ourselves. When we learn to trust ourselves, we can trust our inspirations and the creations we are intending.

Another example, if you are creating a great outfit for a party, know that you are going to start to get help – probably from unexpected places – to bring the creation to you. (I am using a very tangible example for clarity purposes.) Then a friend tells you about this great website that has wonderful clothes. But you dismiss it because you do not like to buy things online. So, you do not even bother to look at the site. But life works in mysterious ways and things are not always as they seem. If you had gone to the site, you might have seen an outfit that you really liked. And the site happens to have the clothes carried at a local department store…but you would have not gotten this information if you did not go to the site.

Once we plant the seeds of our creation, we need to open the doors that come along. We need to follow our inspiration – inspired action! This is when life gets really fun! And because we know we are consciously investing, things will go more smoothly. If things are difficult or hard then that might not be the way at this time. Smoothness and flow are signs that we are on track. If things are hard, maybe it is time to take a break or wait and try again later, or say "that did not feel good, let's find a different way." I am not making the case for quitting when things feel difficult or when there is a bout of adversity. I am making the case for checking in and seeing *why* they feel difficult. Is it because you don't want to do some aspect? Why? Is there another way that feels exciting, interesting, or more effective? Check with your internal guidance – your felt-sense and let that guide you back into flowing and inspired action.

Flowing is like being on a magical journey, with amazing helping friends walking by our side every step of the way (some seen, some ethereal), giving us encouragement, guidance and ideas (the details) to help us realize our creation.

"If you powerfully believe in the value of what you offer the world, your love and passion for it will become an unstoppable force. Then you will attract things commensurate to that force." – Rod Stryker in *The Four Desires*

The table below is a short list of words to help feel the difference between the energy of flow and the energy of efforting.

FLOW WORDS	EFFORTING WORDS
Gentle	Demanding
Caring	Expecting
Smooth	Pushing
Gliding	Efforting
Sharing	Working it
Creating	Worrying
Grace & Ease	Fretting
Loving	Being hard on yourself
Joyful	Grinding it out
Playful	Managing
Enjoying,	"Have to..."
Savoring,	"Should..."
Basking,	"Must..."
Appreciating,	Pain
Enthusiasm	Force
"That would be great"	
"Would love to"	
Satisfied	

"The only way to make sense out of change is to plunge into it, move with it and join the dance." – Alan Wilson Watts

⑥ Investment Tip: Write a Thank You Note for what you are going to receive.

Thank you notes are fun to write because they come from a place of feeling like you are so happy to have received a gift or had a wonderful time. Thank you notes let us relive the experience we had and make note of it to the person with whom we shared it.

So, with this tool you are going to write a thank you note for what you are going to receive. Write a note to *WUW Unlimited Wealth Spring* (or you pick something/someone that feels good to you) and thank it for all the great experiences you just had; like your finances upgrading, your body feeling great, your relationships blossoming, and feeling light-hearted and free.

The key is to write the note from the place that it has *already happened* and you feel just great about it. Then re-read and re-feel the thank you note every day for 2 weeks and see how this feeling of, "Oh, thank you, thank you, thank you" makes you feel amazing.

Pay attention and be on the lookout for synchronicity

Flowing is exciting because we are dancing with life. It brings us to our desire and it brings our desire to us! However, we need to be willing to step into the unknown and let life bring us the help we need. Most of us get into trouble in this phase of Allowing because we get very attached to our wealth creation coming the way we think it should, or expect it to. We become narrow and rigid, looking for only one way—usually our way—for our wealth creation to come into being.

Allowing means being open to what comes our way – usually through synchronicity. When we are in flow, the life of magic really kicks into gear. We see a sign on the road that gives us an idea, we get a call from a friend with needed information, we see a movie that clarifies something. So, we need to be paying attention to the "signs" and the wisdom flowing to us, working with us.

Become excited by new possibilities and new opportunities, because for things to change something needs to change. Our creations are new and different. Therefore, some things probably need to change for them to get to us. So, fall in love with change, possibility, unexpected opportunities and synchronicities. Try new things; when something new or unexpected comes along flow with it...because you know your creation is on its way. It is important to pay attention, be on the lookout for things that just seem to come in from out of the blue; these are coming in response to your investment energy.

"Stay attentive... When you have the urge to say or do something, please go ahead. You are now manifesting in the now moment, so to wait will not give you the opportunity to capture the dream." –
Mystery of the Universes Book 3 by Beverly Thompson

Let go of guilt (and don't feel guilty about not feeling guilty)

What we are talking of in this module might sound crazy. You may be thinking: *"What do you mean I don't need to push and force? That is the way everyone else seems to live. It seems many people experience struggle and difficulty, why should I be any different? Why would I experience flow when they don't? Is that fair?"*

This is understandable. What we are talking about does seem counter to the average life experience. But for every person you see that is having a difficult time of it – there is a person that is having a smooth time of it. There are many different life experiences going on all around us right now and we do not know how or why others are having the experience they are having. It is their lives. We need only honor that this is what is happening *for them*... but it is up to us what happens *to us*.

The only person you have control over is yourself. So, don't judge others' choices and experiences; learn from them and make choices that will work for you. Realize you cannot feel bad enough or get sick enough or sacrifice enough to make someone else's life better. You just can't. The guilt that your life is flowing along smoothly while others are having a tough go of it is a waste of good life energy. Bless them and get back to your own life.

◎ Investment Tip: Marinate in the feeling of lavish all-sufficiency and well-being.

I love marinating things! Marinating is the process of immersing something in a variety of flavors and letting them soak until everything absorbs the flavors of whatever you are creating. What if we took a moment every day to marinate ourselves? What if you immersed yourself in the feeling of lavishness? You will be allowing yourself to soak in the feeling of all-sufficiency and well-being. And you will allow the all-sufficiency and well-being into your body. Taking just a moment to give yourself a bit of time to feel the prosperity that is around you - always and in all ways - relaxing and letting go enough to absorb all that richness.

Today, marinate in the juicy prosperity of life, letting the essence of prosperity seep into the crevices of your being. Spend time allowing the beauty, abundance, love and unlimitedness of life into your body, mind and spirit. Relax, relax, relax...as the grace of life fills you up and enjoy the bounty of just being. How yummy!

You are a magic maker

If you are thinking that this conscious investing stuff is the stuff of magic - you are right. We are learning that life is magical indeed and it is meant to facilitate our experience of our magical, wondrous creating selves. At every point along the way, we can choose to remember that we are magical or believe that we are measly. We can see our power or forget and fall into powerlessness. We can embrace our wholeness or select fragmentation and separateness. This is the joy and challenge of the earth experience and once you start to see yourself in this new Wealthy powerful way, you will not settle for living life in the old way.

The Harry Potter series is wonderful for this. It has planted the seeds of thinking like a wizard. Kids and parents alike, all over the globe, have a magical paradigm opened up to them. Even though the series is fiction it has a great deal of truth to it. Learn to invest your energy and you can create magic!

We all have a bit of muggle in us – but we can always invest in our wizardness. Start feeling your ability to create and then create anything and everything your heart desires by investing in the feeling energy of it. And as each of us comes closer to our true abilities, we transform our lives and the lives of those around us.

Remember Who-You-Really-Are, Power Investor and how magnificent you really are. We can change how we experience life and how we create our world. As we allow ourselves to flow with the Wealth inherent in life, we enjoy the wealth of life. We can create harmony, beauty, peace, joy and abundance – maybe even world peace – yeah world peace – why not! Heaven on Earth! You bet! That is the power in being a conscious investor.

Practice Allowing!

"Practicing feeling good and satisfied IS the work." Abraham Hicks

Practicing allowing teaches us to create a *felt-sense* in our being that is welcoming, playful and trusting. As we practice, we create a mind-body understanding of when we are in an "allowing" state of being or when we are not. And this felt-sense understanding can be used to assess if we are making effective investments or not. We have discussed much of these points in this chapter, so think of this as a cheat-sheet of sorts as to an overview of how to go about moving into allowing.

As we choose to allow wealth to flow to us, we are more willing to…

1. **Trust** – That which you desire, desires you. It is already in the field of possibilities; you are now pulling it to you, attracting it lovingly into your reality. This includes trusting the "how" of how it will come. Sometimes if we cannot see *how* the wealth will happen, we doubt. But, when we invest in wealth consciousness, we know that Well-Being and Wealth are ours. We can trust this and when we do, we feel comforted that the "how" will come also.

2. **Stay Open to Possibilities** – Because you trust your creation is on its way, you can let go of worry, fear, doubt and befuddlement. You are free to *play* with life, co-creating bringing Wealth to you. Enjoy the "discovery process" of how it comes and when it comes. Feel free to be open to unexpected help and unexpected outcomes, dancing in joy and effortlessness to your creation.

3. **Act on Synchronicity** – Be watchful and alert to options that come. If you get an inspiration to do something, do it. If you get the urge to make a call or open a book or take a detour, this could move you forward. Work with what comes into your life by acting on it and trying things that you might not have in the past. Things are not

always as they seem and some things (which you might not expect) might yield results this time.

4. **Listen to your inner wisdom and intuition** - Your body will help you; listen to your gut instincts and honor them. If something feels "right or good" go with it, if something does not sit right or feel right or if it "smells bad" – stay away or find a new way.

5. **Release attachment and expectation** – T.S. Elliot wrote, "For us, there is only the trying. The rest is not our business." Creating is the opportunity to try, to invest our best energy into the experience. Flowing is releasing the outcome and not worrying about success or failure. When we flow, we enjoy the moments, allowing life to inspire us, without the restrictions and constraints of the attachment of "it has to be this way"; "it has to look like this"; "it has to come like this". **Let there be joy in the moment, joy in the journey and joy in the result.**

6. **Be Welcoming** - Make room for your creation in your life and say, "yes, please, thank you" to it happening. Be welcoming of all things that come your way. Do not judge what is happening. Trust that you are on your way. Things are not always as they seem and the things that seem to be not helping are most likely just the right things you need to get you where you are choosing to go.

7. **Continue to give your creation your best energy** and your highest thoughts by re-connecting, reenergizing, and re-feeling your desire. - Spend time (say 5 minutes a day or more if you can) reconnecting to the joyful feeling of enjoying your heart's wealth desire. Get reenergized about it and re-feel what it is like AS you are experiencing it. Feelize it again – visualize it and feel it a bit every day. Don't worry about the details or making it happen more than letting your inner excitement pull the opportunities to you and inspire action ideas.

8. **Take action and actively participate** - Just do it, don't let your mind talk you out of some inspiration because it seems silly or out of the realm of possibility. Nothing is impossible and anything can happen in the blink of an eye. So, trust that little voice inside and go for it. You will have urges: "call Sandy", "schedule an appointment", "make

a reservation" - act on them – please! Because, you *are* in the middle of your creation happening.

9. **Open to the bounty of life and be willing to receive** - Bounty cannot get to you if you have your protective walls up. We are so busy protecting ourselves that we forget to share ourselves and let life share with us. Bounty and abundance are the way of life…so pull down some of your barriers (whatever they may be) and let yourself open to them and let them in; get ok with receiving as much as giving. Every day say, *"I am open to receiving the bounty of life. Surprise me, amaze me, delight me! ASAHP – As soon as heavenly possible."*

10. **Play!** - Play, play and play, with life! Wealth creating is a joy and a marvelous experience…so play with possibilities, dance your creation into being and enjoy watching your dream come to life. Celebrate how far you have come; give yourself a pat on the back. Don't let creating turn into a drag by getting over-invested in it "having to happen" or exchanging the playful, joyful feeling of inspiration, for the drudgery of doing. Remember play is the way to wealth realization. So, have fun and play…

"We are spring loaded for ascension." - David Wilcock

◎ Investment Tip: Get into a state of grace and ease with the Allowing Wealth Meditation

This mediation is a very wonderful and simple process to use. Don't be frightened off by the word "meditation". Let it mean that you are taking the next 15 minutes and giving yourself permission to let go of all that you have to do, to spend a few minutes attracting and allowing wealth into your life.

Lie down or sit whatever feels best to you. Wear very comfortable clothes and feel very comfortable. Don't let any of the rules you have heard about "the right way to meditate" get in the way. Do what you need to do to be very comfortable, very free to enjoy this time of allowing.

Before you begin, you might want to take a few moments and drain your brain. This is a tool we use in creativity training to help business people let go of all the distractions of their day so they can be available right now. To drain your brain, write down on a piece of paper all the "things you need to remember and/or do today". Once you have them on a piece of paper, put the paper aside, so your mind can now relax; everything is logged and accounted for - so relax.

Now that you have drained your brain set your intention. For the next few moments, you are going to slow down and relax; you are making this investment of time to become available for wealth to flow freely into your life. Take a few deep breaths – slowly and gently. Breath in – sip the breath; enjoy the feeling of it smoothly and effortlessly flowing into your body; it feels so good. Then let the breath leave your body; again, it is effortless because after an inhale you naturally want to exhale and feel the release of the air.

We are going to build our energy a bit more by inhaling and then gently holding at the top of the breath. Feel your vitality build, feel your energy waken; with every breath feel more invigorated and alive; feel tension release and peace seep deep into your pores.

With each inhale feel the wave of air flowing in and as you exhale feel the wave of air flow out of your body; you might even feel your body start to move as you become more comfortable with the flow of air through you. The inhale is our opportunity to receive, to enjoy the air that is all around us. Breathe in this wonderful sustaining air, which is always here, always available, always free to you. If your mind starts to wander, that is fine; gently bring it back to the air flowing in and out. As you breathe out - feel how you are contributing your essence to life.

Let your breathing become a whole-body experience; breathe through your hands, feel the cells of your hands breathing in and out; breath through the soles of your feet. Feel the breath coming in as a whole-body experience, not just air coming in your head and out of your head; feel your whole body nourished by the air enjoying the process feeling the warmth and comfort of the air.

Now spend a few moments feeling the air vibrate through your body by verbalizing out loud the sound of "aaahhhhh" put your hands over your ears and really feel the sound of aaahhhh vibrate in your head. We will do this a few minutes more; don't think about anything, just enjoy the ahh.

Aaaahhhhh

Aaaahhhhh

Aaaahhhhh

Three more breaths of ahh please.

Now just enjoy the in and out breath; feel peace and calm like a soft blanket caressing your entire body. Enjoy the sweetness of this.

Now take a moment and intend to reconnect to this feeling of grace and ease a couple times today. Reconnect to it and remember. This feeling is an important part of teaching your mind and body to allow wealth to flow into your life.

Remember...

- Everything is available to you – so relax.
- The energy of what you desire is here *now* and it is in the process of becoming physical, tangible and available to you in a way you can experience.
- When the mind is quiet and the body is relaxed, allowing happens.
- What you desire – desires you.
- Allowing leads to fulfillment.
- There is no rush; you have plenty of time.
- Easy-Does-It

Frequently Asked Questions

1. **You mention "ask" and it is given. Who/what am I asking?** *We discussed this previously, but I want to discuss it again because it is an extremely important question.* And to be honest, I had to do a great deal of soul searching around this concept. I did not like the idea that I was *asking* "something outside of me" for something. It felt very arbitrary if I would get it, and under what conditions? Who decides? It just felt impotent and risky to me. Then I realized "asking" was actually the energetic equivalent of desiring. As I desired, or felt a creative urge swell within me, I was "asking" or launching a rocket of request. And the Law of Attraction - the unbiased, objective, unconditional, always-in-operation, Law of Attraction was responding, vibrational-match-making, so to speak. So, whom am I asking? Actually, no one. There is no big-daddy-in-the-sky, God, Santa-Parent figure we are asking for our desires. It is an objective equation: ask (desire) and it is given (a vibrational match is attracted).

2. **What is the difference between allowing and aligning?** Actually, not much, but for the purposes of this process, we distinguish aligning as agreeing there is a source of wealth and choosing to plug into it. Allowing is where you relax about what you have said

you want to create and let it flow to you in grace and ease. They both involve the choice to agree and feel good and both essentially feel the same. And if you can find that amazing magical place - don't get hung up on the terminology - just enjoy it and let that feeling take you all kinds of cool places. Allowing is the knowing that you have asked (focused on what you want) and are now receptive to it showing up. You can relax knowing it is in the works! Let go and let it flow. Aligning feels more like a practice of sorts. Practicing the feeling of allowing and then consciously being able to invoke it inside you.

3. **What is the difference between allowing and receiving?** Again, not much. I think teachers use the word "allowing" instead of "receiving" because they are trying to get around the mental and emotional issues inherent in the word *receive*. Because we all seem to have such resistance to the concept of receiving, which makes it difficult for us to feel good about what we want and then experience it. But if you have been studying the art of allowing, you notice that allowing is about being receptive and able to receive. And if you have an inherent problem with receiving, then you are going to have a bit of a block when it comes to allowing wealth and enjoying abundance. The crazy thing is you probably don't even realize you have hang-ups with receiving. *What you need to do is find what works for you.* Find the words that create the feeling inside of you of knowing what you desire is already here waiting for you.

"The world is full of magic things, patiently waiting for our senses to grow sharper."— William Butler Yeats

Investment Strategy
I Allow Wealth

Invoke This…

I really like knowing that Wealth is around me always and in all ways. I feel this *allows* me to relax a bit about getting out there and "pushing" to make it happen. I can honor my desires knowing they are honored by All-That-Is.

I see how the Wealth-Energy is abundantly available for me. I find it gratifying to know that as I become receptive and available, I *allow* what I have always desired to finally get to me.

I dance with life in grace and ease and have unlimited bounty. I feel so good, so loved, so cared for. I feel my heart swell and my essence expand…I feel filled, I feel fulfilled. As I allow Wealth to flow to me and through me I become free to be me.

Doing less – gives me more.
How crazy is that?
Flow is totally the way to go.
I am good with that.

A

Awareness
Of Your Past

Alchemize
Your Beliefs

Awaken
Your Power

Align
Your Energy

Attract
Your Dreams

Allow
Your Desires

Amaze
Yourself

Chapter 11: Invest in Amazing!

Amaze and be amazed! The final stage of the Easy-Does-It investing process is where you get to enjoy the payoff of your energy investing. The opportunity is to be amazed at how wonderful your life has become and to amaze yourself with the power you have to create. Hopefully, you are noticing the flow and you are enjoying it!

Prepare to be Amazed

To be honest, I was so busy developing my wealth consciousness by reading, meditating, aligning, allowing, attracting and investing my energy, I did not really notice all the changes that were taking place in my life. Classic, right?! I had developed the process and been practicing over the years, continuing to plow my energy into learning and thus did not fully acknowledge the joy I was experiencing.

That is why I felt I needed to add this AMAZE module. The original process stopped at ALLOW, with the assumption that as you allowed, you would start to see the changes and benefits. What I did not realize is that this investing goes way deeper into your life and transforms it into something you could not have imagined. You might not notice the changes because you are not looking for them. That is why I've included this Amazing module—to help you notice the transformation; notice the passive incomings like great seats, great parking spots, great friends, great fun, just happening now! You get to just enjoy the worldwide symphony that is playing out for you, with you. It is awesome!

I was thinking of calling this module appreciating, but that implies some effort to me. What I have found is that being amazed just happens. You are having so much fun you just look up and say, "WOW, thank you!" That is the beauty of the Easy-Does-It Process. You consciously invest your life-energy to attract your creations, you practice aligning your energy to a felt-sense of wealth, you notice what takes you out of alignment and choose anew, you practice allowing Wealth and then you are amazed at how magical your life becomes. Yes, you will be amazed at how magical your life becomes!

What follows are just a few of the ways you will be amazed at how your live transforms as you invest in your wealth consciousness.

Be Amazed...at what you create

In this stage of the Easy-Does-It process you are really just being amazed at what you create and what you have created. You feel you have arrived on some level because you have this deep understanding and appreciation for the magicalness of all of life. Yes, there are moments of wondering *what was I thinking* – something happens to jar you – but you get back to your wealth center pretty easily and continue on your amazing wealth journey. I was watching a movie the other night and the main character said, "It never dawned on me I could enjoy my life, I was too busy being responsible." In the past, that is what I felt. Then at some point on this journey we notice we are enjoying our life and are having fun *while* being responsible.

> *"I have been a seeker and I still am, but I stopped asking the books and the stars. I started listening to the teaching of my Soul." ~*Rumi

Be Amazed...at how it shows up

I remember back when I was creating having lots of $100 bills. I thought it would be fun to have lots of hundreds, so I did a few creation sessions on it. Well, nothing really happened and I just forgot about it. Then a year later, one of my renters had just dropped off their rent in cash for that month. I put the money on the kitchen island and there was a pile of $100! I remembered back to those creation sessions and a huge smile came over me.

Here is another story of an amazing way our creations show up. A client of mine was interested in deepening his conscious creating capabilities, so we had a few coaching sessions together. He is an artist and was having starving-artist energy issues. We spent quality time and energy focusing on his desires to do meaningful work. A few months after we worked together, his friend told me that he was in Africa shooting a video series about a water purification systems. This had not ever come up in our discussions together that he was interested in going to Africa, but the law of attraction works in wondrous and mysterious ways.

One more story: One of my favorite experiences was when I was at a seminar and a woman got up to the stage and told how she was able to afford her trip to the seminar. She told this great story of how she was having a wonderful time walking in the woods with her friend – they were talking manifesting and enjoying themselves. I was totally into the story – so much so I felt I was walking in the woods. She then said she found a diamond under a leaf! A diamond. She could not believe it. I could not believe it. She took it to a jeweler and found out it was worth $9000! And she was able to purchase a plane ticket and the seminar fee. As if that was not amazing enough. Two days later, I was walking into work and I saw a gleam on the ground. I looked down and found a very large diamond!!! I ran into work yelling, "OMG, OMG, OMG I found a diamond out in the parking lot!" I took it to a jeweler and to be honest it was not worth $9000 but the experience was priceless!

I am always amazed by how what I desire shows up. I have tons of these kinds of stories from attaining a goal at work to getting one of our puppies.

Actually, I am going to tell you the puppy story. About a year ago we got this adorable fuzzy puppy. He looks like an Ewok from Star Wars. One day he was sleeping next to me and I remembered back to when I was around 10 years old. I had this little stuffed animal dog that I carried everywhere, I even put it on the music stand at band practice. I just loved the face on that little thing. Anyway, I looked down at my pup sleeping and his face was the face of that little stuffed animal dog of my childhood. I was just amazed at how all these years later I had my desire fulfilled!

"Fate is kind. She brings to those who love the sweet fulfillment of their secret longing."- Disney, When you Wish Upon a Star lyrics

Be Amazed...at how life gets better and better

This is one you are going to have to just get used to: your life is going to feel so good you might almost feel guilty, or that you do not deserve all the wonder and magic that is happening. Don't. You are investing your energy wisely and now you are enjoying the passive incomings of your investment strategy. You have built a wealth momentum that draws more life-affirming, flow experiences to you...that is just how it works. The better it gets the better it gets...it is the law of attraction working in your favor now. Enjoy the ride; enjoy the feeling of feeling good, alive, free and empowered.

"Something amazing happens when we surrender and just love.
We melt into another world, a realm of power already within us.
The world changes when we change. The world softens when we soften. The world
loves us when we choose to love the world."
– Marianne Williamson

Be Amazed...at how amazing you are

In the amazement phase of your wealth journey, you are going to feel really good about yourself; you have to—self-appreciation and self-worth are key components of your investment strategy and a wonderful result. You are riding on the high-powered wave of All-ness and this feels amazing. Allow yourself to enjoy yourself as you are. Enjoy your desires, enjoy your approach to creating and progressing and most of all enjoy your unique gloriousness!

"It's a whole new world...I'm like a shooting star, I've come so far."
~ Song from the Disney Movie *Aladdin*

Be Amazed...at how you are impacting others

The way the world evolves is based on how we evolve. As we change, our world changes and changes others' worlds. Our prosperity becomes the world's prosperity; our joy sends the energy of joy into the ethers; it's physics. The people around you will notice you are enjoying your life and they will be impacted. I love this about the wealth journey or any inward journey; as you go about creating your wealth consciousness you are actually pretty "self-centered," focusing on centering yourself. But over time, this has a large impact on your outer world. It is just like the song says: "Change your mind and change your world".

◎ Investment Tip: Try not to keep score

The interesting thing about wealth consciousness is that it is easy to reduce the experience to measuring how much money you have and keeping score as to how "wealthy" you are being. This is a slippery slope. The full-hearted, glorious feeling we are looking for does not come because of the "bank account" score. It comes because we are deciding to feel wealthy anyway. When you catch yourself keeping score or feeling like you are not doing well because of the "score," give yourself a break. Remember, Wealth Consciousness is a state of being, an awareness of all-is-wealth that is not contingent on any score.

"It never ceases to amaze me that every second of every day, more than 6,000 billion neutrinos coming from nuclear reactions inside the sun whiz through my body, almost all of which will travel right through the earth without interruption." – Lawrence M. Krauss

Be Amazed...at the momentum you have built

The other night I was reading a journal entry from before I was consciously on this wealth journey...and it was sad. I had a negative momentum going and it just kept me stuck. But after investing myself in this new energy of unity with Wealth, I feel awesome! It started slow and as I invested in the Easy-Does-It process it got easier and easier to stay feeling good and wealthy! This is momentum working on your side. Invest in feeling wealthy and you will build a wealth consciousness that creates a momentum that builds on itself. You have created forward motion—momentum—through your wealth investing that is now paying off the dividends of contentment, peace, wealth and generally feeling good. Keep consciously investing in the direction of wealth and thus enjoying the momentum you create.

"Your life is a sacred journey. It is about change, growth, discovery, movement, transformation, continuously expanding your vision of what is possible, stretching your soul, learning to see clearly and deeply, listening to your intuition, taking courageous challenges at every step along the way. You are on the path... exactly where you are meant to be right now... And from here, you can only go forward, shaping your life story into a magnificent tale of triumph, of healing, of courage, of beauty, of wisdom, of power, of dignity and of love." ~ Caroline Adams

Be Amazed...at your willingness and ability to be unlimited

Les Brown said, *"Life has no limitations, except the ones you make."* The more I live, the more I agree with this. Every day comes with an opportunity to expand and every day I get more and more excited by this bountiful experience. I see possibilities everywhere. And yes, sometimes it can get overwhelming. But that is ok, it is all there for me when I am ready for it. I want to experience the abundance life has available for me, therefore I am expanding my ability to welcome it. And every day, I am amazed at how life can show up to surprise, inspire and delight me.

"Life is meant to be lived at the edge of your comfort zone."
- Neale Donald Walsch

Be Amazed...at how satisfied you become

Usually people seeking little w-wealth never feel satisfied, or that they have done enough. But when you are in Effortless Wealth Consciousness, satisfaction becomes the norm. At our annual Christmas party for our company, I just felt so satisfied! I wanted to share with our team, the satisfaction I feel about our work together, the satisfaction of our accomplishments. And I wanted us to take time-out from "doing" to notice the satisfaction of a job well done. As we develop our wealth consciousness feelings of satisfaction, enoughness and enjoyment flow easily. And the little things and big things of life become moments to savor and be satisfied in...it really is amazing!

Wealth-Noticing is the Opportunity

In order for us to be amazed, we need to notice the amazingness that shows up and is showing up. Remember how I mentioned I was trying to teach myself to win the lottery? As part of that process, every day I noted in my wealth journal the *lottery-like-experiences I noticed* throughout the day. And as I noticed lottery-like-experiences, I attracted more. That is the way the law of attraction works. What we put our attention on grows and what we take it from fades. Again, noticing what we want to see engages the law of attraction to bring more of that. So, the benefit of noticing is two-fold: First, noticing helps you enjoy the wonder showing up – huge benefit. Second, noticing the good draws more of that good to us. Bingo, double ROI!

The opportunity is to notice how things are moving along in your life. Every day, take a moment to notice and appreciate how life is helping you toward your creations and your wealth dreams. Notice what comes along in support of your creative energies, people who give ideas, songs that send messages, books that inspire, unexpected tweets, synchronicities, a phone call just in time, a message in a dream, anything you can think of!

My wealth journal contains all kinds of *wealth-noticings* and inspirations from getting upgraded to first class on my flight to a beautiful dog coming to say hi to me in the hallway of our condo, to a dream I had about a children's book I want to write. The wonderful flow is amazing!

Noticing the wealth of life dancing with us and to us is the conscious way we invest in our wealth and create wealth momentum. In fact, I am going to make the case that if you just start noticing all the wealth in your life – big and small your heart would open and your life become amazing!

"Life isn't all perpetual bliss, nor is it one woeful weeping session. But you can concentrate so hard on noticing moments of one or the other that either a bright outlook or dim expectations becomes your regular illusion."
– Richelle E. Goodrich

Wealth Journaling: *In your Wealth Journal…Notice all the Wealth*

WEALTH NOTICINGS	
Date	*What I noticed today (what surprised me, what inspirations did I have, what was unexpected, what I thought was great, was fun, enjoyable, beautiful, synchronous, satisfying)*

Enjoy, Enjoy, Enjoy!

I heard an interview with Jerry Hicks where he said that once he realized the *purpose of life was joy* everything changed for him. He said he was then able to make different choices, ones that felt like joy.

I feel like that is what I have learned about Wealth.

As grampa says in Willie Wonka, "I never thought my life would be anything but catastrophe, but suddenly I began to see a bit of good luck for me, cause I've a golden ticket." Once I learned that the Wealth-Energy was available for me to live my life in joy, I realized I've got a golden ticket for unlimited possibilities.

And so do you!

It is time for you to enjoy, enjoy, enjoy the wealth of possibilities, freedom and play that is available in every way for you.

Enjoy alignment. Enjoy awareness. Enjoy your power. Enjoy taking inspired action. Enjoy attracting. Allow yourself the enjoyment of the effortless wealth journey and then be amazed at the paradise that has been here all along.

"If you want to view paradise – simply look around and view it. Anything you want to, do it. Want to change the world – there's nothing to it." – Willie Wonka

Remember...

- You are amazing!
- Noticing wealth attracts more wealth
- Be amazed at:
  - All the things you are consciously creating
  - How it all shows up
  - How life gets better and better
  - How amazing you are
  - How you are impacting others
  - The wealth momentum you have built and are building
  - How willing you are to be unlimited
  - How satisfied you become

Frequently Asked Questions:

1. **Are you in this amaze state all the time?** No, nor should you be. It ebbs and flows because our daily life ebbs and flows. But part of life's creative process is to see things you don't really like or want for contrast and use that as fodder for choosing what you do want. That creative contrast (like an unexpected bill) usually takes us out of alignment. Then we say, "well you know what, pretty soon if an unexpected bill comes in I won't care because I have the money to cover it." We align to the wealth experience we are now choosing. And as we are on this path, we see when we are out of alignment and more quickly get back into alignment and better able to notice the wonder all around us.

2. **Is the amazed state "enlightenment"?** Not sure. It feels light hearted and freed from all of the old rules and expectations. So maybe. And again, you will go in and out of this feeling of amazement as you live your daily life. But don't be too concerned about that. As your wealth consciousness increases, you find ways to be in the allowing,

aligned state more and more and not interested in being out of sync with the Wealth-Energy.

3. **You said this process would impact others; can I use this to change others?** No; that is not advisable nor a good investment. Any time we want to change another, we are investing our energy in an area that is not going to yield the highest return. Focus on your own portfolio and let others manage their portfolios.

4. **Now that I have this momentum built up – can I stop investing?** I wish I could say yes, but you are alive and therefore you are energy investing. Actually, if you fall into your old habits – which might happen, you might find your momentum slowing. That is ok...it is life. The key is that now you know what to invest in and you know what to do to realign to Wealth. And your wealth habit is getting stronger and stronger. So, wealthy thoughts will come more easily and are probably becoming your norm over choosing to agree to scarcity. Conscious Wealth investing becomes a way of life.

Investment Strategy:
NOW I SEE

Invoke This...

Now I see...how amazing a creative life I was meant to live!

Now I see...how the creating technologies have been set up to facilitate my molding the wealth-energy of life into my hearts desires – all by just focusing my energy and vibrating as the experience I desire. How amazing!

Now I see...how I am honored and respected as a power creator who is free to invest their life energy in whatever experiences I desire – free and clear of judgements, requirements or preconceived ideas of what is appropriate. Amazing!

Now I see...that I am free! I am free to be me. I am amazing!

And I feel AMAZING!

PRACTICE

Chapter 12: Easy-Does-It Practice Session

A short practice session of the Easy-Does-It investing process will help you focus your energy in the direction of the wealth you desire. You can use this process for anything you wish to create.

Review the Stages in the Easy-Does-It Investing Process

First let's review the stages of the Easy-Does-It process. You can use this process to create anything you would love to experience in your life. It is a powerful process for intentionally molding the energy clay of life into what you want. In this practice session, we will focus on financial wealth. After we use this process on financial wealth, I will use it on an example from work that I was dealing with.

- **AWARENESS**: We begin by understanding where we are at right now with how we feel about whatever we are creating. Invest in becoming aware of what you think, feel and believe **now** about wealth and your ability to have it. This will create a base-line understanding of your current reality, because you cannot change that which you do not know you are agreeing to. It is through awareness that you get clear of where you might be getting in your own way.

- **ALCHEMIZE**: Once you have clarity and awareness, we work through one of the exercises to alchemize the old beliefs. Take a moment to thank them, honor them and transform them; to free up the old energy, making it available for investment in the new wealth experience you are creating.

- **AWAKEN**: Remember all the new wealth consciousness ideas we have been investing in. The wealth habit you have been building by knowing your Wealth is available to you always and in all ways and that Who You Really Are is a powerful Creator Investor that molds energy into reality.

- **ALIGN**: Next align your vibration to wealth. This is really just visualizing and feeling wealthy anyway. Aligning to Wealth is the way we cultivate feeling Wealthy in a conscious, deliberate way. Use whatever tools and processes you have found that align to wealth and get you into a prosperity frame of mind and body.

- **ATTRACT**: The next step is to apply your creation energy to attracting the wealth you wish to experience. In this stage, vibrate in harmony with what you want and stimulate the law of attraction to bring you what you desire by feelizing – visualizing and feeling wealthy in a real tangible way.

- **ALLOW**: Allowing is flowing and dancing with life in grace and ease knowing the wealth you intend to come to you is on its way; agree to it and allow it. Feel you are flowing in partnership with life...welcome your wealth.

- **AMAZE**: Amazing is the excitement of experiencing all you desire. You are amazed at how wonderful your life is and you are amazing yourself as to what is possible for you. As you dance with life, life dances with you and you find your life becomes the glorious adventure you hoped it would be.

The EASY-DOES-IT Session

With this session, you will be investing quality time and energy into wealth creation and shaping the energy clay of life into your desired experiences. This is why there are so many "investment tips" throughout the book. These tips will help you align and create a wealth consciousness that I hope will become a way of experiencing more joy and wealth in your life.

Please set aside around 15 minutes for this session. For the purposes this session, we are going to focus on financial wealth. This conscious creation session will energize your attractive power, helping you feel you have invested in the financial wealth you desire. Please note: this is a powerful experience! To maximize the results, it is very helpful to be aligned with wealth, feeling good about yourself and alive with the excitement and satisfaction of life as you create.

The steps of the Easy-Does-It conscious creation session:

1. Make an appointment with yourself to create your financial wealth experience.
2. Invite in the Wealth-Energy, become welcoming of this energy and become excited by this time to shape it into your financial wealth desires.
3. Spend a moment re-AWAKENING to the Creation Technologies and Who You Really Are.
4. Become AWARE of how you feel.
5. Optional Step - ALCHEMIZE any worries doubts or other resistant feelings.
6. Review the new wealth agreements (see page 57-58) and review your new wealth agreements in your wealth journal if you created them.
7. Feel yourself ALIGNING with WUW Unlimited Wealth-Source all around you.
8. ATTRACT by feelizing being financially wealthy.
9. ALLOW by feeling it is a done deal.
10. As you go about your day, be AMAZED.

The Easy-Does-It session can go something like this:

1. *Make an appointment with yourself to create your financial wealth experience.* Put this creation session on your calendar, so you see it as a priority and as your time to invest your energy into the financial wealth experience you desire. At the appointed time, turn off your

cell phone and close yourself off from the world as best you can, so you can really focus. Maybe you want to go for a walk, or just sit and write how you feel at this point, or maybe go to a coffee shop. Whatever feels helpful so you are available and ready to do this with focus and clarity.

2. *Invite in the Wealth-Energy, become welcoming of this energy and become excited by this time to shape it into your wealth desires.* You may also want to invite in your Cosmic Financial Team (if you created one in Chapter 9, Attracting) and ask them to support your wealth creation session. Remember there is a bevy of talented souls who have expertise in all manner of earth things from event planning to wealth creating – they were here - remember? So, ask for their assistance, they would love to help!

3. *Become AWARE of how you feel.* Do a scan through your body and mind and see if there is any tension or resistance in your body. You might be carrying something around that has been bothering you. For many of us just the to-do list is enough to keep us distracted.

   If this is the case, take a moment and write down all the things on your mind that you need to get done today – drain your brain – make a list from "get milk" to "meet with the plumber". Get down anything that your mind is keeping track of so you can be very present. Then put the list aside knowing the topics are safely noted.

4. Optional Step: *ALCHEMIZE, if needed* – Do this if you are feeling worried or concerned about something on your mind, or if you have other resistant feelings that might stop the Wealth-flow of this session. If you are feeling good, skip to the next step.

   It is here you may want to note anything that has been bothering you around your wealth or financial situation. There might be something like "I am worried my retirement is not going to be enough", to "I just have a general feeling of unease because of the economy." Write that down. Now you can do a short *ALCHEMIZING* process to honor and loosen the energy around this issue. This is a quick summary of the Alchemizing process:

   1. Acknowledge it

2. Accept it – as it is
3. Thank it and become peaceful with it
4. Release it – symbolically and tangibly
5. Replace it by reaching for a vibration that feels better.

- **Acknowledge it** - this thought and notice that it is here. Don't argue about it or feel bad about it – just see it like a bird in a tree.
- **Accept it** – as it is.
- Release it - say something like I see you and I release you. I let you go and open the space for this new wealth experience I am consciously investing in now.
- **Thank it** for what it is showing you; for being here to give you awareness as to where your energy is being invested. See if you can find some things to say to yourself to get a bit of *Peace* around it. Say something like, "I understand this is a concern, but I am feeling better about Wealth. I am doing this process to raise my vibration and align myself to my wealth – yahoo for me."
- **Replace it** – with the new energy you are investing with the rest of this session.

Note: if you have spent time alchmizing, you might want to take a short break and walk for a bit - or come back to this later. The key here is you want to be feeling pretty good and satisfied as you are doing this creating session.

5. *Spend a moment re-AWAKENING to and feelizing:*

- Remember that the creation technologies are at work always through the Law of Attraction. And that how you are feeling, what you are feeling as you speak, do, and think is attracting. *So, feel excited and unlimited right now.*
- Remember that Who You Really Are is a powerful creator that is infinitely respected. You are shaping the Wealth-Energy clay into the financial reality you desire and you are free to create what you

want. *So consciously put your energy, attention and focus on what you want – and not worry about what is not here.*

- Remember that Wealth is around you always and in all ways. Wealth ants you as much as you want it. *So feel at peace and at ease right now.*

6. *Review the new Wealth Agreements (from page 57-58):* You may have also come up with your own new agreements over the course of your wealth journey – review them also. As a reminder these were some of the biggest ones we discussed and what we can now embrace:

- There is *no separation* between you and Wealth.
- There is *no judgment* around the wealth you desire.
- You are *totally worthy* of having wealth.
- Wealth is *un-conditional.*
- Sacrifice is *not* necessary.
- Scarcity and limitation *do not exist.*
- Wealth is *easy to come by.*
- Wealth will impact you *as you decide.*
- Your wealth *does not need to be appropriate* or your possession of it justified.
- Wealth *cannot be withheld* from you.
- You decide.

This feels so good doesn't it? Allow yourself to feel connected and in flow with the wealth energies – right now.

7. *Next, feel yourself* ALIGNING with WUW Unlimited Wealth-Source all around you, always available to you and that is already waiting for you.

Feelize…

- Your perfect shot wants to find you as much as you want to find it.
- You are a Wave in the great Ocean-of-Wealth, forever connected.
- You are a powerful creator who consciously invests your energy.

- You are pre-paving the way by deciding in advance what you prefer to have happen.
- Your desires are infinitely respected.

8. Now just sit for a moment and ALIGN with Wealth and feeling the love of the Wealth-Source and the excitement with which you are creating. This step is so fun, because you do not have to feel alone in your desires for wealth. When you take this step, you acknowledge the love and support, the unconditional love and support that is available to you. So easy!

Remember and feelize...

- Life is on your side
- Life wants what you want
- Life is unconditional
- Life is a YES Machine
- The essence of life is Well-Being and you are surrounded by well-being at all times.

9. ATTRACT *by feelizing being wealthy.* Enjoy the freedoms of being wealthy. Enjoy the play and fun you are having as a part of being wealthy. The opportunity here is to become in mind and body the wealthy person you see yourself as. Review your new wealth story from Chapter 8 and relive and re-feel that experience. Or remember back to a time when you felt the world was your oyster. Re-feel it, talk or write about it in your wealth journal. Feel yourself enjoying your wealth: playing, sharing and creating – like the millionaire heiress story. You might want to get the energy going by speaking out loud the experiences you desire. Enjoy the moment, experiencing yourself AS your desire. Feel abundant, playful, enthusiastic, excited, easy going, glorious and free.

Remember...

- Put your attention on wealth and what it feels like to be wealthy
- Feel wealthy

- Talk wealthy
- Say yes! to your wealth

10. ALLOW by feeling it is a done deal. Marinate in this wealthy feeling – let it seep into your essence and become internalized. Enjoy that all you desire is yours. You might want to do a little wealth dance, twirl around, feel grace-filled and at peace. Feel the grace and ease of the moment; there is no tension in your body and your heart is open in welcoming pleasure.

Remember...

- Everything is available to you – so relax.
- The energy of what you desire is here *now*.
- What you desire – desires you.
- There is no rush; you have plenty of time.

Wealth Journaling:

Next, you might want to journal about your experience and any insights you had as you did this. You also might want to note any actions or inspirations you had, or ideas you want to act on.

11. At the end of the session, say a quick thank you to yourself for taking time out to invest your energy this way. You can thank the Wealth-Source and Infinite Intelligence for joining you. And then go about your day, knowing that you have just invested quality energy into your creation. This is you investing very wisely and the dividends will be far reaching.

12. As you go about your day, be AMAZED at how you feel. Notice that you might feel great, just because. Notice synchronicities and easy flow experiences that happen. Notice that you feel good just because. Be amazed at how amazing things just flow. Amaze yourself that you created this with your investments.

"Everything is already OK. The notion strikes us as radical and it surely is. What it means is that in our essential nature we are already fully awake and enlightened; it means that God is available to us fully in the moment, simply because God is our true nature. We simply have to stop resisting it. There is no distance to travel, nothing special that we have to do to earn God. It is a "done deal". - Stephen Cope in Meditations from the Mat

MAKE PEACE
WITH MONEY

Chapter 13: Make Peace with Money

Make peace with money by investing in a new relationship with it and seeing it in a new light. For most of us, money is at the core of our wealth consciousness and how we feel about it has a great effect on what we experience around it. Now, we are creating a new feeling vibration around the energy and power of money.

Money Awareness

In the business classes I teach, I always include a segment on money. I find it interesting that the majority of business school is dedicated to the creation, management and mining of ways to make money and profits, but rarely do we ever discuss how we *feel* about money. How we feel about it is at the core of our money creation experience. For many of my students, what they think and feel about money deep down is a mixed bag of beliefs – inherited from family, society, friends - and is usually fear/scarcity-based. And if you have been following the logic of this book, you are realizing that if you feel afraid of money or feel and think scarcity as a matter of practice, the money you desire will elude you because we cannot feel wealthy and worry about money at the same time. These two feelings work against each other, as we discussed, it is like driving with the gas and the break on at the same time. Thus, business students are well served by a realignment of understanding around money...and so will you be.

Developing wealth consciousness asks us to create new money feelings and beliefs. Addressing our feelings about money and making peace with it is very beneficial. Hence, we will discuss some Easy-Does-It ways to make peace with money.

Just as an aside: I was discussing this chapter with a friend of mine and she said, *"I don't just want to be at peace with money. I want to have an amazing relationship with it!"* YES – absolutely. I totally agree, and that is where we are headed. But many of us are not on good vibrational terms with money. So, as we make the journey to peace with money, we lay the groundwork for an amazing relationship with it. Maybe money can become your BFF (best friend forever). Wouldn't that be great?!

I also want to reiterate that throughout this book, I have not used money and wealth interchangeably. Wealth – with a capital W – is enjoying the freedom, joy and growth that are your inheritance for experiencing the physical world. Money is just an energetic aspect of Big-Wealth. Money is Wealth-Energy physicalized into dollars…into a particular form. I also think of money as a physical tool that is just one of the many ways we have available to us to create our life experience. (As we discussed in the Awakening chapters.)

And a caution! Many of us do not have a clear healthy relationship with money. Given this fact, this chapter and this whole book is about *developing* and *investing* a new understanding about money and wealth. There is deep and profound work that needs to be done on the journey to making peace with money. Be careful and honest with yourself. This book is not a free pass to go out and spend like crazy cause you read it and now "hey, I'm all good". This is a process, a journey that will take some time. Our thoughts about money developed over time and changing them takes time too.

The reason we have a chapter dedicated to making peace with money is an acknowledgment of the fact that many of us need to develop a new energetic relationship with money – so let's consciously invest in creating a new experience of it and with it.

"The answers are there. Don't run. Look. Because when we welcome what we most want to avoid, we contact the part of ourselves that is fresh and alive. We touch the life we truly want and evoke divinity itself."
– Geneen Roth in <u>Women Food and God</u>

You Decide Your Money Experience

At the heart of this chapter is the key message that you decide how you are going to feel about money. As the power creator that invests, you are the decider about the energy vibrations you give to money and that you have about money.

You give money its vibration. Because money is just physicalized energy that *we imbue with a vibration*...and we can decide about the vibration we want to imbue on it. For many of us we are afraid of it, or we are worried about it, or we feel it is illusive. These are vibrations we have come to feel about money – and for good reason no doubt. But these are not necessarily the vibrations we would choose to feel as we move forward.

Our relationship with this energy form is again our choice. It is now time to take back your power around it. As always it is about how we see ourselves in relationship to anything. If we feel small and victimized – we will experience ourselves as small and as a victim...this is the way the energy laws work...impartially and in total response to our choices. This is why I am so adamant about us remembering who we really are: power creators that invest our energies to create our experiences of the many and various things in our lives including money.

Do not give your power away to anything or anyone – especially to the thing called money. It is like a human asking the pants if they want to be worn...and thinking that the pants have any say in the process. This is backward thinking. In *Rich Dad, Poor Dad*, Robert Kiyosaki makes this point very clearly: learn to make money work for you - not you work for money.

In this chapter, we are going to get a bit more awareness around how we feel about money. If you did the journaling work in Chapter 2 you already know how you feel about money, so let this exercise help bring your relationship with money to the next level. We are not so interested in digging around in the past and stirring up old money feelings and experiences. We have laid a groundwork of wealth consciousness and now it is time to put that into action by creating a new vibration around money. So, in this chapter – we are going to spend most of our time re-aligning our vibration around and to money and thus attract a different experience.

Can you decide your money experience? Will you?

◎

Make Peace with Money

Early on in my prosperity journey, I realized I needed to come to peace with money because every time I thought about it, I would get a sick feeling in my stomach. I did not feel good about it. In fact, I felt more like it had the power and I was just a pawn, a victim, in the money game. That did not feel good at all and so I decided to put myself on a journey to understand money and learn about it.

I read all kinds of books on the topic of money and it was fun. To give yourself permission to explore a topic that you are so interested in is great. The books that came to me were really money energy empowerment books like *Rich Dad, Poor Dad* by Robert Kiyosaki, *Think and Grow Rich* by Napoleon Hill, *Money and the Law of Attraction* by Abraham-Hicks, *Secrets of a Millionaire Mind* by T. Harv Eker, *The Millionaire Next Door* by Thomas Stanely and so many others. In fact, I was so excited by the idea of money, that I decided to do a yearlong podcast on the topic of *making peace with money* from the perspective that as we understand the energy aspect of money, we can forge a new understanding of it and hopefully, at some point, have a new relationship with it. Many of the podcast episodes are on *TheAbundanceCenter.com* website.

It is time to forge a new relationship with money, so you can feel it does not have power over you and your life. Investing in making peace with money is a choice and to realize you are not in service of it is empowering. As you do this, you will free your power; don't and you might always feel small and a victim with respect to it. Looking directly at money and your feelings about it might be taboo to you too, but the journey is totally worth it.

Can you make peace with money? Will you?

Wealth Journaling:

- How do you feel about money right now? What is your vibration when you think about it? What is your vibration when you think about your checking account? Just notice – don't judge.
- Are you at peace with money? Why or why not?

Give yourself permission to look directly at money

I remember how uncomfortable it was to talk about money from the standpoint of wanting it. It is not all that socially acceptable and you feel like you need to add something like, "I want money...*so*...I can share it or help with it" to make it more socially acceptable. But for me, I needed to give myself permission to be really honest about money, how I really felt about it and even to be ok with wanting to accumulate it.

As I gave myself permission to really focus on money, I was breaking my societal taboo around money. If you cannot look directly at something, how can you really know it and make clear decisions? Reverend Ike used to say, "I love money and money loves me!" Does that sentence make you uncomfortable? It did for me, but the journey into that discomfort allowed me to explore my beliefs about money and ultimately create a new experience around it.

I actually gave myself permission to be in love with money...and to feel like money loved me. I gave myself permission to burn money and to want to accumulate it just for the fun of accumulating it. As I went on this money journey, I found that money is just another form of energy and to have it be a negative form just did not feel right.

I realize now that this part of my money journey, giving myself permission to want it – just because, was very beneficial. It allowed me to give myself what I wanted. It allowed me to be ok with wanting what I wanted (to be a millionaire) free and clear of judgment, appropriateness and customary rules society has. This is incredibly freeing. **And I see now, that** this money journey was not so much about the money, but about giving myself permission to want what I want. I needed to honor the fact, that if I want something, then there must be a reason and to deny that fact is a hurtful thing to your inner being, to your inner self-worth.

On our journey to effortless wealth, we find that what we want, our desires, are inspiration from our inner guidance to true Wealth (feeling freedom, joy and growth). And to deny it or filter it, might just be the unwealthiest thing we can do.

"Within every desire is the mechanics for its fulfillment."
– Deepak Chopra

Can you give yourself permission to look directly at money and talk about it freely and honestly? Will you give yourself permission to explore your money desires, free and clear of judgment?

◉

Wealth Journaling:

- If you were honest about money and why you want it...you would say...

"You can certainly have money and still be afraid.
Yet you cannot be rich, truly rich, if you're living with fear."
- Suze Orman from *The Courage to be Rich*

Now that we have a bit more *awareness* around our money feelings and vibrations, we will move on to creating a new vibration around wealth and *attracting* what we want. Before we do this, let's take a moment and *align* to the unlimited wealth-energy around us by using the following investment tip.

◎ Investment Tip: Flip your umbrella from protection to collection

There is WUW unlimited wealth-energy plentifully raining down on us and around us always and in all ways. But most of us have a protective umbrella of sorts up that acts to have the graciousness of life miss us. With this investment tip, we are going to flip our energy umbrella from protection to collection by dancing in the rain!

Stop for a moment, take 3 deep breaths and smell the rain of wealth. Now feel the rain of wealth energy pouring down on you and all around you. See and feel it pouring in abundance. It is so refreshing and revitalizing. You just want to sing and dance in it. In fact – you don't need that protective umbrella at all. As you dance and sing you enjoy the rain so much you want to savor it. Just enjoy the ease and flow of the wealth. Then take the umbrella out and use it to gather the abundance. Let the umbrella collect the wealth and overflow with the abundance of all things good in life. Breathe and enjoy the peace and satisfaction of this wealth-flow.

Create New Money Messages

As part of *attracting* my new money experience, I realized I needed to embrace some new money ideas and fresh prosperity thoughts that aligned with my intention. The old money messages of lack, limitation, exclusivity and fear from my past were just not conducive to the peace and prosperity I wanted to foster in myself. Over the course of many months of reading and exploration, I complied the following list of new money messages that I put into a PowerPoint presentation and had playing over and over on a screen in my bedroom.

New Money Messages:

- There is an endless supply of money
- My money dreams are completely underwritten
- I am worthy of money
- I am a money magnet

- Everything I touch turns to gold
- I create money all the time
- Easy come, easy grow
- Money comes easily to me
- I am wise and empowered with my money
- I am at peace with money
- I attract money faster than I can spend it.
- I so enjoy financial freedom
- Making money is fun and exciting
- It is so simple to make money, have fun and do good
- I love money and money loves me
- There is plenty to share and to spare
- There is a continuous stream of money flowing always and in all ways.

Please go to www.theabundancecenter.
com/money.inspiration and download these
messages with beautiful pictures.

Do you have some new money messages you would like to embrace? Will you create new money messages for yourself that excite you? Please feel free to add yours to the list, and if you like, share them with me. I always love to hear new money messages!

Wealth Journaling:

- Which of the above messages felt really good? Why?
- Which felt really uncomfortable? Why?
- If you were to allow yourself some new money messages that feel really good, what would they be?

Forge a friendship with money

We actually give money its power. Money is just a piece of paper, but it is our collective agreement about it and what we agree it can do that makes it powerful. For many of us, we have a love/hate relationship with it. We love what it can do and we hate what it can do.

I suggest we toss all that aside; just forget about the old money agreements and start to focus on something fresh and new, like forging a friendship with money. **What if we began a new experience of money based on feeling good about it...plain and simple?**

Think of something you feel really good about. How does it make you feel in your body? Excited? Empowered? Loved? Special? Alive? Now, can you parlay that feeling to your feeling about money? This might be a bit of a jump for you at first. But as you go back to thinking about something that you feel really good about and then imbue money with similar feelings, you are transforming your experience around money...investing in a new energy relationship with it.

This reminds me of an idea I have, that the next puppy I get is going to be named *Money*. Then every time I look at my pup, I will say, "Hello, Money. You are so cute. I love you, Money!" and "Come here, Money! You are such a good guy." You get it, right?!

"My best friend is the one who brings out the best in me." - Henry Ford

Can you give yourself permission to see money in a new light? Can you let yourself see money as a friend that helps facilitate your creative urges?

Wealth Journaling:

- *If money were your friend, how would things change for you?*
- *If you were to imbue money with a new energy what would it be?*

Tell a New Money Story

All of us have a money story — something we say to ourselves over and over that becomes our money agreement, our money mode. For some it is as simple and powerful as "there is never enough", for others it is as affirmative as "I always seem to have what I need". I remember Suzie Orman telling how she created a new money story. She was working on Wall Street early in her career and she did not feel like she fit in at all. So, she wrote a new money mantra about the money she was going to create for herself. Her mantra was, *"I am young, powerful, and successful, and I make at least $10,000 a month."* She read and reread that mantra every day, hundreds of times a day, until her mind could say it on its own...and soon she *started to believe it*...and then things took off for her.

The thing about your old story is that you believe it and that is why it is true, for you. I do think it is helpful to get clear about your old story, but not to dwell on it. Just see it and then alchemize it (see the Alchemize chapter) so you can thank it, let it go and move on to this new money story.

What you really want to do is focus on your new money story; *invest in the story you choose now.* That is what you are creating NOW and going forward. Remember, you are a powerful creator investing your life energy, so you get to write your money story, your way. This is your opportunity and your empowered free-will choice to create a new money vibration and lay a new money foundation.

Take some time to create a new money story or statement that is a pure declaration of what you really want. Let it be something that excites you and that you feel good about, free and clear. I created a simple money statement that I could easily remember: *I have more than enough money to share and to spare.*

Now invest in your new story/statement; read and feel it over and over as many times as you need to (like Suzie did) until it feels like your current reality, like it is a done deal! From the great Cosmic Wealth perspective, *it is* a done deal. Allow the law of attraction to work its magic. Soon, you will have created your new reality, but it won't feel all that new because you knew it was coming and practiced it to the point it was not a matter of *if* but when.

"Storytelling is the most powerful way to put ideas into the world."
– Robert McKee

Can you create a new money story for yourself?
Will you feel good about it?

◎

Wealth Journaling:

- Write a new money story/statement that you can be excited about. This is your opportunity to tell the story you want to experience, so tell a story you feel good about. Spend time writing it and allowing yourself to agree that it is a done deal.
- Create a money statement that is easy to remember like Suze Orman did and say it over and over. This will help you start investing in the new story by putting quality attention energy and focus toward it.

"It is your heart that can create much wealth.
Love of self, love of the things you are and joy about all you do. It is the
doubt, the mind-games and hurtful things we say and do to ourselves
that keep the money from flowing." – Shiva, The Diva of Money

Develop money muscles

I like the word *muscle* because it implies we are choosing to develop something in ourselves. There is focus and choice to build this strength. When we develop our money muscles we are choosing to invest our energy into feeling good about money and seeing it in a new way, thus building our perspective about money into strength. Below are some money muscles worth developing.

I developed a deck of cards – Money Magnet Muscle cards - that contain 45 muscles we can develop to help us feel good about our money situation and the power we have to create wealth.

If you would like to purchase the whole deck
*of **MONEY MAGNET Muscle** cards, please*
visit www.TheAbundanceCenter.com.

Below are a few of the money magnet muscles.

Know It Muscle

There is a difference between believing something and knowing something; the first requires faith, the second is a fact. Choose to know that you are not separate from your wealth and prosperity. Know that your money desires are already fulfilled in the universe and so agree to them.

I know that every need is supplied on time with abundance with much to share and to spare! I choose this freely, joyously and playfully.

AND Muscle

Sometimes we give into scarcity thinking by agreeing "I can have money OR freedom, but not both." "I can have money OR my integrity" ...it is OR, but not both. We can choose to replace conditionality thinking for AND thinking: to experience this AND that.

I choose to allow myself to have money
AND the other wonders of life. I choose this freely, joyously and playfully.

Imagination Muscle

If you can imagine it, you can become it. Your imagination is the energy molding mechanism you were given to create the future. Envision your optimal money life; feelize it, live it fully in your mind and body. The more real it feels, the more energy momentum it is creating.

I choose to use my imagination to bring my dreams into reality.
I choose this freely, joyously and playfully.

Pivoting Muscle

Pivoting is the process of taking a not-so-good-feeling thought/ experience and finding a better feeling thought. Pivot from "I could never" to "I could give it a try" or pivot from "I can't afford that" to "I bet I can find something comparable" or "I could if I wanted to."

I choose to pivot to a better-feeling-thought so I can feel good.
I choose to do this freely, joyously and playfully!

Pave-the-Way Muscle

"I am having the best week ever," I said to a friend. He said, "Really, do tell." I said, "Well, I am paving the way for the best week. I am deciding in advance to have a great week." Know that you have the power *to decide in advance* how you are going to feel in whatever you are doing next.

I will decide how I will feel before doing something.
I choose to do this freely, joyously and playfully!

Wealth Journaling:

- What muscle do you feel you would benefit most from developing?
- What money strength do you think you need?
- If you have the **Money Magnet** deck, hold the deck, take a deep breath to center yourself and ask the question above. Then pull a card, see what card you pull and journal about the message you are giving to yourself.

Choose to feel good about money - anyway

Remember: How we feel about money is our choice. Given all of the mixed messages that come in around it, it is no wonder we have such a variety of money feelings. As we are coming to know, we are powerful creators that get to create our money experience by how we invest our energy. We get to decide how we are going to feel and look at money.

I wish for you to use this as your opportunity to feel good about money - *anyway.* Feel good about money even though you see things in the outside world that tell you otherwise. Feel good about money even though some of the people in the world do not have enough. Feel good about money even though you might have had some past experiences that hurt.

Part of our clean slate approach to money is creating a new energy feeling associated with it. One of the most powerful things we can do is to see that we are the deciders about money: how we feel about it and how we look at it. **You are the one who gets to create your experience of money.** Until now, you might not have believed that. For many of us, money seems like something we deal with; our money reality is outside of our control. If you take anything from this – know you have the creative power around your money reality.

Feel good about money; see money in a new way that is playful, plentiful and freely flowing and you will be creating a new reality around it that will knock your socks off.

Can you give yourself permission to feel good about money – anyway?
Can you allow yourself to create a new felt sense around money?

◎

Wealth Journaling:

- What if you felt good about money? Pull out a $20 bill and look at it. Sit with it for a bit until you can just feel good about it free and clear. Write what you notice as you do this.

Feelize Money

If you remember, we discussed feelizing, which combines feeling something in your body and visualizing it in your mind at the same time. Feelizing money is not only thinking about having it but feeling yourself spend it and enjoying it – don't just think about being a millionaire, become a millionaire! One of the best ways to feelize being a millionaire is to walk around a mall or a car dealership knowing you can buy anything you want. At this point, you are doing what most millionaires do – they look around to see what they want and think, "I could get that if I wanted to and feel good about that." As we discussed in the attracting chapter, if you can feel it you can create it. Play with using your mind/body connection to vibrate wealth and feel the peace and ease that comes from knowing you have plenty in the bank. Practice feelizing.

Or feelize walking to the mailbox and having checks waiting for you. Don't just see the checks but get excited that they are there. Feel the excitement, playfulness and fun of having checks in your mailbox.

Another fun exercise is knowing every day you are going to be given $100,000 and you need to spend it – every bit of it. Every day you are going to need to spend the $100K and you do not have to worry, as the next day another $100K will be deposited into your bank account! Awesome, right?! As you *play*[4] with feelizing spending the money – even writing the checks (which I did playfully) you will notice many things. I am not going to tell you what. Please do this experience and see what happens in your psyche after a week or so...and write about it in your wealth journal.

Remember, power creators are expert feelizers.

Can you spend some time visualizing and feeling
an abundance of money? Will you?

⑥

Wealth Journaling:

- Play with writing all kinds of experiences you want to have, seeing them and feeling them as you write and know they are a done deal!
- What did you notice as you played with spending $100K a day? What thoughts did you have? What feelings come up?

Find Money Role Models

One of my favorite money role models is Kimora, Ms. Fabulocity. I love her audacity around money and her expectation that she has it. She just

---

[4] We are *playing* here. If this idea is frustrating or creates any tension in your body – skip it. We want you feeling better and better about money.

expects money. I also love Beyoncé; she just exudes richness and Wealth. I also appreciate money role models like Warren Buffet, the Big-Hearted Oprah and the free-flowing generosity of my husband. One of the ways to feelize money is to feelize yourself as a person (or combination of people) who live, think and experience what you desire. Feelize one or many people who are living the money reality you would like.

You can use whomever you like as your money role models; there is no judgment around who or how much. One thing I will say, though, is that *you are a money role model, too.* And so, please remember to infuse your uniqueness into the envisioning process. Your role models are just that, examples, but you are the power creator and you get to uniquely create yourself into the money role you uniquely would like.

Are you willing to let yourself weave your unique money experience and/or become a money role model? Are you willing to agree you can have money, too?

❧

Wealth Journaling:

- In your wealth journal talk about the money role models you think have it going on and why. Start to weave a money model that feels really good to you. You get to become all of these and more. Play with this and have fun. Give yourself permission to feel you get to have it in your unique way.
- If you are a money role model, what do you want people to learn from you? What do you want them to say about you?

Appreciate Money

Many energy masters talk of the power of appreciation. Appreciation is the fastest way to focus and bring more of what you appreciate into your life—because what we appreciate, appreciates (grows, gains momentum). So, invest your life energy appreciating money.

Money is fun to have because you can create things to enjoy. It is fun to accumulate and know all the fun things you can do with it. It feels good to know you have more than enough to share and to spare. Money is helpful because we can use it to facilitate our family. You get what I am saying here.

Just be mindful to focus on truly appreciating money without the negative underlying feelings. Like the statement: *Money is helpful because it helps facilitate my family* (and behind it you feel bad because you don't feel like that is happening now). It is important to be in an energetic space where you can really just appreciate money and feel good about it *without any of the negative, resistant heavy feelings that can come with some of our statements.*

Try to find appreciation statements that feel easy. *I appreciate what I can do with money. I appreciate that money is here for me to create experiences. I appreciate that money makes exchange of goods and services easier.*

Can you appreciate money for what it is, as it is?

⊚

Wealth Journaling:

- Get in a playful aligned mood and then journal about all the things you appreciate about money and having money. List as many positive aspects of it as you can imagine. Enjoy this, play with this, let the appreciation flow.

> *"Money is not the means to a happy life;*
> *the happy life is the means to the money."* - Anon

Love Money; Money is Love

We get to choose the energy we assign to things – even how we feel about money. Haven't you ever decided to like someone even though others around you find them odd? You have made a decision to like them. And you can make a decision about how you are going to feel about money. One of the most interesting things to decide is to feel that *money is love.* As the money energy flows, so does the love energy. As all things are made of the Love-Wealth-Energy at their essence, so too is money! What if you started to think of money as love energy flowing? What if we chose to connect to the love inherent in money? What if you wrote "love" on your money? Change the energy, change the experience.

When you use money, make a conscious choice to see it as an exchange of appreciation (for what you are purchasing and what went into making it available for you to purchase), respect (for the ability to use the money, respect of the money as a medium of exchange) and love (of you and the seller in an exchange of something needed and something provided).

When we decide to look at money from a vantage point that is aligned with who we are and the wealth we are choosing to see, feel and experience in our lives, we can transform money into a way to share, exchange and gather in a whole new energy. What I am really saying is that when we put money in its own separate category, maybe we could start to see it as just another form of the Great-Love-Source (Wealth).

Can you open your heart to money?
Can you see it as another energy form of love?

◎

"Small shifts in your thinking and small changes in your energy, can lead to massive alternations of your end result." – Kevin Michel, *Moving Through Parallel Worlds to Achieve Your Dreams*

Wealth Journaling:

- In your wealth journal, assign a new energy to money – be it play, fun, love or any other energy that feels good. It would also be powerful for you to spend some time imagining what it would be like if money loved you and wanted you.

"The creation of something new is not accomplished by the intellect but by the play instinct acting from inner necessity. The creative mind plays with the objects it loves." - Carl Jung (1875-1961)

How the Rich Stay Rich

The rich feel rich; they know money is easy for them to come by; they have created the mindset and felt sense of *easy come easy grow* and the law of attraction gives them more of that experience. Make peace with money and then go even farther to feel good about money; know it is yours, get rid of the "unworthy and underserving" crap. Cultivate money messages that align to the truth of life and you too will become rich in mind and body and then the physical riches must flow; it is law.

"It's really important that you come to believe in the Vibrational version of something because the Vibrational version ALWAYS exists BEFORE there is a manifested version of it. "– Abraham-Hicks

Remember...

- Decide to be at Peace with Money
- Give yourself permission to look directly at money
- Create new money messages
- Forge a friendship with money
- Tell a new money story
- Develop money muscles
- Choose to feel good about money - anyway
- Feelize money
- Find money role models
- Appreciate money
- Love money
- Know money is easy to come by
- You are already rich

Frequently Asked Questions

1. **You mention we shouldn't worry about a lack of money (if that's our situation). Should I just trust that money will come to me and feelize it to make that happen?** Here is where clarity about how you *really* feel is so important. If you are worried, trust is not all that helpful. In fact, it probably is going to work against you – because trust implies there is some outside force that will rescue you. There is no outside rescuing force. There is you and your powerful creative self, tapping into and molding the Wealth-Energy. But words to not teach – experience does. And you will need to experience yourself as powerful – you will need to feelize yourself molding the wealth-energy clay and notice what shows up. It is helpful to go back to the awakening chapters to remember *who you really are*. Worry and doubt are scarcity getting the best of you. Take a few moments and randomly open this book to an investment tool and use it to shift you into a different vibration.

2. **So, I can take this advice to mean that I can spend at will, because I trust that new money will come soon?** Ah no. As I mentioned earlier in the chapter, we are on a *journey* to making peace with money and having a new relationship with money. Again, inherent in this question is a miss-alignment of power (of your power) with respect to money. And this is not advice from me to you. It is ideas for your journey. You are at the helm of your ship.

3. **If someone literally can't pay their bills but then goes out and spends money under this notion that more money will just arrive, they can get into an even deeper mess. Should we practice feelizing something that is likely not going to happen? Like getting $100K everyday – this sounds dangerous to me?** Thank you for noting this. The game of getting $100K everyday was meant to be a *game*, so you can **notice** what you would do with the money and **play** with feeling unlimited, copious amounts of money just flowing in, and letting yourself feelize this experience. Letting yourself *play* with this ease and flow.

    The *game* was not meant to imply you can *literally* spend what you do not have - because this really would make you feel worse in the long run. And we are about feeling better. This whole chapter was about *feeling better about money*! And finding ways to feel better about money is the key...these are some ideas. But if they do not work for you, skip the ones that don't work – but try to find ways that DO make you feel better about money and DO help you to create a new relationship with it!

Investment Strategy:
I Am At Peace With Money

Invoke This...I am now ready to be at peace with money.

I am the power creator and see money as one of my creating tools. I get to mold my money experience into one that feels good *to me*.

> And so I am at peace with money.

I am already rich in so many ways...The abundance of life is always flowing to me and I see it more and more every day. The grace and beauty of it all touches my heart to the point I burst with appreciation and joy.

> And so I am at peace with money.

I have unlimited freedom always and in all ways. I am unlimited as I am and I see how I have efforted enough. I am at the point in my journey that I know how to flow with life in grace and ease. I am a powerful creator who is investing my life energy into a new experience of money.

> And so I am creating the experience of being at peace with money.

I see how I can feelize my experiences into being; by seeing them in my minds-eye and feeling the aliveness of them in my body. I am feelizing a new experience of money.

> And so, I am at peace with money.
> And so, I am at peace with money.
> I am at peace with money.
> I am at peace with money.
> I am at peace.
> I am at peace.
> I am.
> I am.

Raise your Vibration using the Prosperity Ladder

"Remember that your real wealth can be measured not by what you have, but by what you are." - Napoleon Hill, Think and Grow Rich

Chapter 14: Practice Raising your Vibration Using the Prosperity Ladder

The prosperity ladder is a practical process for moving from scarcity to prosperity by consciously choosing vibrational energy states that feel a bit better than you are feeling now.

Choose Your Wealth Vibration

If prosperity feels too far from our current reality we might get discouraged and think, "why bother?" Fret not, for in learning to use the Prosperity Ladder, we will learn to vibrationally climb from where we are now to the next vibration that feels better and more prosperous than our current state. Learn what the Prosperity Ladder is and how to use it in day-to-day life to lift your energy and alleviate the discomfort of scarcity agreements. The Prosperity Ladder meets us where we are at and facilitates us to the better feeling thoughts that ultimately lead to empowered prosperity! Yahoo!

Overview of the Prosperity Ladder

Think of the ladder as a way for us to consciously move from the vibrational feeling place we are at now, to a higher (better feeling) vibrational place. So, when we are feeling:

- Like we do not have enough money to pay our bills
- Worried about the economy
- Afraid when we hear of people losing their jobs
- Insecure that we may lose our job
- Frustrated that things don't seem to be getting better fast enough

Use the ladder to feel better

The key to walking up the ladder is to find a better feeling thought...so you feel the *relief of a vibration that feels better than where you are now.*

If we are feeling helpless, hopeless, worried, fearful, angry or overwhelmed, this is a great time to decide to climb the vibrational ladder to a better feeling place. It is very simple, actually: find a thought or feeling that feels just a bit better and gives the slightest bit of *relief.* Don't try to jump from feeling like you don't have enough money to pay your bills to *"I am a millionaire."* Your mind will shut down and be like, *"Yeah right, you know that's not true."* This does not feel better and it might make you feel worse.

Find one *thought* that takes you from *"I do not have enough money to pay my bills"* to something like, *"I do have money to pay some of my bills,"* or *"I notice that I am a responsible person who wants to pay my bills."* Then check in. Does this feel a bit better?

The Ladder has 6 Basic Levels, From Highest to Lowest

1. At the highest rung: **Prosperous**: We are feeling empowered, prosperous, secure and joyous. We know we have the power to create and see life as an opportunity to create our desires and dreams. It is the *feeling* of prosperity.
2. **Positive Expectation**: We are feeling enthusiastic, eager and optimistic and we can find positive aspects of the situation. We see how things can be; we have a feeling vision of what we want and are moving there. It is the feeling of excitement.
3. **Possibility Oriented**: We are feeling overwhelmed, pessimistic and impatient. But we can see there are things we can do and actions we

can take; feelings we can create to move toward where we want to go. It is the feeling of hope.

4. **Money Frustrated**: We are feeling frustrated that what we do just does not seem to add up. We try, but it is like rolling a bolder up a hill over and over again. We are tired but not defeated.

5. **Money Angry**: We are feeling forgotten by the system (victimized), blaming the outside world like our boss or the government for our financial situation. We cannot stand it anymore. We are angry (pissed really) and worried. This is a very powerful place to be because we can use our anger to jump our vibration up to seeing possibilities and giving us the drive and energy to break free to a new level. Feeling money angry can create positive movement and momentum. So don't feel guilty about feeling angry...use it to your benefit.

6. **Scarcity, Hopeless, Helpless**: We feel vulnerable and insecure; depressed, really, like we are powerless and very afraid. We feel like we are inadequate in some way, deficient, and lacking.

How to Use the Ladder

It is important to start with where you are. Be honest. What are you *really* thinking and feeling? Sometimes, I don't want to admit how I am really feeling, or I don't even know. I just feel crappy. I just feel worried, or have anxiety...but as we practice trying to get a sense of where we are at, we will get quality information and build an internal competence that will always serve us in good stead. At the end of this chapter there is a detailed list of feeling states (from prosperous to scarce) that might help you pinpoint where you are on the prosperity ladder.

Once you have identified where you are at, you can walk yourself up the ladder. The *way to walk up the ladder is to find a thought or feeling that gives you a bit of relief.* You are looking for relief from the vulnerable feeling of not having enough money (the *hopeless helpless* level), to finding a better feeling thought like, "I am able to pay *some* of my bills." (The *Possibility Oriented* level).

So let's take an example where we will start at the bottom of the ladder—Money Scarcity—and walk up to Prosperity.

Scarcity - Hopeless - Helpless:

1. This is how you honestly feel: "I am exhausted and afraid, really afraid. I feel that I am in trouble as I cannot get my financial footing. It feels hopeless, I feel hopeless. I don't know what to do and I am scared. I can't do this anymore."

2. Now find something that you can think/feel that makes you feel *money angry* (the next rung on the ladder): "You know I am sick of this shit. Other people not nearly as talented as me are making more money. I have worked hard, I deserve better."

Money Angry:

1. This is now how you feel: " I am so angry at money. I am sick of my money situation and the amount of time I spend earning it and thinking about it. I could just scream I am so enraged about how frustrated I feel."

2. Now find a thought/feeling that moves you up to *money frustrated* (the next rung on the ladder): "I am paying my bills and somehow I manage. I am a hard worker, I try, really, I do. I keep at it. And I know that I have launched many a prayer for my money situation to change. Something has just gotta change. I always seem to find a way, I am so ready for things to change and for money to flow to me!"

Money Frustrated:

1. This is how you feel now: "I just feel like I have tried and tried to make ends meet. It seems the harder I work, the farther behind I get. Bills pile up but money does not seem to pile at the same rate. This is so frustrating!"

2. Now find a thought/feeling that moves you up to *Possibility Oriented* (the next rung on the ladder): "I am ready to have things go better. And I know I have had money flow into my life. I have had jobs that paid me; I have been able to earn money in the past. In fact, I know

people who don't really work hard and money flows into their lives. That is what I want! I can see my money situation getting better."

Possibility Oriented:

1. This is how you feel now: "I can see how the economy is picking up. I am reading this great book on Effortless Wealth ☺ and somehow Laurie seems to think Wealth is available and could be effortless. I am investing in seeing how the fundamentals of life are abundance based, prosperity promulgating and well-being oriented."

2. Now find a thought/feeling that moves you up to Positive Expectation (the next rung on the ladder): "In fact, I have noticed my ability to engage the law of attraction on my behalf. I can direct my thoughts, words and actions to be aligned with a new money reality and wealth really. I am telling myself my new money story and it is pretty awesome!"

Positive Expectation:

1. This is how you feel now: "I can see that I am creating an experience of wealth in my life. I am a powerful creator who has created much and will continue to. I put my creative power into creating the experience of wealth and money flowing to me. There is enough. I am enough!"

2. Now find a thought/feeling that moves you up to *Prosperity* (which is at the top of the ladder): "I love that I can do so many wonderful things with my wealth and prosperity. I have many talents and capabilities. I am excited to enjoy an abundance of money and all good things in my life. I know there is plenty to cover all my needs with plenty to share and to spare."

Prosperous:

"Boy do I feel good. I am so very satisfied with myself and I feel very prosperous. I feel free and peaceful. I know that all is well and there is tremendous wealth in my universe. I feel full and filled with gratitude. I feel really rich. I feel satisfied and in many ways at peace."

Bam! You have just walked yourself out of a scarcity slump into a prosperity place. This will take some practice. Probably the only "effort" you will need to exert is to practice noticing how you are feeling, walking yourself to better feeling thoughts and allowing yourself to stay in alignment as much as you can. Simple, huh?!

Let's take one more example with money and paying bills.

I cannot pay all my bills - again this month. (Hopeless)

- I am sick of this! (Money Angry)
- I want something to change! (Money Angry)
- And you know what, I do pay *some* of my bills. (Feeling a bit better.)
- In fact, I can make payments, even if not full payments, on many of my bills. And I always try to pay my bills. (Now you are feeling more empowered and hopeful).
- And, I can see how the economy is picking up. (Now you are feeling possibility.)
- And, I see how I will easily be able to pay my bills. (Oooops, your brain says, "What! No I don't!" Ok, try something else, like: I am *making progress* toward being able to easily pay my bills. (Now feeling stronger and eager to make progress.)
- I *see how I can do this.* (Now feeling empowered.)
- I am a powerful investor! (More empowerment)
- I will spend some time marinating in well-being today and let my wealth in. (Positive Expectation)
- I can see feeling wealthy is actually quite a powerful thing. (Optimistic)
- Isn't life great?! (Prosperous, Joyful)

Remember our emotions are an indicator of our degree of alignment with our Wealth Source energy and that the better we feel, the more we are allowing our alignment with the things we desire. The more scarcity we are feeling the more resistance we are feeling and the less aligned we are to what we want and the Wealth that is flowing. **How you feel matters! It is important information from your internal guidance system.** Many of us stuff or ignore how we feel or disregard or discount our feelings, but our feelings are our guidance system letting us know if we are headed in the direction of wealth or not. When we feel bad, we are moving away and when we feel good we are moving toward.

> *"I find that all life comes from our living hands, shaped by our loving hearts and minds."* Antibus, The Magic Man of Craziness.

You are in the driver's seat – You are the investor

Because how you feel is within your power; you control how you are going to listen and respond to your feelings. Are you going to resist, or allow? Are you going to listen, or ignore? Are you going to find a way to feel better, or just ignore how you feel and keep re-creating more unpleasantness? The Prosperity Ladder is a powerful tool for you to take an affirmative, proactive investment action for finding a better-feeling thought. And you can do it right here, right now. There is great value in using this simple tool for re-alignment.

What are you really "saying" (vibrating)?

As we have discussed in previous chapters, many of us think we are focusing on what we want. But really, we are sending out a feeling vibration that is the exact opposite of what we really want through our body vibration.

For Vibrational Example:

We may say, "I want more money." But what we are really feeling and what the law of attraction is feeling and getting from us is:

- *I am **not** happy with my financial situation.*
- *I feel embarrassed by not having money to pay my bills.*
- *I feel disappointed that I don't have more options.*
- *I feel jealous that my neighbor has more money.*

- *I feel angry I cannot afford the things I want.*

Or

We may say, "I want a raise." But what we are really feeling and what the law of attraction is feeling and getting from us is:

- *I am angry because my employer does not see my value.*
- *I feel unhappy with my current salary.*
- *I feel frustrated that I cannot get them to pay me more.*
- *I feel angry I cannot afford the things I want.*
- *I feel trapped because of the economy.*

In both of these examples, we are saying what we want, but we are feeling and vibrating its direct opposite.

When we can consciously understand our current vibrational state of feeling, we are in the driver's seat to make conscious investments to a better feeling state, which moves us closer to our destination.

Many of us stay stuck in this never-ending loop of wanting something (like more money) but unconsciously focusing on the money we don't have. Feeling angry, frustrated and trapped **creates more** anger, frustration and limitedness.

There are 2 powerful reasons to move to a better feeling vibrational place:

1. To bring us what we really want via the law of attraction
2. To reduce resistance to what we really want

Shift to feeling better using the prosperity ladder

Take the "I want a raise" scenario.

1. First it helps to get clear about what you really want. Yes, you want more money, which is fine, but is there something else that money is a stand-in for? Do you want more security? Do you want more recognition? Do you want more authority? This clarity will help you move up the prosperity ladder more effectively.

2. Ask yourself how you are really feeling. Perhaps it's: *I am angry because I am unappreciated at work.* Now think of a thought that feels just a bit better, like: *Everyone is so stressed out lately, I don't think anyone is paying attention too much.* Then check in to see if that helps you feel a bit better. Is there another thought that can elevate you to possibility orientation or positive expectation?

3. Find thoughts and feelings that can move you up the ladder and give you a bit of relief from where you are right now. Learn to check in and see how each thought makes you feel and see if you can find a different thought that gives you relief.

4. Practice, practice, practice raising your feeling vibration until you get really good at sliding up the prosperity ladder in a matter of minutes.

⊚Investment Tip: The Because Tool

The Because Tool helps us vibrate in the direction of what we want by focusing on why we want what we want. *I want it because ...*

For example: I want more money...

- *Because...*I enjoy paying my bills on time
- *Because...*It makes me feel like I have more control
- *Because...*I like being able to share it with causes I feel are valuable
- *Because...* I enjoy using it to go out and have nice dinners
- *Because...* I feel free to do what I want when I want.

Keep the list going as long as feels good. The Because tool helps elevate your vibration to what you desire instead of focusing on what you don't have—thus taking you up the prosperity ladder. Play with this and see how relieving it is to focus on why you want what you want.

What is our money desire really about?

As I mentioned, much of the time we use money as a stand-in for what we really want. We really want to feel secure, or feel confident, or feel the excitement and anticipation of life. We want to feel powerful, joyful and prosperous. And instead of feeling these things, we think we need money *and then* we can have these. Thus, we have agreed to the notions that:

- When I have money then I can *do* _____ and then I will *feel* _____.

For example:

- When I have money then I can quit my job and then I will *feel free*.
- When I have money then I can buy liposuction and then I will *feel beautiful*.
- When I have money then I can ignore what my boss says and then I will *feel powerful*.
- When I have money then I can buy my house outright and then I will *feel prosperous*.
- When I have money then I can pay my bills and then I will *feel secure*.

Notice what we are saying...we want to feel *free, beautiful, powerful, prosperous and secure*. And you know what? We can invest in feeling those things NOW, without the pre-condition of money and without whatever effort [action] we believe is required to feel that way.

Find ways to feel what you want to feel - NOW!

For example, what can we do to increase the level of security we feel right now?

Something to think about: As children, many of us feel vulnerable. We are young and usually feel we need our parents to take care of us or provide for us. This unconsciously creates a feeling of insecurity and vulnerability. We just feel we are at the mercy of life and can be victims of the system or situations. We carry these feelings of vulnerability with us into adulthood. Victimhood is synonymous with insecurity – no wonder many of us have money problems. We feel insecure. And then we go out and buy stuff to help create that sense of security, which makes us feel less secure! Yikes.

But now things are different. We have new understandings about our strength and power, creative power. We are born investors and as we focus our vibration energy in the direction of our desires, we can attract what we want. We do not have to feel powerless like we might have when we were a kid. Nor do we have to feel we have to dance to someone else's music or agree to someone else's life agreements. This is the excitement of being a wealth investor. We can create our own life and our own security. We are in charge now!

And essentially what I did in the previous paragraphs was walk myself up the prosperity ladder.

And as we have been discussing throughout this book, there are many ways we can shift our vibration to better align to the wealth vibration we desire. If you notice, the investment tips throughout this book, are essentially ways to move you up to the higher rungs of the prosperity ladder and can help you shift into a new feeling place.

It's about consciousness & awareness

Hopefully what you are noticing is that there is a level of conscious awareness that we are developing. We are courageously checking in with how we are feeling and then finding a better feeling thought to allow the life force of well-being to flow effortlessly and unrestricted through us. We are realizing that when we feel angry or scarcity-minded we are not aligned to Well-Being and thus restricting and limiting our natural prosperity.

It is like a woman I know who did retail shopping therapy. She would routinely go shopping when she was bored or angry or upset. She would see the clothes or whatever and purchase it in an effort to feel better (a.k.a. move herself up the prosperity ladder.) In reality, she started out in a bad-feeling place and was using shopping to try to elevate her vibration, but this elevation did not last too long. And she was left with not feeling any better and the guilt of the bill for it – effectively sliding herself down the ladder.

But over time, as she was checking in with how she felt, she realized she was shopping to deal with not-so-good feelings. Then one day, when she was about to purchase something she stopped and said, "Do I want to do this? Do I really need this?" She found she had a new awareness and consciousness around her shopping and did not make the purchase. She felt empowered and stronger for her choice and she moved herself up the prosperity ladder with that realization and subsequent new action!

Remember...

- Practice, practice, practice – checking in and raising your feeling vibration
- Ask yourself: *How am I feeling right now?* Check in using the prosperity ladder: Are you feeling hopeless, helpless? Are you feeling angry? Are you feeling possibility oriented? Are you feeling positive expectation? Or are you full-out joyous and prosperous? Make up whatever words you want – just get a gage of where you are at, so you can find a next feeling that feels better.
- Use the prosperity ladder to walk your feeling vibration up just a bit toward feeling better. This does not have to take years; it can happen in minutes.
- Use the "Because" tool to focus on the positive aspects of what you want.

  I want _____ because it will make me feel_____.
- Ask yourself: *What do I really want?*
- Ask yourself: *Am I using money as a substitute for some other feeling or experience I really want to have?*

Practice With the Prosperity Ladder!

Walk your way up the Prosperity Ladder[5]

1. Ask yourself how you are feeling now.
2. Look for a thought or feeling that takes you up to the next rung on the ladder. Don't try to jump too far up and create cynicism or discouragement.
3. Go as far up as feels good.
4. Practice moving yourself up the ladder as much as you can.
5. Once you get to the top rung, "prosperous", stay there and milk it. Enjoy that feeling and keep it going as long as you can. You are aligned.

---

[5] This table is adapted from the Emotional Guidance Scale discussed in the book Ask and it is Given by Ester and Jerry Hicks

PROSPERITY LADDER

Prosperous	**Joy, Appreciation, Empowered, Free, Love**	I am so very satisfied with myself and I feel very prosperous. I feel free and peaceful. I know that all is well and there is tremendous wealth in my universe. I feel full and filled with gratitude. I feel really rich.
	Passion	I love that I can do so many wonderful things with my wealth and prosperity. I have many talents and capabilities. Enjoying an abundance of money and all good things in my life excites me. I know there is plenty to cover all my needs with plenty to share and to spare.
Positive Expectation	**Enthusiasm, Eagerness, Happiness**	I can see how the universe reproduces my thoughts of abundance. I am excited to experience it. I am eager to share my good fortune.
	Positive Expectation, Belief	I can see that I am creating an experience of money possibilities in my life. I am a powerful creator who has created much and will continue to. I put my creative power into creating the experience of money flowing to me. There is enough. I believe in my ability to engage the law of attraction on my behalf. I can direct my thoughts, words and actions to be aligned with prosperity.

	Optimism	I am talented and capable. There is no reason I should give into the idea that I cannot experience money in whatever amount I would like. I have access to all and I am noticing there are many times when I receive, like_____, _____ & _____
	Contentment	I can find aspects of my life that I feel contentment about. I can choose to feel the sufficiency in my life. There is enough, enough for me to partake of.
Possibility Oriented	Possibility	I have had times in my life when money flowed and I can see that it is possible again. Plus there are others out there that experience prosperity and money all the time – look at _____. (Pick someone who seems to feel contented with their money situation.)
	Hopeful	At least, I have had money flow into my life. I have had jobs that paid me; I have been able to earn money in the past. I am paying my bills and somehow I manage. I can see my money situation in the future getting better.
Money Frustrated	Pessimism	I am not even sure I know how to have more money flow into my life. I can only experience it If I _____. I just feel I have no hope or confidence in the future.

	Frustration, Irritation, Impatience	I am frustrated, I have tried so many ways to get more/earn more but nothing has worked.
	Overwhelmed	I am overwhelmed by the need for money. I work but the bills just keep piling up and all the money needed to live overwhelms me.
	Disappointment	I am disappointed I don't have enough money. I feel sad and displeased because my hopes and expectations are not being fulfilled.
	Doubt	I doubt my relationship with money, or my ability to have more of it in my life. I doubt my ability to earn more if it.
Money Angry	Worry	I am worried I will not be able to pay my bills or have enough money to do what I want to do.
	Blame	If it weren't for _____ (my boss, my job, my parents, the government, etc.) I would have more money.
	Discouragement	I am discouraged at my money situation. I cannot see how it is going to get better.
	Anger	I am so angry at money. I am sick of my money situation and the amount of time I spend earning it and thinking about it.
	Revenge	I will figure out how to get mine; I will take it.

	Hatred, Rage	I hate money and I hate the fact it has such a huge role in my life.
	Jealousy	I feel jealous that others have more money than I do.
Scarcity, Hopeless, Helpless	Insecurity, Guilt, Unworthiness	I am not worthy of money; I don't deserve it.
	Inadequate	I feel that I am not enough. I feel limited and inadequate. There is just not enough money, time, or energy.
	Fear, Grief, Depression, Despair, Powerlessness	I feel powerless with respect to money and it is ruining my life. I just feel hopeless about it. I feel really poor.

The Effortless Wealth Journey

I once read this wonderful poem by Portia Nelson, *Autobiography in 5 short chapters*, which I think captures the essence of the effortless wealth journey we have been on. But this is the way I see the prosperity journey and our evolution from scarcity to wealth consciousness.

- Phase 1 – I walk down the street I fall in the scarcity hole - I agree to scarcity and feel limited - it takes me a long time to get out of the hole.
- Phase 2 – I walk down the street I *see* the scarcity hole but I still fall in - and feel there is not enough but I get out faster because I am open to something new.
- Phase 3 – I walk down the street, I see the scarcity hole and try to avoid it but I still fall in - I get out even faster because I am investing in my wealth consciousness.
- Phase 4 – I walk down the street, I walk around the scarcity hole and don't fall in. I know I am wealthy.
- Phase 5 – I walk down a different street avoiding the scarcity hole all together - I agree wealth is unconditionally flowing to me always and in all ways.
- Phase 6 - I realize the hole (scarcity) does not really exist and I am free.

APPENDIX

Appendix 1: Remembering: Summary From Each Module

Investing Remember...

- Expand your definition of Investing to mean that it is a way to consciously focus your energy.
- Expand your definition of Wealth to include it is an abundance or profusion of anything and everything.
- You can develop the ability to be in that wonderful state that makes wealth inevitable.
- Wealth does not require hard work and difficult effort.
- Wealth Consciousness creates a wealthy reality.

Easy-Does-It Remember...

- The Easy-Does-It-Process will help you powerfully develop your wealth consciousness.
- You are investing in the eyes to see the wealth all around you.
- It is not so much what you do, as it is how you feel as you are doing it.
- A journal will help you document your journey and help you capture insights, observations and new understandings.
- It is ok to keep this journey your secret for now.
- The more you expand your wealth consciousness the more you expand the pie and make more pies for everyone.
- Easy-Does-It means effort-less and enjoy more.

Awareness Remember...

- There is *no separation* between you and Wealth.
- There is *no judgment* around the wealth you desire.
- That you are *totally worthy* to have wealth.
- Wealth is *un-conditional.*
- Sacrifice is *not* necessary.
- Scarcity and limitation *do not exist.*
- Wealth is *easy to come by.*
- Wealth will impact you *as you decide.*
- Your wealth *does not need to be appropriate* and your possession of it justified.
- Wealth *cannot be withheld* from you.
- You Decide.
- Easy-Does-It: assume-less and choose more.

Alchemize Remember...

- Alchemizing is the process of transmuting energy from "lead" (old scarcity belief) to energy available for reinvestment in a new golden wealth agreement.
- Alchemizing is easy and does not need to take a long time.
- It is ok to let go of your scarcity baggage.
- It is ok to feel how you feel.
- It is ok to be wealthy.
- You are a powerful investor who moves energy to create.
- You have the power to alchemize scarcity thoughts and feelings into wealth feelings, effort-lessly.
- Be gentle with yourself as you do this powerful process.
- The Alchemizing process is 5 simple steps: Acknowledge the old scarcity belief that does not feel good, accept it as it is, release it to create space and surrender it to allow for something fresh, thank it and come to peace with it, and reach for something greater (invest in a new Wealth agreement).
- Be gentle with yourself as you do this powerful process.
- Easy-Does-It: less scarcity, more prosperity

Awaken To The Creating Technologies Remember...

- You create by engaging the law of attraction.
- How you feel (vibrate) attracts more o that vibration
- The creating technologies are always at work, impartially.
- Choose to invest in wealth
- Feel Wealthy
- Talk Wealthy
- Think Wealthy
- Vibrate Wealthy
- Easy-Does-It: worry-less and allow more.

Awaken To Who You Really Are Remember...

- You are a powerful creator who creates by investing your energy.
- You are a glorious soul having a human experience.
- Create your wealth habit by deciding to feel wealthy – anyway.
- Pre-pave the way by deciding in advance what you prefer to have happen.
- You are a sure thing.
- You are worthy of good things.
- You are infinitely respected.
- Your life experience is your creative opportunity.
- Life is unlimited abundance, unconditional prosperity and ever-flowing everything available to you – just because - no worthiness or earning necessary.
- Easy-Does-It: react-less and remember more

Awaken To the Wealth Inherent in Life Remember...

- There is WUW Unlimited Wealth Inherent in Life.
- Life is Abundance.
- Life is friendly.
- Life is on your side.
- Life wants what you want.
- Life is a YES Machine.

- The essence of life is Well-Being and you are surrounded by well-being at all times.
- Wealth IS and it is experiencing itself AS you.
- Life is always evolving.
- The nature of life is flow.
- Life has all the resources you need.
- The earth is your creative playground designed for you to experience the fulfillment of your desires.
- All outcomes are already in the infinite field of possibility
- The Law of Attraction is the foundation of the Creative Playground.
- Effortlessness is the way fulfillment was meant to happen.
- You are dearly loved.
- Easy-Does-It: fear-less and know more.

Align Remember...

- Easy does it.
- Your perfect shot wants to find you as much as you want to find it.
- You are a Wave in the great Ocean-of-Wealth.
- Do more of the things that help you feel aligned (feel good).
- Do less of the things that move you out of alignment (feel icky).
- Easy-Does-It: less pain – more gain.

Attract Remember:

- Attracting wealth gets easier and easier.
- Feelize it – don't meditate on wealth, meditate AS wealth.
- Be the wealth you seek.
- Put your attention on wealth and what it feels like to be wealthy.
- Do things that make you feel wealthy.
- Notice the Wealth you do experience.
- Feel wealthy today.
- Talk wealthy today.
- Employ your cosmic wealth managers.
- Say yes! to your wealth.
- Easy-Does-It: do-less, feel more.

Allow Remember...

- Everything is available to you – so relax.
- The energy of what you desire is here *now* and it is in the process of becoming physical, tangible and available to you in a way you can experience.
- When the mind is quiet and the body is relaxed allowing happens.
- What you desire – desires you.
- Allowing leads to fulfillment.
- There is no rush you have plenty of time.
- Easy-Does-It: push-less, flow more.

Amaze Remember...

- You are amazing!
- Noticing wealth attracts more wealth.

Make Peace with Money Remember...

- Decide to be at Peace with Money.
- Give yourself permission to look directly at money.
- Create new money messages.
- Forge a friendship with money.
- Tell a new money story.
- Develop money muscles.
- Choose to feel good about money – anyway.
- Feelize money.
- Find money role models.
- Appreciate money.
- Love money.
- Know money is easy to come by.
- You are already rich.

Appendix 2: The New Wealth Agreements

#1 – There is _no separation_ between you and Wealth

#2 – There is _no judgment_ around the wealth you desire

#3 – Your worth and _worthiness_ of wealth is not in question

#4 – Your wealth is _un-conditionally_ yours

#5 – _Sacrifice is not_ necessary

#6 – Scarcity and limitation _do not exist_.

#7 – Wealth is _easy to come_ by

#8 – Wealth will impact you _as you decide_

#9 – Your wealth _does not need to be_ o⌐

#10 – Your wealth _can never be_

Appendix 3: Consulted Sources

- Assanti, Angelina. "The Lottery Heiress" The City of Palms Publishing Company; 2 edition, August 11, 2013.
- Braden, Gregg. "The Isaiah Effect: Decoding the Lost Science of Prayer and Prophecy" Harmony, Revised edition, July 10, 2001.
  - Choquette, Sonia. "Your Hearts Desire: Instructions for Creating the Life You Really Want", Potters Style, March, 11, 1997.
- Chopra, Deepak. "Seven Spiritual Laws of Success: A Practical Guide to the Fulfillment of your Dreams" New World Library / Amber-Allen Publishing, November 9, 1994.
  - Dyer, Wayne. "Manifest Your Destiny: Nine Spiritual Principles for Getting Everything you Want." William Morrow Paperbacks, February 17, 1998
  - Dyer, Wayne. "The Power of Intention." Hay House, Inc. December 15, 2005
  - https://www.GoodReads.com
  - https://www.BrainyQuotes.com
  - Hicks, Ester & Jerry. "Ask and It Is Given: Learning to Manifest Your Desires" Hay House, October 1, 2004.
  - Hicks, Ester & Jerry. "Money and the Law of Attraction" Hay House Inc.; Pap/Com edition, August 12, 2008
  - Hill, Napoleon. "Think and Grow Rich: The Landmark Bestseller Now Revised and Updated for the 21st Century." TarcherPerigee, August 18, 2005

- Housden, Roger. "For Lovers of God Everywhere: Poems of Christian Mystics" Hay House; 40825th edition, November 1, 2009.
- Kiyosaki, Robert T. "Rich Dad Poor Dad: What the Rich Teach Their Kids About Money That the Poor and Middle Class Do Not!" Plata Publishing; Second edition (April 11, 2017)
- Price, John Randolph. "The Abundance Book" Hay House Inc. Revised edition, July 1, 1996.
- Price, John Randolph. "Nothing is Too Good to Be True" Hay House, February 1, 2003.
- Roth, Geneen. "Women, Food and God: An Unexpected Path to Almost Everything." Scribner; First Edition, later printing edition, January 1, 2009.
- Slatter, Jean "Hiring the Heavens" New World Library; March 10, 2005.
- Schiffmann, Erich. "Yoga: The Spirit and Practice of Moving into Stillness" Pocket Books; 1st edition, December 1, 1996.
- Stryker, Rod. "The Four Desires: Creating a Life of Purpose, Happiness, Prosperity, and Freedom." Delacorte Press, July 26, 2011
- Talbot, Michael. "The Holographic Universe: The Revolutionary Theory of Reality" Harper Perennial; Reprint edition September 6, 2011.
- Thompson, Beverly J. "Mystery of the Universes, Book One, Two, Three." The Gathering Press (March 29, 1997)
- Walsch, Neale Donald. "Conversations with God, Book 1." G. P. Putnam's Sons; 1st edition, October 29, 1996.
- Walsch, Neale Donald. "Friendship with God (Conversations with God Series)" TarcherPerigee, October 1, 2002
- Williamson, Marianne. "A Return to Love: Reflections on the Principles of *"A Course in Miracles""* HarperOne; Reissue edition March 15, 1996.
- Yogananda, Paramahansa. "The Autobiography of a Yogi." Self-Realization Fellowship; Reprint edition (January 5, 1998)
- Yogananda, Paramahansa. "The Law of Success – Using the Power of Spirit to Create Health, Prosperity and Happiness." Amazon Digital Services LLC, May 25, 2010.

About the Author:
Laurie LaMantia

Laurie is a successful entrepreneur, professor and artist who shares her wisdom about developing wealth consciousness to her many students. She has been developing her wealth consciousness from a very young age and has learned both how to allow wealth and repel it.

She teaches Leadership, Creativity in Business and Entrepreneurship at DePaul University's School of Business. She is also the co-author of *Breakthrough Teams for Breakneck Times*, a book on unlocking the genius of collaboration.

As the marketing and sales director of her manufacturing company, she sees the opportunity daily to foster wealth and prosperity in the company, which is an exploration in deeply held business agreements about prosperity.

Laurie is the Chief Prosperity Officer for The Abundance Center. She has an MBA from Northwestern Kellogg School of Management, an MS-IOE from University of Michigan and bachelors in Electronic Engineering from DeVry.

For more wealth resources please visit:

www.TheAbundanceCenter.com
Also check out her ProsperityAtWork.com BLOG

Remember...live long and know
you are always prospering

Other works by Laurie LaMantia

- Effortless Wealth Workbook: *A Journal Experience for Developing Your Wealth consciousness*
- Investment Tips for the Soon To Be Wealthy: *Unconventional Tips for Creating Effortless Wealth*
- Curious Guide to Money & Prosperity
- Make Room for Innovation: *Cultivating Innovation in Your Company*
- Success Dreaming: Entrepreneurs Guide to *Investing in Success*
- Prosperity At Work: *Fostering Prosperity Consciousness in your place of business*
- Money Magnets: *Cards for Attracting Wealth*
- Breakthrough Teams for Breakneck Times: *Unlocking the Genius of Creative Collaboration*
- Collaboration Cards: *Building your collaboration muscles*
- Making Peace with Money Podcasts
- Sweet Dreams: *Pillow Top Inspiration Cards*

For all these and more visit us at:

www.TheAbundanceCenter.com

Easy Does It ☺

A

Awareness
Of Your Past

Alchemize
Your Beliefs

Awaken
Your Power

Align
Your Energy

Attract
Your Dreams

Allow
Your Desires

Amaze
Yourself

Printed in Great Britain
by Amazon